GROUND-TRUTHING

Caitlin Press Inc.
8100 Alderwood Road
Halfmoon Bay, BC V0N 1Y1
www.caitlin-press.com

Text design by Benjamin Dunfield
Copy edited by Kathleen Fraser
Cover photo by Richard Droker
Photo on title page and back cover by Lowell Brady
Printed in Canada

Caitlin Press Inc. acknowledges financial support from the Government of Canada through the Canada Book Fund and the Canada Council for the Arts, and from the Province of British Columbia through the British Columbia Arts Council and the Book Publisher's Tax Credit.

Library and Archives Canada Cataloguing in Publication

Denholm, Derrick Stacey, 1969-, author
       Ground-truthing : reimagining the indigenous rainforests of BC's north coast / Derrick S. Denholm.

ISBN 978-1-927575-70-3 (pbk.)

       1. Rain forests—British Columbia. 2. Forests and forestry—Social aspects—British Columbia. 3. Nature–Effect of human beings on—British Columbia. 4. Human ecology—British Columbia. I. Title.

GF512.B7D45 2015   333.7509711'1   C2015-900551-5

GROUND-TRUTHING

REIMAGINING THE INDIGENOUS RAINFORESTS
OF BRITISH COLUMBIA'S NORTH COAST

DERRICK STACEY DENHOLM

CAITLIN PRESS

ACKNOWLEDGEMENTS

Thanks to Laurie Ricou, Lorraine Weir, Robert Budde, Jason Wiens, Annie Booth, Kevin Hutchings, Rita Wong, Ken Belford, and Alistair Schroff for direction, critical support, and inspiration. Thanks to Kathleen Fraser for her sharp-eyed copyedit. Thanks as well to Lisa Szabo-Jones, who published a wild fragment of this book in *The Goose*, the journal of the Association for Literature, Environment, and Culture in Canada. Warm gratitude to Andrea and Kristy Rasmus, Donna Ablin, Sean Neufeld, Elin Price, and Chris Ashurst for routine social grounding. Thanks to Richard Droker for the cover image and Lowell Brady for the image on the title page. And thanks beyond words to Lisa Funk for patience and support through the six years of research, writing, and crossing of mountain ranges that went into this project.

for Toni Lutick,
who opened this door into out

CONTENTS

To speak thoroughly and accurately about this countryside is impossible in English.

—*Desskw*, Walter Blackwater, *Git͟xsan Wolf* (1990)

POC (point of commencement

home,
perhumid,
Indigenous.

FOREST SCIENCE MANUALS CAN BE HIKED BY POETS, JUST AS REGIONAL cookbooks can be taken as cultural guides by anthropologists. Similarly, the sapwood and heartwood of streamside conifer trees can be read as ledgers, as they are the economic record of a tree's productivity under the success and failure of annual salmon runs. It's all written out between the lines of growth rings just as it registers within the fibres of so many other plants in the riparian zone (the area of life that thrives along the edge of a river, stream, or wetland).

The passive reading of words on a page can be like counting growth rings to discover a tree's age, while interpreting and gaining a critical understanding of the depth of the ecological information that is encoded within a tree is quite a bit more complicated and challenging. Undertaking work of this intensity demands a certain kind of person, or perhaps a particular kind of perspective. Gaining a proper understanding of human life from the perspective of the environment in which we live may seem counterintuitive, but here on the North Coast it is imperative to consider such a concept, as even the foggy indeterminacy of our normal weather patterns can work to either sharpen or dissolve the resiliency of human beings on a day-to-day basis. These challenging complexities can be seen as either barriers to growth or opportunities of various colourful descriptions. And whatever perspective you take can inspire larger questions and answers or merely dispense with them.

While thick mist and rain may dampen the productivity of field procedures performed by research biologists working in the *Khutzaymateen*—day after day after day, to the point where they give up and limp home to hide in the office—there is also a way that these endless fogbanks and the perpetual force of drizzle can clarify and strengthen the focus of human beings. For example, on the long winter drive to *Kitamaat* Village, shuttling commuters may become one with the steering wheel and concentrate with an intense enthusiasm, weaving their vehicles slowly around ice patches and fallen trees, through walls of fog and curtains of rain mixed with snow, always anticipating the unexpected headlamp dazzle of either an oncoming commuter around a curve or the slow-moving mote of a Sitka blacktail deer foraging for scraps of lichen torn down by wind. Perhaps the daily routine of intensity becomes so stressful and aggravating that a person moves back to Edmonton, which is a place where the idea of normal holds a wholly different kind of intensity.

On the North Coast, this daily challenge of mustering may create a mute, clean slate of the mind or perhaps a heightened awareness, as when a pair of Tlingit halibut fishers dreaming *Taant'a K̲wáah* (Ketchikan) may persevere on into the timeless perpetuity of a grey winter sleet, or, likewise, be filled with such annoyance and frustration that they return home empty-handed. For some, the ongoing repetition of inclement pressures can transform the harshest extremes into an accepted ordinary actuality, perhaps even such a thing as the extreme weather that is routinely experienced along the North Coast, but I've yet to meet more than a handful of these kinds of people.

For the many entities of the Wild, it is "second nature"—perhaps "first nature"—to shrug off the worst conditions as normal and proceed with the daily routine. A wet eagle crouching atop a hemlock snag in the nearly perpetual winter rain of *Metlakatla* may be pressed by a long stretch of hunger to fly away, even far away, yet it will wander only a certain distance from the magnetic force of the instinctual map that persists within its genetic memory and evolutionary habit—unless of course the *keta* or *kisutch* (chum or coho salmon) do not return. Amazingly enough, even in the darkest, raging depths of a Prince Rupert winter, when hardly any human being would dare go outside without damn good reason, I have witnessed gangs of eagles and ravens playing rapturously in the midst of fierce evening storms. Amazed, I have watched these giant birds flap headlong into the gales that blast up the face of a cliff, where they are tossed a hundred metres upwards, ass over teakettle, ending up high overhead in a drenched freefall of tumbling wings. And each one of these birds just flaps around for a quick rest and another round of fun.

As far as challenges go, this book does not have either the tough waterproof paper or the hard plastic cover that my field notebook must have. This book is made for the living room couch, or the bus, or for a park bench in fair weather. But for most people, the tasks of the everyday—never mind reading, thinking, and getting through the hard work of seeking a critical understanding of the unknown perspective of the Wild—can be similar to the experience of ravens and eagles flying headlong into storm gale updrafts blasting off cliffs in downtown Prince Rupert. If we can find a way to approach things with a degree of fearless joy, then many of the complex and overwhelming challenges we face every day can become profound experiences and vivid memories of growth that compensate for the uncertainty and pain that accompany every difficult process of change.

These mountains and rainforests, wild inlets and rivers of perpetual rain, the fierce winds and dense mists, they are all incredibly beautiful to witness, but they also represent living situations that are incredibly stressful—and then when they all come together on the same day, or for months on end, the resulting situation can lead any person trying to live here to ask some fairly strong and direct questions. How much do I accept and embrace that which is around me: the weather that often runs from unpleasant to brutal; the disquieting remoteness and the stifling isolation; the potential and reality of material and cultural poverty, and perhaps the promise of a precarious opposite? And even a more pointed question, how much do I love myself? Of course, there is always the offset psychological benefit of living within an overwhelming richness of spectacular landscape and awe-inspiring wildlife. Truly, this place can be a hellish kind of heaven on earth, as all of its prized wild qualities are also the source of its human miseries. Blurred together by weather into unimaginable varieties of green, they reach to sprawl within a series of nearly impenetrable rainforests, each of which combines to envelop a dizzying procession of unbelievable mountains—forest-choked barriers of stone that plunge haphazardly into the even wilder breadth of the Pacific Ocean. Cast along this bewildering spectacle of wild green, there are many small towns and remote villages where the concept and reality of human culture can be—depending upon where you find a space to stand in the social strata—either ancient or ephemeral, and perhaps both at the same time. As places embedded within the farthest torn edges of the Wild, the social atmosphere can be far more civilized or stretched far beyond thin, and often at the very same time.

Now that we are a bit storm-battered and dizzy, we need a way to find our bearings. *Ground-truthing* is one important method of investigation utilized by scientists as they attempt to uncover the biological facts that hide within the profuse material confusion of any given situation within the unknown. Ground-truthing is the practical activity of gathering technical data through field observations in order to provide statistical evidence for the interpretation of theories and the determination of hypotheses that had been established by statistical or laboratory investigations. At its most direct, ground-truthing seeks to grasp and clarify where something *is* and where something *is not*, which it can often achieve by looking as closely as possible at the material that is present within the field of investigation. Essentially, this kind of work can help to uncover the truth that exists, right in the ground.

Within this book, in addition to staying true to this kind of scientific method, I will also attempt various kinds of social, philosophical, and literary ground-truthing. While truth for human beings can be based on any number of perceived values, particulars of culture, or plain old individual opinions, truth in ecological science is meant to be based on pure, statistical fact; yet we shall see that each kind of truth can be complicated by distortions.

My own version of ground-truthing will look closely and from a studied distance at the tripartite relationship that exists between the North Coast rainforests, their diverse groups of First Nations peoples, and the recently arrived populations of industrial Canadian society. As a writer who is also a forestry field worker, I will run a kind of literary baseline along the breadth of my creative skills and work experiences within the wild, rugged, and wet complex of habitats and communities that make up the North Coast. As we hike together through words on the page, the rigour of the social and ecologic landscapes we encounter will be transected by personal memories as well as by relevant scientific data, all of which will hopefully provide context for a deeper, more intuitive understanding, and all within the arm's-length reach of the book.

Along the way, I will introduce a triad of relatively obscure, non-charismatic flora species from the rainforest: the mountain hemlock (*Tsuga mertensiana*), the devil's club (*Oplopanax horridus*), and the blue chanterelle (*Polyozellus multiplex*)—three wild species that have continued to bewilder and excite me over the entirety of my life and work in northern BC. (Charismatic species are things like orca whales and kermode bears—species that easily captivate the human spirit. Non-charismatic species are the ones we are slower to notice but which are just as important, if not more so.) I chose three species in order to highlight the relationships we often perceive between forest plants: those under our feet, those we meet face-to-face, and those that reach high above our heads. Of course there are many more conceptual layers I could describe, but I limit myself to three in order to mirror the components of the North Coast relationship of rainforest communities, First Nations peoples, and immigrant Canadian society.

One thing that I believe is that ecological truths exist, and that they are the most reliable templates for human truths that we have. Out in the bush, where every step can be a misstep with unforeseen consequences to more than individual well-being, I believe it is the same for ideas, which is especially true within activities of writing and reading. With sensitivity to time spent in observation of forests, people, and the page, my literary baseline will traverse an intuitive as well as a forensic path through the ways in which these three non-charismatic species—the mountain hemlock, the devil's club, and the blue chanterelle—all work and interact productively within their community relationships. Inevitably, over time, these connected story-paths of the wild realm have influenced my own, and will no doubt do so here, taking me out of the lived experience of the rainforest and back along the winding gravel backroads that lead to the asphalt of Highway 16; from here, even more paths diverge through the villages and towns that punctuate the undulating network of coves and riverbanks that make up the North Coast.

Engaging with what is fundamentally local, wild, and Indigenous, this investigation will be contextualized from time to time with a brief postcolonial history of North Coast First Peoples and the impact of the recently arrived European industrialists and their many settlements, not just as they have transformed the lives of Indigenous peoples but also as they have altered the ecology of the Wild. Hopefully, this tripartite experience of observing, wondering, and writing will lead to both new and renewed perspectives, not just of our view of the rainforests and our many human neighbours, but of the view we have of ourselves.

To get our minds supple and primed, one of the things that the North Coast does best is make *perhumid* rainforests. Perhumidity is a temperate quality, one that characterizes much of the territories of the Tsimshian, X̱aaydaa, Tⁱingit, Tahltan, Heiltsuk, Haisla, and so many other peoples. Perhumid describes a climate with a humidity index value of +100 and higher. Although the North Coast did experience a climate of relative drought up to about five to six thousand years ago, today the region rarely, if ever, has any shortage of rainfall. And, thanks to anthropogenic (man-made) climate change, this place will only become more perhumid, if such a thing is even physically possible.

From the perspective of BC forest science, the region is dominated by the coastal western hemlock zone (CWH): a submaritime, coastal to montane region of forest lands and all of the species, climate variations, hydrologies, and geographies they encompass and influence. These are lands where the predominant western hemlock (*Tsuga heterophylla*) and western redcedar (*Thuja plicata*) burst up in vast, thriving communities, starting right from the salt water at the sandy tideline and the edge of oceanside cliffs. Here they are often joined by Sitka spruce (*Picea sitchensis*), the diminutive Pacific yew (*Taxus brevifolia*), and robust shrubs that grow to the size of trees— such as red and Sitka alder (*Alnus rubra* and *Alnus crispa*). There are so many other species, all of which can grow their communities up to five hundred metres in elevation, where we enter the more obscure, darker zone of the mountain hemlock, which shares its much colder and much wetter duties with communities of Pacific silver fir (*Abies amabilis*), Alaska cedar (yellow-cypress, *Chamaecyparis nootkatensis*) and many other high-elevation species.

Throughout *Kxeen* (which is the Tsimshian name for Kaien Island, and which is much more than the townsite of Prince Rupert) there are so many unnoticed and priceless wild things, all of which contribute to the expression of the region's biotic integrity, its cultural æsthetics, and so many other qualities of life that are relatively inscrutable, intangible, and difficult to express with English words. These often uncounted, sometimes priceless wild things are all part of the many subtle, hidden, minute and even large-scale entities, both living and dead, that might be found with a microscope, with an idea, or with the conscience. These are some of the things that are often invisible to newcomers or those who just spend too much time rattling around in town. Yet these many little things, subtle concepts, and qualities are all as essential to the thriving of life as are the mild weather and heavy rainfall, and the North Coast cannot be defined without appreciating their values, however they might manifest themselves—whether falling unseen from the top of a tree or hiding within moss.

While a tourist on board the cruise ship *Norwegian Pearl* may quietly rancour in ignorance, if only to himself—preoccupied with the pressures of unresolved settlements and legal procedures that sit at the forefront of his mind but that are half a world away—distracting himself over how much *this* will cost and what *that* is worth—his eyes might focus upon but not actually see that which exists within the length of the rainforest archipelago that stretches darkly before him. From high upon the textured metal decks of such an incredibly luxurious vessel, the lolling green backdrop that looms beyond the tidy corral of his vast, floating holiday will be an entirely different experience from what is witnessed directly from the flared butt of a crumbling Pacific silver fir, out on the remote stretch of coastline that he sees briefly at a distance. From the roots of this rotting hulk of wood, the *Norwegian Pearl* itself would be a tiny knife of white, but the human being on the moss and rock would be equally small, standing below a dead tree that reaches as a massive rotting sentinel above the long, wild, and currently uninhabited shore, the wooden ears of its thriving bracket fungi having heard not much more than the sounds of water, wind, and the songs of raven for more than a century.

While it appears dead, this crumbling tree is even more alive, and yet this slowly collapsing spiral of redrot wood might remain battened up above the rock and surf with roots that, even as they continue to decay, will function admirably, possibly for another hundred or more years. Secure for now against the blunt granite plunge of the rocky coast, at least until the next big windstorm, the slowly disintegrating fibres of this snag provide stable perches for more and more small organisms and various kinds of plants—such as villous cinquefoil (*Potentilla villosa*) and Unalaska paintbrush (*Castilleja unalaschcensis*), both of which can thrive as they face directly into the rough salt spray, spilling in green expressions of life directly out of the sheltering lap of tree roots that daily turn into more and more dirt.

For the tourist who peers distracted out from the fifteenth deck of this immense, all-you-can-eat smörgåsbord and floating adult daycare centre, this conifer snag on the horizon may be just one of so many million rainforest signifiers of ideal, pristine beauty—objects that blur the real into the imaginary—ideas that have been rationalized as necessary to experience, not just as cultural badges of status and success, or to justify the high price of the ticket, but for other things, like proving to oneself that the long life spent working in an office in a dingy city has added up to some kind of exotic, if brief, payoff. Perhaps this distant silver fir snag is just another romantic tree dabbed onto a romantic backdrop with a mental fanbrush, and perhaps it is much more.

Taking a lesson from the seventeenth-century Japanese Buddhist poet Bashō, linguist and poet Robert Bringhurst advises us all, truly and treely: "if you really want to understand the wood, the water, the minerals, and the rocks, you have to visit them at home, in the living trees, the rivers, the earth" (*Tree* 169). And, as I will continue to reveal and describe them from the perspective of close experience, the perhumid rainforests of the North Coast are a complex of temperate, successional forest ecosystems (which also include the fresh marks of so many recently industrialized swathes of second-growth clearcuts), and are also the Storied Lands of a great diversity of First Nations peoples. These are not just wild rainforests, but ancient human homelands, and as mysterious and breathtaking as they are, they also possess long and complex anthropogenic, ethnoecologic, and ethnobotanic histories.

As forester A.K. Hellum perfectly describes them, these are *Indigenous rainforests*. This phrase gets closest to considering the deeper breadth of recognition and significance that these particular places have witnessed, experienced, and given back—all of which is retold profoundly in the annual story layers of the sapwood and heartwood that grows and collects within so many millions and millions of trees (39).

What *Indigenous* means is to fundamentally belong to a place or to occur naturally in a region, yet there is much more to this concept than a pithy Western definition can hope to explain (OED s.v. "Indigenous"). Indigenous forests used to exist throughout the world across the breadth of human history, as these were the kinds of forests that adapted in the ecological conjunction of long interactions between both human and wild communities. As such, the Indigenous rainforest is also a social concept, linking the history of these perhumid rainforests with the long cultural histories and biological evolution of the long-standing cultures of the North Coast's many First Nations peoples.

Bringing forward issues of social justice and the slow work of decolonization, there are Other aspects of the Indigenous rainforest that should be recognized by Canadian society, one being the fact that these old-growth forests and the long histories of their human residents have evolved together in the same place—an idea that itself still meets with resistance from both individuals and the loci of power in Canadian society. But the word Indigenous demonstrates the idea that there are those who have the potential to possess knowledge of better ways to live in this place than those who are non-Indigenous. In the most ideal sense, an Indigenous entity spontaneously treats the local as a permanent home much more than the foreigner or the immigrant, those who sometimes treat the local as an arbitrary position of opportunity or as a temporary site for exploitation, or even as nothing more than a launching pad to somewhere else, as they are always heading to some better place around the corner. Reflecting sensitivity to the kind of impact that European settlers should have had upon the North Coast in the last century, literary critic W.H. New writes: "as Western technology enters the Indian way of life, so an appreciation of the indigenous cultures must invigorate, strengthen, and give metaphysical depth to the empirically-oriented white society" (xii). This idea of Canadian settlers being influenced in profound ways by First Nations peoples and cultures has yet to manifest itself, except as it has within a few activist strains of contemporary society, those that work along the fringes of a mainstream that tolerates and yet looks down upon their activities, allowing this dissident behaviour only so long as the mainstream itself remains free to continue with its business-as-usual frontier-era strategies of progress and profit-taking.

Bringhurst gives a studied view of how Western society should learn directly from the wild source, telling us that "any healthy and sustainable human culture in North America has to rest, region by region and watershed by watershed, on indigenous foundations" (*He Who Hunted Birds* xii). This idea can only be true, as there must be a willingness on the part of the newly arrived to educate themselves about the dimensions of their new home. And, if such a prospect is to grow, there must also be a fostering of shared understanding and the acceptance of differences, as well as many genuine expressions of personal affirmation. In order to create an enfranchising relationship between the various distinct cultures of the North Coast's human communities and to create a social atmosphere that expresses an equal respect for the wild realm they live within and are dependent upon, it is we as settler and immigrant Canadians who have to make the most allowances and change many of the habits of our activities and especially our minds. But it is simplistic and wrong to assume that what we want is a general unity of viewpoint for a new cultural direction, as what is necessary is the creation of various solidarities between multiplicities and a shared willingness to work toward the sustainable coexistence of what will always be a complex dynamic, one that encompasses the ancient entities of the Wild, the long-term Indigenous human residents, and the recently arrived settler and immigrant Canadians. Often, somehow, there will have to be an acceptance of differences, one that does not act as a barrier to the growth of trust. What we require for prosperity is what philosopher Alphonso Lingis calls "the community of those who have nothing in common"; where what is of primary importance is a willingness to find the means to both protect and celebrate the various qualities of Otherness that exist all around us (3). Where yesterday we turned difference into a flashpoint for conflict, hopefully tomorrow we might nurture the acceptance of differences in order to live richer, more dynamic lives.

If we can accept the fact that there are such things as old-growth rainforest human beings, then we must also accept that there are such things as noxious alien invasive human beings. The latter are most often (although not exclusively) the most recent arrivals, mostly the colonial-era settlers and their offspring, those whose presence has been overwhelmingly harmful to Indigenous life. With one example from the Wild, historically, _Xaaydaa Gwaay_ has been a place of glacial refugia for many rare and endemic plant and animal species, but Europeans have introduced a number of species that have disrupted the balance and breadth of this unique diversity. Biologist Todd Golumbia tells us that the current surge in populations of alien invasives is "one of the more important threats to the ecological integrity of the region...which place many unique species or natural communities at risk" (327). Alien invasive plant and animal species are recognized globally as the second-greatest threat to biodiversity, but in addition to their effect upon wild eco-systems, the human alien invasives that have swept across the North Coast rate as the number-one threat to the breadth and diversity of its wild entities, just as they have been to the histories, lives, languages, and cultures of the region's Indigenous peoples (BC MNRO). Expressing the entwined, layered perspective of an Other, much more integrated way of being, Tlingit Wolf Ernestine Hayes proposes one basic principle that must be considered and respected for the well-being of us all: "Who loves this land better, the eagles, the ravens, or the people? How can they be separated from one another? How can they be separated from the land?" (133).

In terms of both human and wild history, many thousands of pages and even hundreds of books could not begin to describe all that occurs and has occurred within the Indigenous rainforests of the North Coast. As they stand, bewilder, droop, fall, arc, and skew, eventually falling flat to dissolve back within the rainforest floor, much of the physical evidence of these perhumid rainforests, these Storied Lands—year after decade after century after millennia—has been buried within the rich layers of a biomass that is as quickly decomposing as it is accumulating. Covered over, along with the slowly disintegrating shellfish middens of the earliest communities of coastal peoples, the majority of this evidence transforms into other elements but is at the same time recreated over and over again with more old-growth human culture, Indigenous presence, and an overall perhumid persistence. This is all happening under the shadows of gulls, ravens, and eagles and is represented not just by the giant green growths of rainforest trees and the myriad variety of smaller plants but by all of the small scuttling lives that surge along the tideline on bird, crab, and even smaller legs, as well as all of those intertidal lives that uncork themselves in and out of the surf in the form of mussels, clams, oysters, barnacles, whelks, and dogwinkles.

If we try to think about everything together, the world becomes overwhelming and too complicated. The problem is that the world is overwhelming and complicated, and if we simplify our knowledge systems too much, without making an effort to recognize them as enduring parts of an enormous whole, we do ourselves and our environment serious harm.

—Nancy J. Turner (2005)

transect 1

the North Coast triad:
larger-than-human, First Nations peoples,
and immigrant Canadians.

IF WE LOOK IN THE RIGHT PLACES, THE ANSWERS TO SO MANY HUMAN questions might turn out to be given freely from within the Wild world that spreads out around us.

The Wild, that most fundamental of the various realities we exist within, is what a great many people have unwittingly turned against, whether or not they believe or even realize that this is true. For so many more, the Wild is something they have never even had the opportunity to experience directly or come to understand, either obliquely or even vaguely. The dearth of experience so often leads to the creation of imaginary scenarios that become myths and lead to institutionalized activities that propagate concrete neglect and abuse. If we can accept the idea that the Wild is essential to life and health and has answers to real questions, and if we pause and imagine that it could, what might the Wild tell us about itself and what it requires in order to function and thrive? And if anyone could hear, how might we listen to this dialogue and glean something of its meaning?

To go further, are there senses or directions that might lead to a more respectful means, one that allows human beings to prosper and yet still allows for the rainforests, the mountains, the rivers, and all that they support, to thrive in their own way—a way that allows the stories of the North Coast to play on as they must?

Play, after all, is serious business.

Around here, every year, wind and rain throw massive trees down mountainsides and tear the roofs from buildings. On a daily basis, tsunami debris from Japan reminds us that the Wild is ready at any moment to play hardball. But the play of evolutionary forces also gives us all of the stuff of life, throwing Pacific salmon out of the ocean and up rivers where they spawn and die and drift back down in smaller and smaller pieces of themselves, dispersing in a slurry through the moss, eventually percolating through sediment to the finest roothairs of plants and all the way up into the spring branch tips of giant conifer trees. Here, and in the same way, human gestures, serious and not too serious, should be long-term commitments enacted with the same intensity of blood being shed in the water and green limbs being thrown upon the ground. Human transactions should not be written only with the blood of wild animals, the fibre of trees, and all of the other gifts of the earth that we utilize, but should be balanced with an understanding or even an equal proportion and commitment of our own.

As is clear to be seen in the stripped zones where human settle-ments have cobbled themselves together—here, where every year our immigrant grandfathers spent the winter cutting down a small patch of trees and used the salmon streams as skid trails to move logs down to the bay—here, where most of the best growing sites are now paved over with parking lots and are contaminated by railyards and industrial sites—here, where a small municipal library shaded by Norway maple and Scots pine stands on what used to be a wild Indigenous rainforest, a place where wild leaves were once inscribed with a multitude of local stories—here, the balance of human take and Wild give long ago stopped being anything near proportionate. As poet George Stanley pushpulls it, this is where "the system, the tangled boundary / (that has no place in what we learn / as place—we can't see what we name) / deflates, at every encountered point" (*Opening* 96). And it is here where, all too often, to rename something may be to alienate, just as to grasp for something is, perhaps, to also unknowingly obliterate.

Within such a wild place as the North Coast, many questions and answers and more injustices become lost all too easily within the regular annual cacophony of spreading, surging green. This is a place where, within the few weeks of a spring flush, lady fern, salmonberries, and a sprawl of alder can rise to engulf and disappear a cast-off living room couch, basically forever. In Prince Rupert, I once found a *Boletus edulis* mushroom fruiting from a smashed computer monitor that had been thrown off a roadside and become hidden within mouldering leaves under a glade of cottonwoods. Here on the North Coast, covering everything, there is both the hypersense and the hyperreality of always everything everywhere evergreen.

When we step back further to see the North Coast in a way that most of us can hardly perceive, as Peter Sutton tells us, we can realize that "the land is already a narrative—an artefact of intellect—before people represent it" (19). This idea might make people consider what they presume to know about the place they live and about how they live there, perhaps with the individual eventually coming to understand that what we have taken as facts are actually various kinds of disingenuous projections or outright lies, and, hopefully, that from here on our time will be spent within an intensely selfless activity of righting these wrongs and giving back a proportionate amount of gifts and respect.

The North Coast is a place of fast recycling, where many of the earliest human activities within the Wild have become lost in green and are rarely found by the more recent activities of human curiosity. I'm talking here about those activities and industries that were transcribed for generations through Indigenous cultures, spoken with words that to this day still mimic the sound of waves stroking back and forth through black rocks encrusted with barnacles, coral leaf, and bryozoa. This is a place where sentences still slip with perfect fit through endless warm rains sieving down through serpentine trees, where human phrases mix with the intricate annunciations of ravens that pop and click and scrape through the crackling of firewood and the incense of wood smoke. This is a place where local words still sound like literal reflections of salt water streaming from the blades of canoe paddles. It might sound terribly romantic, yet these details are authentic, ordinary aspects of daily reality. To dispel the romanticism, the truth is that many of these languages are quickly becoming extinct.

What's real: From the perspective of wild communities in the coastal rainforest, there are millions upon millions of stories, all with their own biotic questions and as many organic answers, so many of which are still standing, some as conifer trees, "drenched in height," moss-sewn from moss-crown to moss-earth (Avison 95). As well, there are all of the grey and fallen dead (all still very much alive, in their own way)—rotting bulks of the older denizens of the rainforest, those that the newer, robust green of youth stand and thrive upon. There are the leafy annuals—a steadily unfurling eruption of ever more and more green: plants and plants and more plants, all unravelling daily sun compasses of jade and emerald by community interval and chance opportunity. All will eventually fade under the weight of their own seasonal gravity, crumbling to feed the next generation. There are the mostly untold and unstudied stories of thousands of varieties of micro-organisms, fungi, and invertebrates, and so many animal stories of the land and air and water, those who mostly live and die and rot quickly enough that only the ever-present algae can make small green paraphrases of themselves upon their ephemeral remains, found here and there in the form of a green forked spiral antler, a green corduroy of shell, a green diaphanous fish scale, and even at the base of lichen-swarmed trees near the shoreline, where I've found eagle feathers that were more green than they were black and white.

Getting closer to the landscape-scale breadth of things, all Indigenous life on the North Coast persists within locally interconnected phrasings of its own *eco-logic*. Eco-logic is, at its most basic, the daily formation of wild pragmatics. Eco-logic is the habitat-sensitive, multidirectional work performed by various means, always for overall community persistence. Eco-logic is the survival-thrival modes of so many experienced individuals in the process of *becoming* and in the state of *being*. Eco-logic is the natural reason why most Indigenous things live and die, and it is the means by which most things also replenish the spent field of their existence with the accumulated wealth of their life's work and the broken-down remains of their essence. As everything that grows here must be given back to that from which it came, Northwest or Southeast, the coastal rainforest reveals its eco-logic with robust expressions of abundance—not just with the obvious immense exclamations of living growth that we see from the roadside but also within the more substantial and yet inscrutable works that we hardly perceive: its gifts of food, shelter, medicine and healing, clean air, and clean water, all of which provide essentials we require for the lives we live.

Spread out within the multitude of living green stories, there are two other, often very different narrative flows. These are human cultures, both of which combine with the wild landscape to create a tripartite schema of more stories. Although the deepest, most complex and profound of these stories comes from the ancient cultural experiences of the old-growth rainforest itself, there are also the accumulated millennia of cultural experiences of so many different Indigenous peoples, as well as those from the recent arrival of European colonizers and the tides of even more recent global immigrants.

Represented within numerous First Nations groups, the traditional legacies and contemporary persistence of Indigenous peoples along the North Coast are expressed by a dozen related or distinct languages within what we have already come to understand are *Indigenous rainforests*. To give them something that is still not even close to their due, while trying to describe their persistence as succinctly as possible, the qualities of North Coast cultures perfectly define what it means to be an old-growth rainforest human being. Within the diverse circumstances of a past where people lived without smart-phones, electricity, central heating, or hunting rifles, traditional First Nations peoples were important components in the maintenance of these old-growth perhumid rainforests. Not so long ago, people lived embedded lives within the coastal rainforest fringes and up the shores of the many great rivers, linked with the land to such an extent that they attained an eco-logical form of symmetry, proportion, and harmony within what we should rightly call the *larger-than-human* world. The larger-than-human is everything: the realm of animals and plants, of weather and geography, of time, consequence, as well as all that is influenced by human activity and presence. As it stands and flows to this day, the eco-logic of the wild lands of the North Coast concentrates and is plainly evident within the gathered perspectives, philosophies, and knowledges of the many groups of people that have taken the time, the aptitude, and the good sense to observe, consider, and synthesize. This is a vital concentration that only a few still possess and understand and that even fewer still understand within the depth of their original languages. Thankfully for us all, the larger-than-human is well equipped to remember and perpetuate itself on a much larger than human scale, and there is more than hope that it can continue to adapt, renew, and thrive in a variety of future forms.

Where the cohesion of wild communities on the North Coast starts to splinter reveals itself with the impact of the relatively recent incursion of European colonizers. Comprising the generations of settlers who have since swelled to engulf the entirety of Cascadia, from *Siuslaw* to *Kenai*, these newcomers have carried with themselves a complex overculture of settler-immigrant experience and habits. As it has been only 143 years since British Columbia became a province of Canada, comparatively, what we call Western or industrial-consumer society or just plain old Canadian culture is a relatively new system. Establishing imperial and colonial restrictions of interpersonal and community repression within an ever-widening means of regulated force, this third, newly arrived element in the North Coast relationship has brought incredible change in a very short period of time. Starting with eighteenth-century fur traders, then nineteenth-century fishermen and cannery workers, more recently there have been repeating waves of settlers, farmers, and larger importations of industrial and technological workers from all over the globe. As they come now from just about everywhere to the rich bounty of western North America, international immigrants have altered vast areas of the Indigenous temperate rainforests of Oregon, Washington State, British Columbia, and Southeast Alaska, transforming Cascadia into a string of zones of intense resource extraction, areas of large-scale industrialized farms, and urban housing developments, and as it "progresses," this positive-sounding activity crowds out and often overwhelms the First Peoples and other Indigenous beings who call these places home.

Despite recent transformations of heavy industry, surging populations of immigrant workers, and the spectrum of good and bad they bring, the only reason that the Other-wise flourishing of the larger-than-human realm (when brought together with the philosophies and activities of First Nations peoples) cannot reclaim its rightful position as the model for individuals, communities, and the flourishing of all life on the North Coast is due mainly to our collective unwillingness to allow it to happen. The United Nations states that there are up to 370 million Indigenous peoples worldwide; yet, with 180,000 Indigenous peoples currently living in BC and with a population that is steadily growing, First Nations are increasingly expressing their frustration with government inaction and repression. And this frustration is matched by First Nations groups' equally increasing desire and ability to take matters into their own hands (UNPFII, Muckle 4).

The Indigenous rainforests teem with so many complex wild histories and daily stories, all being re-remembered and retold by leaf, feather, and fur, by season, by decade, by century, a great many of which are also woven deeply within the ancient narratives of North Coast peoples, communities who find their personal origins within many historical marriages with the mammals, birds, and fish who have shared their homelands for millennium. Although the recent European settler-immigrant population acclaims its own history of conquering and subduing the Indigenous wild, both here in BC and in Canada overall, when compared to the earlier histories of rainforests and First Peoples, these most recent newcomers hold the shallowest narrative about their new home. Most have one or another version of a recent flight from conflicts in the Old World, or an escape from the earliest outward trial thrust and failure of European industrialization and globalization. Some, like myself, don't even have this much to tell, as our parents and grandparents, for various reasons, never saw the reason to bother with sharing the truth of our origins, or much else. Living *here* in the *now*, this personal tragedy is no longer anything to be publicly ashamed of, yet the ahistoricization of First Peoples' heritage by both government policy and the cultural force of society is a serious matter that describes a large-scale, multi-generational injustice. For colonial immigrants and settlers of mainly European descent, there are the fleeting sepia-tone images of railroads, coastal canneries, high-grade logging shows, and various remote mining operations—most of which were built and run briskly and which have been abandoned just as quickly. Unfortunately, what we have also done within and between the lines of these brief and brave stories of arrival, hard work, and transformation is to declare, legislate, and enforce so many means by which the previous, larger, Indigenous histories are meant to become irrelevant and meaningless, with its people doomed to assimilation or extinction.

As much more than one of the wettest places on earth, these rainforests of the North Coast must become, once again, more than just a location for so many newcomers to start from and arrive at, and from which they so casually continue to come and go. This place must rebecome a home with deep interconnections and not continue to be just another patch of gravel scraped clear for another round of temporary industrial work camps. Offering much more than logs, minerals, and meat, the Indigenous rainforests of the North Coast are already first and foremost a home to many important and mostly undervalued communities, all of which manifest themselves by moment, by season, and by millennium. For thousands of years, the physical, experiential, and philosophical interconnections of the larger-than-human realm have been aggregating themselves into a multitude of questions, ideas, and concepts that are as large and strange as they are small and banal. All of their answers and subsequent lessons are here, standing, flying, and swimming, as mysteriously within reach as they are deeply entwined and often lost from sight within green green green.

When the sky is no longer a roof
one's eyes are finally open:

—Jan Zwicky (1998)

transect 2

questions of here and there,
eco-logic and Real Work,
participatism.

WHY, REALLY, DO ANY OF US CLIMB A MOUNTAINSIDE OR HIKE THROUGH a forest? To exercise the body, the mind, the spirit? To get away? To drag out some quick cash? Perhaps to remind ourselves that there are Other worlds and ideas out there, worlds and ideas that are every bit as important as those we find behind our work desks or that we fantasize about within our minds? But at the same time, perhaps the better question is, why *shouldn't* we climb a mountainside or hike through a forest?

Within the ordinary, imperfect everyday—the blunt reality of errors we live hurriedly and unavoidably within—this place where minds drift to meet either human walls or tree trunks—can a bored Heiltsuk high school student, or a hardware store clerk who is also a mother of three, or perhaps a nurse from Calgary on his day off— can any of us as relatively ordinary Canadians find our way off the sidewalk, out and up through the tangled, mostly impenetrable crush of conifer trees, climbing all the way to the montane schoolroom of gnarly roots and lichen, into the lecture halls of crumbling cones and drifting fog? Here, out of our element within the shadow of a moun- tain hemlock tree, can we do more than gasp and stumble beneath the sticky subalpine fir and storm-battered cypress sway of the north-slope rainforest? Here, where there might seem to be not much more than the dark, cold, inhuman, pungent hanging drip of green and grey over steep heaves of moss and rot—can we also find a way to reach beyond this thwacking branch edge to the bright mist opening of the higher rainforest ledge—can we reach to gather a renewed sense of purpose and perspective, one that can be a force of change within the day-to-day lives that we live down below? Or will this exercise bring only aches and pains, torn rain pants, scrapes and blood, a hundred festering slivers, even the near-death experience of almost falling off a slippery bluff into a jagged scree swarming with devil's club, where we bring back to town nothing but the frustrated, seething decision to stay, ever afterward, safely down on the sidewalk?

As exhausting and frustrating as most human experiences can be within the depths of the rainforests of the North Coast, can we still find the means by which to live both a satisfying and an ethical life, not just in the daily routine of small-town streets and buildings lost in fog, but with consideration of these moss-dripping places, these wild surroundings of rain-run slopes and moss-drenched heights of blowdown timber? Can we all find a way to live a life that inscribes its own ethical and purposeful momentum with a daily routine of critical thought and active participation, can we live a life that works to nurture both a more productive and a more diverse reality? And can we find the means for all of this here, starting within these thin, smooth pages, here where small marks of inky idealism plot themselves out on paper? As poet Ken Belford hopes within his own essential *lan(d)guage*, I would like to find a way to live and work "without the flavour / of sentiment, writing in invisible ink, living / on an invisible river" (44). This is the aim of the "Real Work" that eminent poet and ecocritical writer Gary Snyder champions the revival of when he tells us: "Get real! Get a life!" (*Ecology* 4). Real Work is not just what the Wild does with each trickling breath of water and each green blossom that unfurls out of the riparian zone. Real Work is what most of our ancestors used to live and breathe on a daily basis, back before large-scale industrialization transformed both human and larger-than-human life all over the planet.

Real Work is the basic activity of protecting and providing for biotic health—it is one of the tasks that we all need to reconsider finding our way back to within the distraction of our technologically driven lives. As Snyder describes, Real Work is the activity of living well and respectfully in relation to the earth. As the most essential form of participation, Real Work is the activity of "manifesting in ourselves the integrity of the wild;" it is the force within which we make choices and construct our daily and lifelong means of thriving and prospering; and Real Work is all of the thoughts, gestures, and activities that "check the destruction of the interesting and necessary diversity of life on the planet" (*Ecology* 10, *Real* 82). This is what social theorist and psychoanalyst Félix Guattari considers with his own vision of the "logic of intensities, or eco-logic," when human work and thought become concerned "only with the movement and intensity of evolutive processes," which is a concept that can lead to activities that renew the health of the biosphere just as they protect and promote the "words, phrases, and gestures of human solidarity" (30, 29).

Ecologic and human health, as we are coming to perceive, are linked not just in thought and in word but in the tasks of our material duties—in Real Work. Ecocritic Randall Roorda considers the breadth of this social, ecological, and political dynamic of theory and practice through the activity of nature writing but also, just as importantly, through the activities of those who read it. Roorda points to the strength that lies in what he calls the "participatory-ecocritical," which is summed up in the concept of *participatism* (73). Roorda proposes that we all seek to take on this initial, readily available transformation within our lives: where passive readers learn how to become critical thinkers and gradually educate themselves until they become active ethical and political witnesses. Once here, Roorda urges these more enlightened readers to become active participants in their own writing or in performing direct, practical activities of relevance and consequence, both of which can lead to changes in our personal realities as well as within the greater wor(l)d (74). Roorda's concept of participatism encourages the interchange of information into knowledge and the formation of ethics and principles that can bring the formerly passive reader into the realm of the activist, and then into the supracommunity of "wildness"—the philosophical space where they "grow up" and take on the responsibilities of a biocentric worldview (77).

And all of this should be the everyday concern of anyone who lives in a community, has a family, or has a pulse.

I tell myself such cold stories, ice
rain everywhere, electricity gone

a hearsay of the land I live in
a breath I did not even feel

in what I see is a pocket of world
stopped in its tracks by the unsaid

an undiscovered coastline, without
roads or paths or even maps

where I can call to no hearing
and ask so strange questions
            —Krisjana Gunnars (2002)

transect 3

land of the hemlock,
biogeoclimatic history,
lan(d)guage.

LOCATE. COMPASS. PERAMBULATE.

Back when I was a bit younger, within the "on season" I pretty much spent all of my time in the bush, not just at work during the day but in the evenings as well, and so I became a bit of a hermit, and, yes, slightly mad, as my friends will nod and even describe in detail. There were the normal signs, and I saw them: I cringed at the sound of the telephone, I noticed that I talked to myself an alarming amount, I lolled in and out of cabin fever at the end of winter, and I almost always had a crazed appearance—like a bookish werewolf. But I was also a chainsaw whiz.

I entertained bats in my living room, and as I did not have a dog, I lived alongside of a great many deer, moose, crossfoxes, and bears, and an annual family of woodchucks lived their lives just twenty metres outside my kitchen window. Along the way, I learned to accurately predict the weather, to the point where some of the few people I still talked to would call me up out of the blue for short-term forecasts (even though I cringed at the sound of the telephone). As I did live pretty much out in the middle of nowhere, I recall many occasions when I hunkered down in the wild rhubarb when the rare sound of a vehicle came anywhere near my driveway. Once, a pair of German tourists pulled up on mountain bikes to gawk and take photographs (all from a safe distance and without speaking a word to me) while I cut firewood in the ragged spruce just off the road. On a regular basis, I had pretty interesting conversations with local raven gossips and, yes, even songbirds perched on my shoulders. I spent hours sitting on remote rocky hillsides playing one chord over and over again on a banjo—basically, most people would say that I wasted years and years of my life on a whole bunch of things that don't pay.

Throughout this period, I was also a kind of forestry worker, as I am today. What this means is that I get paid to run errands in the bush, performing various tasks related to the forest industry's "hard" values (e.g., how "natural resources" are transformed into products that are then sold for money). Yet throughout most workdays, I always let the forest distract me as much as it wanted to, allowing it interrupt me from activities such as collecting data from sample trees, hanging orange ribbons in cutblock layout, or establishing riparian management areas around streams. First off, I didn't become a forestry worker because I admire two-by-fours or heavy machinery but because I was endlessly captivated by the intricate biologic functions and bewildering conceptual presence of the forest itself. To me, the forests of northwest BC give us all the daily opportunity to re-experience the kinds of earthly realities that we have now constructed our modern human societal structures in order to avoid having to deal with altogether.

Thankfully, here in BC, so many layers of these earthly realities remain intact, and the rainforests of the North Coast in particular give us a complex series of physical perceptions and mental realities that can be as overwhelming and inhospitable as they are restful and soothing. When I was younger, I didn't understand much of any of this, except on the most intuitive level. When I started working in the forest, I meant to learn as much as I could, both first-hand and otherwise, not just about the unavoidable "hard values" of the industry but about the mostly ignored "soft" values (e.g., how "non-timber values" are crucial components of home, community, health, sanity, etc.), values that the forest is always ready, willing, and trying to teach us, just as it is always living and expressing them, each and every day.

While out at work in the forest, I am always looking to the left and right, down and around, up and up at whatever is going on around me (which is always quite a lot), while I am supposed to be moving as straight and as quickly as possible from one witness tree to the next—eyes forward, intent on my task. Of course, this is also for the sake of the ledgers of one or another multinational corporation and, of course, to flash some rent and grocery money into my bank account. This work has added up to more than twenty-three years of what was at first seasonal labour but slowly built up to a full-time job that I still can't properly call any kind of career. What I did and still do (among many things) is finger the marks (designate who will fall and who will stand) and perform a shakedown (measure, categorize, and inspect the trees for pathological defects). Most of the time, I have been a timber cruiser—essentially a "tree pimp," which is the name my old silviculture friend Cory used to call us, even though he earned his own bush paycheque from a man who was, in fact, the very same Man.

In addition to timber cruising, I've been a treeplanter, a silviculture surveyor (like my friend Cory), and a stream and watershed assessor. I've chased wood for both conventional and high-lead logging shows, where, on the coast, I hunted out viable *pockets* and *fingers* of acceptable-quality *merch*, established tentative boundaries with *recce* lines, located potential yarding decks on accessible benches, and ran deflection lines up and down the mountainside in order to create geometric slope profiles that located the most workable cabling lanes for moving logs to the landing. I've also done both old-school tight-chain and modern GPS traverses of falling boundaries and proposed logging spurs. I've scouted and laid out countless in-block roads, ribboned out wildlife tree patches, and selected and established the design of caribou migration corridors in sensitive management areas. I've done mountain pine beetle probing, multi-story surveys, silviculture pre-scriptions—if it involves walking around in the bush, taking notes, and hanging ribbons, I've done it. Although I don't deal with machines larger than a pickup truck or with tools bigger than a hatchet, when I was younger I did a lot of miserable grunt work: I've spent weeks on my knees scraping the dead bark off of the cut stumps of beetle-killed trees, I burned slashpiles, and dug the deep snow out from around the butts of trees on steep slopes so that handfallers could cut them down. Nevertheless, there was always the daily opportunity to listen to wolves or coyotes howl (or howl myself in order to coerce them to respond), gobble up wild berries, collect wild mushrooms, take pictures of vultures that were a thousand kilometres out of their range, eat my lunch by a stream full of spawning sockeye, trip over caribou antlers in the moss, view amazing trees, watch bears sleep in patches of fireweed, come face to face with screeching sandhill cranes, discover rare hybrid plants, bump into surly wolverines, and come eye to eye with tiny owls on snow-laden branches. Always, some aspect of even the most terrible bush work has the potential to leave you with a memory to be cherished for a lifetime. Misery and joy: these two words best define the life of a field forestry worker.

In any average week, I may spend more time out in the forest than most people will spend in a whole year, and in an average month I will experience the inner workings of more remote forests than most people will see in their lifetimes. Although I might attempt and assay something similar here with words on paper, I know that I stumble across the forest floor with more direction and meaning. After all, it is all of these years of walking and thinking that have led me here to this page. You could try to follow me (and some of my co-workers) as we scramble over the slick blowdown, stacked up to eight logs deep, as it sometimes is, and usually from here to the crack of Satan's ass, all of it choked with entangling alder, elderberry, and devil's club, most often on daily treks that lead up to four kilometres away, way up into the relief of the dank and dark subalpine, where we somehow manage to make it back down to the pickup, and most of the time in one piece.

I might be one of the rare people who still have the opportunity to enter and explore intact, wild forests for a living, but if we reflect upon what Canadians believe about their rights and entitlements— those which enable us to go out carefree and enjoy woodland trails and wilderness areas for our leisure—we should also consider, for example, recent studies undertaken by the University of Calgary on deer/wolf population dynamics. It has been shown that both industrial activities within woodlands and the activities of leisure seekers at the municipal-forest interface substantially disrupt the predator/prey relationship. Whether it's hikers on the trail or the noise and activities of machines, these interruptions often disallow wild predators many of the few opportunities they have to hunt, just as, in turn, these interruptions allow the weaker prey individuals they seek more chances to avoid predation. Biologist Tyler Muhley writes that these interruptions in the form of human intrusion have negative impacts upon both predator and prey, leading to weakened characteristics on both sides of the relationship. And here I am, a field forestry worker, urging my readers to find a way to engage with the knowledge of the Wild and to seek wisdom from its source.

But the fact remains that as Canadians, and especially as rural British Columbians, whether we work in the forestry sector or as teachers in elementary schools, whether we hold day jobs as computer technicians, veterinarian assistants, restaurant cooks, or social workers, we live relatively comfortable lives due to the wealth generated by a foundation economy of large-scale resource extraction. If you live in any kind of house or apartment building, if you buy consumer goods of any kind, if you are reading this book, you have, to some degree, been involved in deforestation; and if you live anywhere on the earth and travel from place to place, either in a vehicle or on foot, you are negatively interfering with and adding stress to the already difficult lives of so many small and large living things.

At this point I will restate the idea that humans must always be respectful of the Real Work of the Wild as much as possible and consider the influence their activities have upon the interplay of local communities and their various wild economies. Winter, spring, summer, or fall, any well-fed Canadian out on a pleasure cruise down the highway or partaking of a rejuvenating walk along a forest trail can harm or destroy a multitude of wild lives with what may appear to be the most casual of activities. At the same time, the most harm that may come to me if I don't pay close enough attention while walking in the rainforest is that a mass of drenched fern might obscure a very wet Derrick-sized hole, and I might get poked by a few sticks on the way down. Once back in town, I won't starve to death because of the steady stream of traffic that rings day and night through the streets and out onto the highway that bisects the wild forest lands. In fact, all of this noise and activity, while it continues to disrupt the lives of a multitude of beings in the Wild, is actually bringing me my dinner, my new boots, and my evening's entertainment.

If we choose to look back, there are all too many incidents that demonstrate how the combined effects of industrialization, global economic pressure, and the building of Canada as a nation have also greatly disrupted the lives of local Indigenous peoples. First of all, we know that First Nations communities have survived and thrived along the North Coast for thousands and even tens of thousands of years. Anthropologists James Andrew McDonald and Jennifer Joseph tell us that evidence of shellfish middens in the Prince Rupert harbour indicate that human occupation dates back at least thirteen thousand years, which takes us to the time of the retreat of the Cordilleran ice sheet (193). Just as the first seeds were blowing in and plants and trees were sprouting up across dusts that were settling to form new soils on bare stone behind the retreating glacier, so the earliest human residents were arriving, establishing economies that focussed upon local flora and fauna. Historic examples of this kind are evident everywhere along the coast.

Focussing upon one location in particular, archaeologist Roy Carlson describes the ancient Heiltsuk site of *Na'wamu*, a cove shielded by redcedar (whose name roughly translates into "everything is close by") and the ancient village site of *Mah'was* (the "loading place") that persisted within the cove's point of shelter (quoted in Glavin, 17). Most recently referred to as Namu, this site contains midden caches of shellfish, mackerel, and salmon bones that stratify more than eleven thousand years down into archaeological history (Glavin 17). Journalist Terry Glavin describes how the perishable local commodities of the primarily marine harvest at *Na'wamu* were successfully transferred into non-perishable wealth and status through an elaborate system, one that was sustained by the local people for thousands of years, a system that was based on a long-term understanding of the necessity for the sensitive harvest of resources, which was based upon the complex economic concept of reciprocity (20).

With the arrival of European-owned canneries in 1893, marine harvest patterns that sustained local First Nations cultures were disrupted and *Na'wamu's* life as a site for human industry and habitation was over (17). Sadly, *Na'wamu's* last days were in the 1980s, when it was reduced to a gas station for the international industrial fishing fleet.

It should be fairly shocking to consider how, after many thousands of years of careful use by local First Peoples, both the human and the wild shellfish communities of *Na'wamu* were exhausted less than one hundred years after Western industry entered into this relationship. Due mostly to the effects of industrial overfishing, *Na'wamu* was abandoned in 1988, as were so many other locations when the entire Northwest fishery was consolidated, centralized, and rapidly stripped of its assets by the largest industry players. *Na'wamu* is just one of so many communities throughout the region to experience this kind of disruption and upheaval, all of which is just one small manoeuvre within the ongoing neoliberalist management strategies of post-globalization—a powerful, life-denying force that continues to transform not just the wilds of the North Coast but the world as a whole (31). Speaking to McDonald, *Sm'oogyet Hataxgm Lii Mideek* (Alex Bolton), a Tsimshian Tribal Council leader from *Kitsumkalem*, gives his commentary about these and other similar issues as experienced by the Tsimshian, the Gitxsan, and many other regional groups: "They have the same problems there. Their lands also are being wiped out, all their resources wiped out, all their land has been occupied, all their traditional foods are being depleted" (12).

This underlines the very real questions of who has the most right to movement, ownership, and activity within the coastal rainforests of the North Coast; who has the privilege of speaking with real authority; and who has the true entitlement of freedom of movement. If we were to take (or give) things literally and directly upon the merit of biological history and success, then it really is as biologist Michael A. Dirr writes: this is Canada, "land of the hemlock," and if anyone can be said to possess this "Crown property" it is the trees that have built it with their own quickly accumulating biomass, those Indigenous beings who grasp it for dear life with so many thriving and rotting roots, most of which are older and far more substantial than any municipal bylaw, federal omnibus bill, or act of Confederation (1187).

Fundamentally, as this is the Land of the Hemlock, it is the human beings of English Canada who would do better in appreciating the legacies and lessons of these forests and the many other Indigenous entities who live within the Storied Lands that the trees have helped create and perpetuate. On a purely perfunctory basis, if not a prescient one, the forest science arm of the provincial government long ago designated the North Coast as the coastal western hemlock zone (CWH), even though the perspective of most foresters is that the hemlock is a weed, a tree that is usually too diseased, too wet, and too rotten for boards or pulp or anything else of value. To the most recent foreign arrivals in this land, the hemlock tree is often an obstacle of cumbersome junk that stands in the way of progress.

But from another, unequivocal standpoint, some threads of science are in and it turns out that quite the opposite is true, as the hemlock tree is just one of many local Indigenous species that demonstrate their abilities for sustainability as integral players in the long-term biotic management of perhumid rainforest ecosystems. Hemlock communities are as strong as the storms and waters and mountains that have worked for millions of years to create the droop of their serpentine, languid-branched forms. Hemlock trees and their many associate species may not get to vote or write vociferous letters to their MLAs in the Skeena–Bulkley Valley regional district, yet their deeds of entitlement are all there to be read within billions and billions of vascular bundles of gymnospermic Braille, written up and down as they are within living sapwood and marked out in the testimonials of centuries within the dormant structural support of their heartwood, just as they are sprawled out in thousands of years of direct evidence within the earth that surrounds their roots—earth they have built themselves with hundreds of thousands of generations of dedication to place. Their larger-than-human right to thrive stands in the layered warp and weft they punctuate as they climb, tree by tree, up and around all of the bedrock upheavals of the North Coast, describing and adorning the mountainsides with the jagged green-grey millions of their hanging branches and whiplash crowns.

Looking forensically at these values in deep time, botanist Hebda and geographer Whitlock write that it was fourteen to fifteen thousand years ago that the Cordilleran ice sheet retreated from much of the North Coast region (227). The tree species that we see here today didn't spring up as foreign migrants before the crumbling calves of the most recent retreating glaciers. Most of them had been thriving here for hundreds of thousands of years and had simply been pressed southward in their community ranges by the earlier advance of the glaciers or were left isolated in areas of glacial refugia (in areas such as X̲aaydaa Gwaay and a few of the outer islands along the coast of Southeast Alaska). Shortly after the retreat of the ice, lodgepole pine was the first to recolonize the tundralike terrain that was being revealed farther and farther up the coast, and after about two thousand years a mixed forest of pine, hemlock, true fir, and spruce had re-established itself (241, 243). Western redcedar and yellow-cypress had also expanded nearly to the limits of their current ranges by only four to five thousand years ago—a very short time considering the time frames we could imagine necessary for tree communities to migrate (246). At about this time, the hemlock once more became the dominant species, and the varied community types that we see today came into their current composition only over the last two millennia (247).

Despite so many recent large environmental, social, and economic injustices, in the Wild, hemlock trees continue to spring up everywhere, as their own green economies require little more than a narrow space of damp mineral soil, consistently temperate weather, and a few scraps of sunlight. Here, these members of the oldest and largest remaining citizenry will continue to overwhelm the highwayside ditches, growing faster than government contractors can mow them down, along with all the other Indigenous weeds. Hemlocks will continue to surge up and over the first round of stumps that were cut during the fervour of nation building and the many shattered fragments of rotting wood that remain, still growing strong long after the first wave of handfallers have died and been forgotten. In another hundred years, after the last Cascadian gravel road warrior is dead—perhaps still curled over the mossy jerry can he died for, his mouldy overalls overgrown with algae, moss, and lichens—it is likely that a tiny hemlock tree will find economic advantage and use the hummock of his remains as a nurse stump. Then there will be yet another one of these millions of serpentine pronouncements of perhumid lan(d)guage, stating its rightful green ownership over this, the Land of the Hemlock.

I am the blood brother from
the river up the coast, the cousin
once removed, the trash in
the truck, the descendant
begrimed in the raff and rags
of language. I am the kind who
licks the meal of the marginal
land. One of these days you will
say goodbye and travel north.

—Ken Belford (2013)

plot D1

mountain hemlock:
outliers in transition.

THE FIRST MOUNTAIN HEMLOCK TREE I EVER SAW WAS IN THE SOUTHERN
reaches of Witsuwit´en territory while timber cruising north of Tweeds-
muir Park. High above Whitesail Lake, we were a logging barge ride
and then some across Tahtsa Reach, negotiating a series of blocks in the
transition zone between coastal and interior climates. Below us, upon
the shores of this large network of man-made lakes, the grey spires
of dead, drowned conifer trees marched below the shore, their tops
eventually disappearing to reveal a markless surface of black water, the
pattern repeating up and down the shore for a hundred and more kilometres to the east and west. Back in the 1950s, countless ecosystems
and a number of First Nations villages had been flooded for Alcan's
Kemano power plant, which also served to provide an easy float for
log transport to the Eurocan mill in Kitimat (which recently became
the site for a new liquefied natural gas export plant, and which is the

planned site for a supertanker port and the end of the Enbridge pipeline). Back in the Whitesails, while the first mills and a dozen others are all long gone, this whole series of man-made lakes and their ecological and social tragedies remain.

As we drove up and down the winding gravel roads, a few caribou launched themselves here and there from around brush-choked corners, startled by the lawnmower-like buzz of our rusting "rice-burner" (which is what the logging truck drivers on the two-way radio called our Toyota pickup). In this region, a typical morning trip to the block was a winding ascent up denuded hillsides through mist and strips of ghostly trees that partially revealed themselves and disappeared, the way hemmed in by steeply falling rock bluffs down one side and abrupt cliffs that reached up with jutting roots and silver-flat stumps on the other. Wet eagles and ravens hung aloof at eye level on broken snags, sweeping in and out of sight along the side of the road, the birds seeming as unfazed by the noise of these invading red vests as they were by the miserable autumn weather.

Once up and inside the subalpine forests, I found tiny mountain hemlock trees growing in climatic supression below the thick green wings of late successional subalpine fir and hybrid spruce—much larger overstory trees that were up to four hundred years old and often over forty metres tall. For much of their lives, these smaller trees in the understory had spent almost nine months of the year within the depth of snowpack, all but disappeared from view from October to June. Each one of these hemlocks was stunted and none stood more than four metres tall, having achieved little more than the stature of a sapling after fifty to one hundred years. Struggling along amidst the hardier, cold-climate species that best typify the region, these were outsider resiliants, diaspora holdouts from the warmer rainforests to the west, flung here into the drier, colder interior as misplaced seeds upon mountain-scaling updrafts.

As struggling migrants, these mountain hemlock were signposts of change along the transition to the coastal climate zone, and they are still my favourite kind of tree. Wherever they grow, mountain hemlock are tough, beautiful trees that hold fast as proximity markers along the interface of ecological boundaries. However slim their successes might be, as vanguards out of their depth in the realm of stress tolerance, these tiny hemlock of the Whitesail were struggling to adapt to combined evolutionary circumstances of random chance and harsh climate. Discoverees, these stunted trees were marvels of unexpected survival. When you walk month after month through lodgepole pine, hybrid spruce, true fir, aspen, and cottonwood, to find one of these strange, unexpected hemlock trees is to be reminded that there is much more to life than what we see in the small experience of our daily routine. Arranging rare glimpses of these ecologic longshots together in the black and white halves of my young mind, I had one of my first expansive glimmers of green and became overwhelmed by wonder in the refraction of this interspecies, cross-cultural parallel, and—as someone who has always been adrift without roots—I immediately felt closer to home.

Warped by weather and stress into graceful, arresting compasses of living essay (as the meaning of essay is "to try"), these small mountain hemlock trees were more than just inadvertent drifters along an eastward flow of the breeze, and I was no longer just another accident of place, brought in from the westward pressure of an uneducated, broken family and the dislocation of an increasingly technologically materialistic society, seeking sense in wilderness and a way to earn something more than pocket change.

*All the efforts of the Dominion must be devoted to production
and economy. The vast resources of Canada, to which the term
'illimitable' has been so frequently applied, because of lack of
knowledge, must be turned to some useful purpose. Untilled
fields, buried minerals or standing forests are of no value
whatsoever except for the wealth which, through industry, can
be produced therefrom.*

—H.N. Whitford and R.D. Craig, from the
Canadian Commission of Conservation Report
Forests of British Columbia (1918)

Mountain Hemlock: *Tsuga mertensiana* (Bong.) Carr. (view 1

A GIANT OF THE GENUS, MOUNTAIN HEMLOCK WORK HARD TO SURVIVE. Like huckleberry and salmon, redcedar and marmot, devil's club, mountain goat, skunk cabbage, and many other species of the rainforest, mountain hemlock give back plenty in return for the privilege of living, receiving various versions of respect from those who see the value of their gifts. Expressing community service and sacrifice as part of their everyday routine, these trees protect the steep, unstable subalpine slopes with their extensive root systems, and they add the greatest amount of biomass of any tree or plant to the nutrient-poor soils that nurture them. Hemlock are called *giik* by the Tsimshian, *k'aang* by the Xaaydaa, and *yán* by the Tlingit (Dum Baal-Dum; Turner Plants 93; Thornton 206). Tsuga mertensiana are more frost resistant, shade tolerant, and flood resistant than all other conifers besides their lower elevation sister, western hemlock, yet their nutritional requirements are far lower (Krajina, Klinka, and Worral 24).

As a different within the dense, mountain hemlock find their home upon the steepest north slopes, climbing much more than a tree length higher than cypress, fir, and spruce can muster. And after establishing this, they still crawl higher, up and out to the edge. An important and crucial long-term component of subalpine ecosystems, *giik* also serve as the primary protective cover for the upper reaches of watersheds and form dense structural systems within the steepest, most unstable slopes.

Gymnosperms (conifer trees) develop through seasonally triggered energy sinks that ordinarily operate in directed stages to build length upon branches and roots, to add girth through new layers of sapwood, and to boost themselves in height by propelling a new top leader, also taking time to grow small clusters of cones and flowers for sexual reproduction. For mountain hemlock, these energy sinks can often delay for hundreds of years while saplings just "wait" in the dim understory for an opening of light to break from above. Mountain hemlock also improvise to harness energy in unique ways, adapting to strain and reach odd stems of growth outward in asymmetrical configurations that follow the trajectory of daily *sunflecks*. Sunflecks are small but crucial patches of light that are created where various holes in the dense canopy allow small strokes of light to track in oddly angled beams within the predominant shade of the rainforest. Being immersed in a vast shadow for eight months out of the year and sometimes more, mountain hemlock spend most of their time just waiting to grow, either hidden or stalled within deep snow, enclosed, as George Stanley writes, within "glaciers in the arms of trees" (*Opening* 40).

Torpified where they squat in the zone between survival and thriving, some contorted saplings will scrunch supplicant for one hundred years or more, waiting in darkness. Stalled where they stand buried except for July, August, and September, while these small saplings are protected under solid rafters of white darkness, they will also remain mostly hidden in the summer, lost as they are under a profuse puzzlework of densely configured, sometimes completely closed crowns that may receive direct light for only a few weeks of the year on the steepest northern slopes. Waiting. Working. Slowly. Working. Waiting.

The morning consisted of presentations made by prominent
environmentalists, who droned on about p.b.m.'s, chloroform
counts, soil erosion, and so forth—none of which was
understood by the Native people there…At the end, an old
man got up and said he would like to give an Indian point of
view. Gratefully, the environmentalists bent their ears to listen.
The old man spoke for three hours in his language, then sat
down.
  The Natives cracked up. The environmentalists sat
confused.

— Lee Maracle, Stó:lō author (1992)

transect 4

storied lands and kincentrism,
the superorganic, vanguard salmon,
the value of names.

IS IT THE OBJECTIVE OF THE ENCYCLOPAEDIA TO INSTIL WONDER IN THE
individual about the nature of the universe, or is it the nature of the
universe to instil individuals with objects of encyclopaedic wonder?

As dizzying as it can be, literary logic twine has more in common
with how ecosystems work than we might like to admit. The contents
of a simple handful of dirt from the roots of a hemlock tree are highly
complex and have more interconnected layers than the literary output
of Jeff Derksen, who looks back at the habits of our thoughts from
the depth of the cosmos, wondering if the vastness of the universe
itself is "structured as a language" (40). Similarly, wherever we stop
to observe a thriving biotic system, there will always be things that
don't make sense to us but which always do to themselves by their

own eco-logic, and not just because change and adaptation are two of the most constant forces at work in systems like ours, those that possess such immense powers of healthy biocomplexity. In this light, *transitionality* is one of the most common pragmatic concepts of North Coast ecosystems, where considerable alterations in climate, hydrology, elevation, and aspect not only have occurred over the last ten thousand years but also occur within the hour or two it takes a seed to be carried east upon a breeze. Transitionality is also an evolutionary process, whereby disrupting pressures force individuals and species to make vanguard excursions from otherwise ideal habitats to distant fringe locations where they might only attempt to survive and fail. This is a wild, local form of immigration and colonization, where relative foreigners enter into new realms to see if they can establish a new community within a new set of parameters. Unlike the schemes of human colonization—in which new habitats are invaded more than entered, with the plan to alter them as necessary to suit the unchanging form of the alien's established habits—usually wild colonization by locally neighbouring species will succeed or fail within the limits of a set of pre-existing biotic capabilities and adaptabilities.

Although we might consider this wild method of colonization as random, unconscious, and purely instinctive, a species like the mountain hemlock is undertaking its own schemes of wild strategy, as its seeds are structured in such a way that they can blow up into the more inhospitable upreaches of the rocky alpine and trickle their way down into the colder and drier rain shadow of the next valley. They are trying something new by the whim of the wind, and their seeds have evolved wings and tiny size in order to go after the important question of "what if?" that waits in the next valley. Although it cannot be compared to choice in the way that people make decisions, it is a mode of strategic planning within the larger-than-human realm, as those trees that have evolved this particular kind of seed have also been the most successful at dispersing themselves.

With this example as an initial concept, let us consider similar ideas about the activities of spawning Pacific salmon. Fisheries research biologists Gordon H. Reeves and Peter A. Bisson tell us that there are always a few individuals of wild salmon populations that either consciously or instinctively choose to diverge from the usual cycle of returning to the exact natal stream of their origins, migrating instead to new streams where there is no previous history of spawning (74). In this case, as yet another aspect of a species' evolutive capability, impetus breaks from established patterns and enters the open realm of improvisation. Here, adult fish that have just returned from two to four years in the open ocean head blindly into new freshwater streams and seek out potential gravels for new spawning beds and new communities. As incredible as it sounds, this activity occurs on a small scale within almost every window of opportunity with just about any species, as habitat conditions everywhere are always in states of perpetual change and disruption. To illustrate this: an intense winter storm may create a heavy load of runoff that a small gulley cannot contain. Next, a landslide may break down a slope and cut off a stream that has been used for hundreds of years by many thousands of salmon. But, luckily enough for the population, there are always a few individuals "thinking ahead" who, for some inscrutable reason, decided earlier to diverge from the old route to the natal stream of their birth and instead try out a new streambed, one that perhaps just a few decades earlier had never been deep enough or cool enough to properly raise a hatch of eggs from alevin to fry to parr. From a broadly historical perspective, logically, if it were not for these outlier modes of experimental behaviour, there would be no salmon anywhere—or any life at all, including our own. Improvisation and experimentation by a vanguard few are the only reasons such a diversity of life thrives in any, let alone every, nook and cranny of the earth.

From a Western social perspective, to anthropomorphize such adventitious biological activities and interpret them as purposeful or conscious (like human decision making) will likely be viewed by most rational thinkers as absurd, yet these purposeful divergences from the mainstream demonstrate that there is always present the evolutive necessity and persistent will to break from normative modes. To cling fast to institutional patterns that deny difference can only result in numerous forms of atrophy and a very dead end. In most cases, the Wild has its own set of spontaneous methods and gut instincts for knowing when to break rules and defy expectations. Somehow—genetically, or who knows why, but likely humans never will—even creatures that most people consider stupid (like fish) understand, perhaps in the very fibre of their being, that change is *all*. This is not to anthropomorphize but is just a sign that intelligence and decision making as realized, understood, structured, and performed by human beings is not necessarily the be-all and end-all of cognitive capabilities on earth.

In contrast to a secular, contemporary Western dualistic system in which humans are elevated above and separated from the rest of the world, a strong emphasis upon anthropomorphism remains a key element within local First Nations cosmology. For First Peoples who live aspects of traditional ideas, there is a belief that animals, plants, and humans all have a common ancestry and a shared fate. This is a concept that ethnobotanist Nancy J. Turner and other anthropologists refer to as *kincentrism*. Within this openly inclusive view, people are just one side of a "large and diverse family of beings and entities, including both physical and spiritual realms" (*Earth's* 93). Turner writes that the historical narratives of First Nations peoples describe an earlier time when there were no barriers to communication or communion between living things, emphasizing that all creatures were and are still capable of "taking on human form and performing human actions" (69–70). To negate the possibility of decision making by entities other than human beings or to discount the idea of rational planning within the wild as being nothing more than incidents of random instinct or the statistical probability of evolutionary chance is to continue to reinforce a strict duality between humans and other forms of life and deny basic rights of life to anything that is not human. Even the most rational thinkers within the scientific community describe that there are many deeper complexities within all aspects of life, the molecular, and the cosmos, which outlines an entire strata of unknowns that science can neither reach nor explain.

The traditional concept of knowledge being passed from animals to humans is held by Indigenous peoples the world over and has been brought to light by various anthropologists, such as Dr. Enrique Salmón of Mexico, who characterizes this idea most aptly as a "kincentric" view, which is a perspective and worldview that expresses the importance of the deep interconnections that exist between the human and the larger-than-human world (quoted in Turner, *Earth's* 70). Engaging with her own understanding of the kincentric worldview, Linda Hogan tells us that animals and plants can hear, in an old voice from somewhere within a gene or a cell, a message that impels an instinct, an intuition, a necessity: "Some current of an inner language passes among them, through space and separation, in ways that we cannot explain in our language" (157). Hogan tells us that plants and animals are all travellers and settlers possessing much more collective experience than we have, and that they know the proper ways of living (155). Along the forensic line of the pragmatic difference between the human and the Wild, I have met people who have spent their entire lives in places like Prince Rupert, yet who have never stepped off the pavement, either physically or mentally. I have known people who are unable to identify a bald eagle on the face of a postcard, even though these birds fly all day by the dozen over the streets of their hometown.

Forest biologist Robin Wall Kimmerer runs her own thoughtful compilation of this phenomenon, writing that "the average person knows the names of less than a dozen plants, and this includes such categories as 'Christmas tree.' Losing their names," as Kimmerer tells us, "is a step in losing respect" (101). Admittedly, many people wouldn't know a mountain hemlock tree (or a spruce, or even a pine) if it fell on them, as the brief window of opportunity for life on earth is crammed with so many urban, technological, and social distractions, all of which demand priority within some people's thoughts.

We also live in a society where most of us don't even know our human neighbours down the hallway or along the same street where we live. From birth, most of us have been surrounded by ever-enlarging ripple effects that are tragedies of unknowing disconnection. Fundamentally, a wilder and more sensitive way of being should be as normal as breathing. Even though the process of bewildering is both riddling and exhausting, it should be an automatic reflex of adaptation to the condition of the *now*. These can be gestures and activities that reach to the level of the *superorganic*, yet there is nothing stopping any individual human being from rediscovering their own means for operating within the life-blood intensity of this kind of interbeing.

The superorganic is how anthropologist and folklorist Alex Olrik describes the autonomous process whereby every culture generates itself, which is also how abstract patterns and principles such as evolution and instinct come to govern the processes of life (130). The superorganic is composed of intense combinations of experimentation, trial and error, sensitivity to deep time as well as to the moment, the unconscious ability for wild decision making, and the possession of a well-honed instinct. This is how male Sitka blacktail deer (*Odocoileus hemionus sitkensis*) have learned over millennia to know what plant (deer fern, *Blechnum spicant*) to seek out and rub their forehead upon after they have shed their antlers, to receive medicine from the juices of the crushed leaves (Pojar and MacKinnon 420). This is also how traditional ecological knowledge and wisdom (TEKW) has been synthesized and accumulated over the thousands and thousands of years that First Nations peoples have thrived on the North Coast. Through era after era of observation, experimentation, and error, countless generations of local peoples learned how to respectfully utilize the myriad gifts of food, material, and knowledge that the Wild provided. They watched how animals did things, and in many cases animals told them directly how various wild materials worked, as well as what wild foods were good to eat and which wild medicines were good for what ailments. All of this knowledge was gathered together and improved upon, with necessary adaptions arising as conditions of climate, ecology, and culture changed over time. All of this was passed down, generation after generation, through rituals and ceremonies within a complex oral tradition of storytelling.

Whether you are a salmonid, an ungulate, or a hominid, success in transitionality must always start as an ordinary and everyday form of improvisation, one that usually requires a willful persistence, one that can be arduous and even debilitating, as it demands an incredible amount of patience to carry one through a series of physical failures and numerous mental dead ends. There must also be a sense of innate curiosity, sometimes to the point of obsession, with a propensity for undertaking intense critical analysis, which is often balanced by an almost offhand, contradictory detachment. The immediate intuition of the gut combined with the studied reason of analysis. For human beings, the superorganic process can and does lead to the creation of medicine and magic out of the rust of mental static and a good quantity of plain old dust. More than anything else, this process is part of a heightened awareness and fierce understanding of the vitalities of inevitable upheavals, which can be seen as both damaging and nurturing, depending upon one's perspective. Ordinary people can all perform their own Real Work, even on the level of the superorganic, as we all face the daily opportunity to re-engage with our larger-than-human responsibilities. For chum salmon and silver-tipped black bears, saprophytic fungi, Steller's jays, and hemlock trees, Real Work on the level of the superorganic requires nothing more than the instinct they already possess. But for human beings, Real Work on the level of the superorganic requires difficult decisions, as we must turn in the opposite direction from the neurological patterns we have been building since we abandoned the natural patterns of the world; habits that we have been fervently attempting to make more concrete and metal and technologically profound over only the last hundred years, habits that go against the grain of our being, as we have become the world's most gifted and yet most failed students of the potentiality of the world.

For those who hold neither Western scientific nor Enlightenment-era perspectives of rationality, there are Other perceptions, paradigms, and philosophies. On the North Coast there are many alternate living models for ethical cultural and industrial production, just as there is a whole series of ancient names and stories within these Indigenous rainforests, as well as a series of kincentric patterns and paths for travelling safely throughout the complex and dangerous layers of these coastal geographies, all of which are found internally as ways as much as externally as paths.

However, the English language has hardly begun its apprenticeship into the realm of understanding and knowledge on the North Coast, even if only a few of its many local speakers realize this fact. Personally, I should state here that I was not born into or raised within a traditional knowledge culture, and, as a non-Indigenous male of European descent, I can never gain a full understanding of First Nations knowledge or culture, or the subtleties of perception that are particular to the diversity of peoples that have survived and thrived here on the North Coast of British Columbia. While this text may be part of my small attempt to begin to understand, it may also become its own problematic failure to reach for or express respect for the many land-cherishing, tree-conversing, and river-listening cultures that have sustained themselves here for thousands of years.

But within these Lands better designated with a capital L, Storied Lands are the hereditary territories of Indigenous peoples; they are diverse aggregates of ancient, owned properties, each including overlapping sites of significance with human-landscape connections that go back, in some cases, much further than ten thousand years. The rainforest-covered mountains of the North Coast are not as they have been generally perceived, as an empty wilderness waiting for the direction of Western industrial management. Storied Lands are the legacy and presence of an ancient heritage of human experience and knowledge embodied in the kincentric forms of animals, oceans, landscapes, and rainforests. These Storied Lands were and are highly specialized and complex anthropogenic places with hundreds of long-standing village sites that were and often still are venues for seasonal cycles of local industry and cultural production. All of these rainforests on BC's North Coast have been occupied, utilized, and managed for thousands and thousands of years, often being shared within gestures of open civilization as much as they were claimed from other groups by brutal force. Some individual sites within these Storied Lands have had their ownership and management duties gifted or exchanged after an expression of serious need was communicated, and some areas were also presented to others as amendments for past wrongs. All of these cultural conflicts and accomplishments are continually being retold by First Nations peoples up and down the coast, most often within the official governance and cultural drama of diverse, often overlapping narratives of historical stories.

As anthropologist Fikret Berkes tells us, for traditionally minded Indigenous peoples, "meaning and values are rooted in the land and closely related to a 'sense of place,'" and "stories and legends are part of culture and indigenous knowledge because they signify meaning" (6). As they are represented within the importance of story, the method-sense for finding the deeper, interdependent meaning and value in the local places of everyday life and their deeper philosophies serves as an initial explanation of what it means to live in *interbeing*. Giving the briefest definition: interbeing is a state of deep connectivity, dependence, and an intensely realized experience, that which is found within the multiple facets and elements that make up the whole of the environment, which includes concrete reality, personal thoughts, and the communal philosophy of kincentric interpretation and teaching. In terms of history and geography, reiterations of interbeing within Storied Lands have been experienced, retold, and re-remembered through oral histories amongst the breadth of the many North Coast cultural groups, peoples who were, per capita, more culturally and linguistically diverse than the Canadian immigrant population who live here today. Unfortunately, it is the Canadian immigrant population that still requires a great deal of education about these ideas and concepts and for which there still exists the necessity for the wildest twist of conventional logic.

As ethnoecologist Leslie Main Johnson describes, Storied Lands are qualitatively rich, lived-in homelands, places in which oral history and ancestral ownership interlink with intergenerational and interspecies conceptualizations (*Trail* 17). Storied Lands are more than the backdrop location before which we bide our time as we wait to live out our future lives someplace else. As sentient beings, Storied Lands are keenly aware of our lack of respect and they recognize and remember all of our acts of abuse: Storied Lands are thoughtful, judgmental and forgiving, instructive and loving. And, for traditionally minded First Peoples, these Lands know and understand them much more profoundly than the people themselves can ever possibly know the Land.

As we reach and think our way nearer to interbeing, we must try to understand that traditionally minded First Nations people view the Storied Land as a living interface of physicality and communication with their ancestors and the various kincentric forms that persist with them, often residing all at once in the combined mental presence of the present, future, and past (29). Anthropologist Keith H. Basso describes Storied Land as a vast store of knowledge and experience set within an earth-structure recall system of *mnemonic pegs* (17). Mnemonic pegs are those significant cultural landmarks whose unique geographical forms act as memory triggers within a people's experience of their traditional territory. Imbued with the ability to draw forth the memories, stories, and lessons of ancestral events, this living effect of interbeing within Storied Land reveals itself where the environment "becomes charged and responsive to the movements of time and history and the enduring character of a people" (ibid.). Within this sense, we can now understand and accept that so many of the local, seemingly ordinary places that we call wilderness are actually sacred spaces. These are rich places where individuals of any number of variable talents, sensitivities, and perceptions can all come to view, to remember, and to realize, synthesizing meaning to their own degree of cultural complexity and thus transforming their thinking, feeling, and living, all with stories and memories arising from a hillside, a cove, a river bend, a mountain, or a grove of trees. As important as it is to culture, interbeing is lived simply and directly within the everyday patterns of waking, sleeping, and work, being linked emotionally and intellectually to the momentary joys and sorrows that come from the earth and that are experienced both with and within it.

We should try to understand that any view of the life-giving elements of Storied Lands by traditionally minded First Nations people will be markedly different from the way that Western ecological science has perceived the productive and degenerative processes of ecosystems. In addition to oral and memory-based methods of cataloguing and synthesizing biotic data within TEKW, Storied Lands are imbued with a combination of human and larger-than-human consciousness. Speaking always in the here and now about the past and future—about times when animals, plants, and people lived and loved, planned, worked, and quarrelled together within hierarchies that could be reversed by the most ordinary gestures, all for the necessity of finding solutions to real-time problems in communities that recognize the importance of reciprocity and long-term consequences—the complex perceptual idea of Storied Lands reveals the need for human beings to interact with all of the entities of the world just as they would with the most precious loved ones in their own families.

Within an attempt to see the pragmatics of interbeing in the plainest terms, here on the North Coast, as elsewhere, First Peoples named all of the places they interacted with in direct response to the routine of day-to-day processes that filled their lives. As experiences of success and failure are equally worth remembering and learning from, over time both the locations for successful hunting and gathering and places where tragedies occurred became significant and were made into their own ceremonies, rituals, and stories, becoming cultural forces that took on larger purposes in societies that have been steadily evolving in the same location for many thousands of years. After a time, when these places and their cultural signs and stories had become imbued with generations of cultural memory and evolved to hold and express deep vibrancies of kincentric power, the two became entwined—place and cultural concept. The pattern of pedagogic repetition enriches each place, its name, and its individual story with deeper purposes, eventually encompassing, representing, and having the power to reinforce various social concepts, philosophical and material lessons, and cultural meanings within the community. All of this can then be realized with the mere sighting of this landscape feature, and, for some, even by the merest flinch of its recollection. Then, and even now, with each new day, people remember multiplying layers of interconnected histories, their lessons, and their mental cohesion with the past into the present and carry them on to coming generations.

The events or circumstances that name a place can be as simple as the fact that a spot provides a good site for harvesting a particular food, or that the site's geography may visually resemble some roughly familiar human form. Over time, a relevant anthropomorphic detail of its features or history is elaborated upon and is made more complex and important. Transformative details complicate the everyday tasks and seasonal visits with story lessons and simple reminders that reveal one or another important protocol of life and how to live it. As Basso explains, what these stories that tie people directly to the Land have likely "done for centuries, is fashion possible worlds, give them expressive shape, and present them for contemplation as images of the past that can deepen and enlarge awareness of the present" (32). Basso tells us that "what matters most is *where* events occurred, not when, and what they serve to reveal about the development and character...of social life," which draws the lesson or story out of the abstract and here into the realm of the concrete, immediate now, where the awareness of thoughts, actions, and consequences is potentially heightened (31).

As it is reiterated through the series of kincentric connections that are created by our personal experiences in life, place can become recognized as the locus of wisdom. For those who hold the ability to think and act within this deeper breadth of consideration, there exists the gift of realizing that wisdom is always given to human beings from the larger-than-human realm, and thus respect for life beyond the human is protected. And it's true, as all of our wisdom comes directly from the trees, the birds, the plants, the mountains, and everything that supports and sustains us—even entities that we consider pests, such as insects, bacteria, and rodents. Superorganic forces such as Storied Lands are critical to TEKW, just as they are to the overall strength and continuity of the vital distinctiveness of the breadth of First Peoples' cultures as they persist and thrive here on the North Coast. Although so many people find conflict, fear, and trauma within experiences of meeting with difference, it is the very quality of difference itself that is most important in all aspects of providing and maintaining a healthy life. Values of cultural diversity are as important to health and well-being, innovation, and adaptation in human communities as values of biocomplexity are to the health and well-being of wild communities. Both spheres depend in relative measure upon these same qualities in each other for survival and prosperity. Biotic success is not just a situation of the last man standing but is most usually represented by a shared capacity to demonstrate a willingness to utilize various systems of intense interdependence.

In contrast to Indigenous forms of place naming, the social and landscape depth of interbeing, and the lesson-power of stories, most European place names in the colonial world are abstract signifiers that reinforce or punctuate the hold of the distant empire, usually in the form of an aristocratic tribute or ownership by an elite individual. We now understand that the original First Nations place names along the North Coast are usually more regionally intimate, culturally specific, and socially meaningful than the recent European names that have displaced them. Indigenous languages on the North Coast developed to utilize more verbs than nouns, created as they are through the grounded work of community life and the pragmatics of cultural histories that retain larger respect and deeper ties to the earth and a recognized link between environmental and human interactions. By contrast, European names of colonial tribute in Canada most often tend to symbolize aristocratic lineage, reinforcing distant power structures represented by economic and political forces, structures that are usually detached from the tangible, essential workings of daily life.

Cree anthropologist Shawn Wilson interprets First Nations place names this way: "Objects themselves are not named; rather what they might be used for is described," among other things (73). People on the North Coast gave a bay its name due to its wealth of herring roe, to a creek mouth because it was a good place to catch and dry salmon. They gave a name to a hillside for its berry patches or its marmot hunting. *Hagwilget* is the name of the village site the Gitxsan gave to the Witsuwit'en after a landslide blocked the river upstream, the name for which translates into "quiet old man," given in veneration for the mountain that rises above, who, as some know, has not always been so quiet (Johnson 50, 219). The Witsuwit'en also named a small lake *Ts'en co Tanedilh*, which literally and poetically translates as "swans land in the water," while European immigrants to the region ignored or denied the reference to this seasonal visitation and called it Toboggan Lake (Johnson 52).

One profound example out of the diverse breadth of the story practice of First Nations people is found in the cultural experience of Tlingit elder *Sèdayà* of the *Yanyèdí* (Elizabeth Nyman), where she describes the cosmology that surrounds the kincentric history of two mountains that stand on either side of the *Taku* River. Her story stresses the larger historical narrative and life lessons that people would remember and retell over and over again while travelling past a particular point while going up and down the river. *Łkùdasêts'k Shàtí* (The Head of the Giant) is one mountain on the south side of the river; on the opposite is *Łkùdasêts'k* (The Torso of the Vanquished Giant) (264–65). A sheer rock face above the river contains the site where this ancient giant was decapitated, and the waterfall that runs down its face is his windpipe (264). Here is a brief summary of the story that unravels a lesson within its commemorative place-name: Two giants lived in harmony for a very long time, agreeing about all of their decisions. After a while they began to take one another for granted, and both became greedy about their shared rights to the river. Eventually, quarrels and insults flew back and forth across the water and soon they began to fight over their entitlements to the *Taku*, during which one of the giants went so far as to kill his former partner (264–66).

Today, without any stretch of the imagination, these two mountains still visually represent just such a scenario—their geological features easily fit the details of *Sèdayà's* story. The human lesson rises up for all to see within the geologic scale of the rocky landscape, held up as a morality play within these giant mnemonic pegs, a story which has long instructed river travellers to get along with each other as well as with strangers and to always try to share respectfully instead of turning to violence. Even today, as people travel upriver, they can see the mountains and read the thrust, cleave, and drop of the broken mountain's telltale features. Importantly, travellers can also remember this story, wherever they might be, and, if they have the talent for it, they can also weigh and consider this old story of conflict to contemplate better strategies for interacting with people. It's simple, and it's as huge as a pair of mountains and glaciers on either side of a river.

These days, most of the day-to-day lessons that young people receive come from the overwhelmingly bland milieu of media culture, streaming through the predominantly white industrial societies of our small northern resource towns. Far from being the isolated hinterlands they were even just fifteen years ago, small rural communities have now become places where technology can transmit the same variety of positive and negative values, through the internet, on the ubiquitous smartphone. These days, young people in either Old Masset or *Gitanyow* can access the same online world that young people explore in large urban centres like New York, Sao Paulo, and Tokyo. But these are values of another entirely new world, one that, for people in northern BC, is still physically beyond reach, a world that can usually only be imagined and is thus subject to projections and distortions. Unlike the influence of parents, family, traditionally minded elders, and teachers in local communities, the dominant problem with flashy ultramodern devices is that the western technologists who control the means and distribution of information on the internet are not necessarily as trustworthy and do not always express themselves as being either thoughtful ethicists or moral teachers.

While there is a great deal of beneficial, productive, and admittedly essential activity on the internet, some of which could even be called Real Work, for the most part, technologists tend to develop technology for the benefit of technologists, and mostly for the sake of shareholder profits. If we consider the kinds of issues that are created as much as solved by the powerful but distracting technologies we possess today, where so much useful and useless information comes at us through tiny plasma screens in a torrent of entertainment, ancient traditional stories of jagged mountains facing each other across a river are in danger of becoming as obtuse as the stone the mountains are composed of, while their human qualities erode away under the neglect of growing indifference. While technologies are constantly changing in order to catch our attention and collect our dollars, out in the remote Storied Lands of the *Taku*, the mountains that rise on either side of the river remain as they always have, standing and giving their knowledge, freely. But who goes upriver today?

High on a fire-killed fir, black against the sky
a sombre raven sits in judgement.
How long until the account is rendered
payment on demand
for all this squandered wealth of mine and mill
of farm and forest,
for a life span of man-hours brought to nothingness?

—Hubert Evans (1977)

transect 5

Highway 16,
colonial history,
idle no more.

ARRIVING FROM THE EAST, SLOWLY, INTUITIVELY, AND SOMEWHAT TOPO-logically, we reinterpret the accepted landmarks of the west, reacquainting ourselves with the mythologies that we thought we knew, but which unfold in strangely disorienting patterns. These lands are filled with stories: those simple few we grew up with as Canadians—bumper-sticker slogans, most of which are positive spins watered down out of lies; and then there are those stories that we might never know, those that are told in hundreds and even thousands of languages, none of which have had positive enough experiences with the English language to do more than flinch at the sounds, thoughts, and activities that it generates. These are some of the undeniable aspects of the relationship that we have no choice but to accept as we enter into these new and yet very old Indigenous rainforests of the North Coast. As the bewildering mystery of this place is unquestionable, I imagine that this feeling will shadow me until I die.

Looking around, the trees and mountains all seem to stand pretty much as they did when I first saw them back in 1991, but over the last twenty years my own personal geography has been thoroughly revised by the extreme social, historical, and hydrological forces of the region that have been at work upon my conscience. While the frontier wilderness postcards of my Canadian youth got me this far, in light of all I have seen since then, they now seem cheap, imaginary, and destructive.

Ascending and hopefully descending to better understandings of ourselves and these lands, the way to the North Coast follows only a perfunctory route up and down Highway 16 and is made much more real when it takes us along a series of hard-knock thought-trundles through more than the spectacular gaps that rise within the dizzying treewalls of the sweeping rainforest. With even just a bit of sobering education, the mystery and bewilderment of this place can begin to reposition perspectives. Now, each glimpse of life thriving within every shade of unimaginable green is observed differently. Each giant, dripping upheaval of life and geography that plummets into view can carry us beyond our accepted, coherent descriptions of colour, scale, and form, rattling us into a place of humility that we have never before encountered. It is the Indigenous power of this place as a hypermaritime explosion of life that creates the kind of unique experiences that we encounter nowhere else, those that demolish levity and bring us, dizzy and quiet, beyond the previously accepted bearings of our wonder, leaving us to ask unknown questions of green out of indescribable stone and water. And it is often at this point that we discover within ourselves new perceptions of respect that we had previously been unable to imagine we were capable of, all because, before this moment, we were not.

Slowly, slower, my eyes breathe long breaths as these not-quite-unalterable mountains spin, enlarge, and distort, eventually turning their massive, scraped backs behind the tree- and lichen-crusted shoulders of their equally massive sisters and brothers. Truly, these enormous upheavals and protrusions of stone stand not entirely eternal but are actually always fidgeting, cracking, and crumbling, sliding around amongst themselves like children crammed into the back seat of a car. The Coastal range is actually lunging beyond itself, expanding upward with more than the phenomenon of postglacial rebound. Upwards, outwards, these mountains actually do grow larger with more than lack of understanding as we ourselves shrink to become a living idea momentarily whizzing along an auspicious asphalt thread, one that the mountains will someday lift, warp, crumble, and brush aside.

As our tiny white truck follows Highway 16 west, streaking by and streaked over with bursts and lines of colour where actual arthropods have met the windshield, my thoughts also colour with details from the history and recent news brought in upon these two small, opposing lanes of speed and mobility. Whether we notice it or not, we are all marked again and again by what limps away, flies, dashes, or is dumped beyond the denuded cut of this industrial right-of-way, this highway of tearing. It really is as poet Ken Belford writes: "These roads suck blood. / The better the highway / the worse it gets" (*Ecologue* 20). And I wonder: as the first Europeans arrived and were confronted with such overwhelmingly wild biologic, climactic, geographic, and Indigenous human power, did the subsequent increase in alien awe and confusion bring on a corollary retreat into fear and create the harsh sense of superiority that so many chose to embrace? Or did some of these righteous Christian devotees come here with this already in mind?

Admittedly, in the not-too-distant 1980s, I myself was living a dream of youthful exuberance and joy about my someday-life of immersion in "real wilderness," yet I recall what I have more recently read in Margaret Atwood's *Survival*, Northrop Frye's *The Bush Garden*, *Woodsmen of the West* by Martin Allerdale Grainger, and other books about perceptions of early Canada: those were dark, rugged times. From out of the literary wilderness that was Canada in the 1940s, Frye describes the poets of his era having an unusually exposed contact with nature, but this view of nature was as a vast and dark "unconsciousness" where humans cast within the wild zone lived "a kind of existence which is cruel and meaningless," and where the Wild itself was "the source of the cruelty and subconsciousness stampeding within the human mind" (141–42). As Frye interprets the psychologic flash point of his era's flinching literary conscience, he pronounces that if there are any positive glints of vision gleaming upon the literary frontier, they are a rare, recalcitrant bluster, typified by "a refusal to be bullied by space and time" and "an affirmation of the supremacy of intelligence and humanity over stupid power" (142). It seems that most of the poems Frye reviewed in those days were depressing versifications of suffering following the collapse of the European spirit in wartime, most often describing a misplaced spirit thrown mercilessly under the absolute brutality of the Canadian landscape.

Understanding that the 1940s were a particularly dark political and social period out of many preceding generations of dark times—these days, when anyone who has eyes, buttocks, hands, and feet can glide smoothly from gas station to gas station down Highway 16, smiling and even dozing in comfort through the now-subdued terrors of the mythic violent wilderness, the thought of so many historical acts of oppression and genocide can seem preposterous. But incidents of this kind were routine parts of the many extreme, tertiary activities of nation building and were passed off as growing pains while the vast timberlands were levelled and the cliffs were blasted down to manageable rip-rap for the construction of bridges, pack roads, and rail lines. Tough enough, the first colonialists and settlers of the North Coast were camped out within unmanageable fields of smouldering stumps, surrounded by drizzle, trying desperately to imagine a life that brought more than meagre foodstuffs to a raw plank table. Still, the policy and practice of human cultural erasure was a routine activity for many explorers and early government officials, as it was for later company employees and the waves of settlers who arrived by ship and rail throughout the early times of colonial expansion.

Denying or being ignorant of the Indigenous names that had persisted here for hundreds and thousands of years, European explorers gave new names to almost everything they encountered, presuming themselves to be entitled to take ownership of landscapes that God, within his grand design, had so generously set before them alone to discover and profit from. As Eliza R. Scidmore points out, this practice of colonial naming usually paid tribute to "some inconsequent and now forgotten statesman whom it seemed officially desirable to flatter at the time" (128). Scidmore's critical words of conscience might seem exceptional, coming as they do from 1896, but they demonstrate that we have not so much risen out of the social backwardness of the past through any amount of current social enlightenment but that we have always possessed the power of conscience to see and make ethical decisions about how we respect other peoples and their cultures.

Haysport, Cunningham Peak, Smith Island, Mount Elizabeth, Port Essington, Balmoral Peak, Kennedy Island, Mount Hayward, Inverness Passage: all representing blatant genuflection, these few out of the many ahistoricizations marked by map and road sign venerate not just a Canadian history of oppression and exploitation but also the illegal seizure of property, the denial of heritage, and direct cultural erasure. As they represent more than just the steamrolling force of capital and the leveraging of political power, at the local level these names are blatant acts of contempt and disrespect, not just for the families and individuals who lived at the time but for the memory of ancestors that reach back thousands of years, and also, importantly, these names work as a denigrating force within the lives of future generations, those whose origins and cultural history have been stripped away before they are even born. It may be difficult to consider this context today, as these European names continue to exist within the dignified history and official routine of Canadian life, yet it is important to realize that these are not just historical mistakes, as these names embody the contemporary perspective and law of the nation. As ongoing mechanisms of legal intimidation, these European names continue to repress and diminish, operating today under ubiquitous powers of nationalism, nostalgia, and conformity. I won't pretend to imagine how, from an Indigenous perspective, seeing foreign names posted everywhere across your people's territory might feel, especially considering recent federal government apologies for injustices of the past that have since had no follow-through with meaningful changes within federal policy. By the very fact that they persist at all, the European names that stand everywhere in their thousands across these Indigenous Storied Lands continue the insidious work of empire, pushing steadily forward to an imagined future of complete homogeneity and assimilation, a time when the original people of this land have all been either forgotten or extinguished.

Back on September 25, 2009, Canada's prime minister, Stephen Harper, was down in Pittsburgh for the 2009 G20 Summit. Throughout his address, he listed various reasons why Canada was the envy of other G20 nation-states. After giving numerous recently compiled statistics as long-standing facts to support his assertions, he closed with the eye-popping statement that "we also have no history of colonialism" (Ljunggren/Reuters). Absurd as this statement might be to the ethical historian, many good-hearted Canadians still hold their patriotic heads high as they commit their own similar acts, day by day, utilizing similar versions of this very kind of subtle, gentle ahistoricization. Indeed, there are many nationalistic "historical" societies that promote the fact that Lord such-and-such sent Crown representatives and governors all this way and is due the respect of having a mountain or a river or a valley named after him, because building a country up from nothing is hard work.

Today, the general response is that we have more important things to do than spend time and resources correcting the mistakes of the past, mistakes that were made many generations ago by people we have no connection to, people who just didn't know any better and were just doing their best. And so we sit, held within a congealed mass of complacency, distracted by our hockey games and other Canadian pastimes, which serves only to increase the scale and nature of our disgrace. We rationalize our way out of complicity by telling ourselves that whatever harm was done in history is excusable in light of the freedom, happiness, and prosperity we experience today.

The common view of Canada's appropriation and ownership of these Indigenous Storied Lands was that all of this formerly untouched and underutilized wilderness has now been progressively "improved." This was the official adjective used to describe both settler and industrial transformations of what was actually a much more sustainably managed landscape under the stewardship of First Nations people. Recently, while living in Rupert, I was having an online chat with a friend in the UK who was shocked to hear that this province is still called British Columbia. Still, as a small sign of hopeful changes, on December 11, 2009, just two months after Harper's blatant lie to the G20, the X̱aaydaa Council finalized negotiations for reclaiming their own original name of *X̱aaydaa Gwaay* for their historic homelands (CBC News). Now comes the unsavoury task of the BC government to actually break with old familiarity and stamp the original, traditional name upon its signs and documents, and without also attaching the colonial-era tag "Queen Charlotte Islands" (which was just the name of a colonial-era ship) before the inaccurate but accepted, anglicized form of "Haida Gwaii." I suppose that, for so many Canadians with names like Honomi Watanabe, François Léger, Tariq Zulfiqar, Gerður Mjølsnes, Jaswinder Singh, and Xingjian Tian, the words *X̱aaydaa Gwaay* must appear quite foreign.

And what of BC's colonial past? Whether they were businessmen, settlers, or labourers, many of the Europeans who came to the North Coast quickly, directly, and often silently dispossessed First Nations peoples of their lands, usually while the local people were off at their fish camps, smokehouses, weirs, or other distant seasonal locations where they undertook their cultural life. Either way, European settlers took over all the best sites for their own fast-growing communities and quickly applied for official land permits, which they promptly received, and when the families of Tsimshian, Gitx̱san, or various other groups returned in the late fall with loads of winter food stores, they found their homesites occupied and transformed by white strangers, all of whom were safely under the protection of the Queen's laws and the clockwork routine of RCMP patrols.

Historian William G. Robbins writes that this emigrant population "overran and pushed aside an already decimated native population," most usually from the most valuable lands, which were almost always the few ideal locations for settlement, either upon river terraces or protected within harbours along coastlines (317). Summarizing the polarized sensibilities of many new arrivals, Robbins adds that these European immigrants "imposed upon their freshly established homelands new bounds for reckoning the landscape, new definitions for natural phenomenon, and new perceptions about a common environment," views that were contained within "a commercial ethos that viewed the natural world in terms of its commodity potential" (317, 317–18).

Government initiatives developed quickly in order to legalize these otherwise illegal acts of seizure and theft into sanctioned policies of Canadian entitlement, policies that continue as normative behaviour to this day. As historian Margaret Ormsby points out, Governor Douglas created a land policy in the 1860s that allotted 160 acres to any British subject who would occupy and improve the land (quoted in McDonald and Joseph 199). And, as anthropologists McDonald and Joseph reveal, First Nations were disqualified from this privilege program and could claim no preemptive rights in response to their lost homes and lands (199). Gunboat diplomacy was also used on the North Coast as part of the government's socio-economic strategy for demonstrating who had more privilege and entitlement. Providing a show of force that was meant to intimidate the local chiefs, in 1872 two naval gunboats were sent into the delta of the Skeena, right up to the village of *Metlakatla* (198). This was in response to a transport blockade that was set up farther upriver by protesting groups of First Nations peoples after the village of *Gitsegukla*, with its twelve longhouses and twelve totem poles, was destroyed by a fire set by American prospectors who were idling on the riverbank while travelling through to the northern gold fields (ibid.).

As decades of settlement and development continued, First Nations did manage to become nominally involved in the canneries, logging shows, and other aspects of the new economy. By paying humiliating wages amidst a social agenda that included the open, pervasive denigration of First Nations cultures, many European settlers used both despicable and illegal strategies to dominate and control the socio-economic activity, thus maximizing their own profit-taking to the fullest while they diminished the economic health of local peoples (199). While not every European newcomer sought such unfair advantage, a general practice existed for limiting, disrupting, and negating the opportunities and prosperity of Indigenous peoples. But, as McDonald and Joseph reveal, none of the complex restrictions set down in terms of policy and regulation nor many of the oppressive social norms were passively accepted by local peoples (ibid.).

Even though most of us would rather reflect upon the past and remember something else—something *nice*—these colonial injustices continue, perpetuated today within the ever-complicating strata of Canadian Law, enacted each day across the country with numerous ordinary acts of repression, assimilation, and negation. Within recent years, Bill C-31 was legislated into being, first upon the promise of its ability to end discrimination against First Nations women who married non-Indigenous people. Yet hidden within the bill in section 6 are clauses that mean to continue to extinguish First Nations entitlement. This is achieved by the process of legislating status Indians out of existence by a more veiled means, in this case, when their children are born within circumstances of marriage that exclude them from the status of full-blooded heritage. Passed as it was into law by the Canadian government in 1985, Bill C-31 takes away even more than it was meant to give back, asserting on the one hand that it means to return rights and freedoms to First Nations women who married non-Indigenous people, while section 6 works counter to the spirit of this idea by stripping the status from particular categories of children born of marriages between status and non-status people. Bill C-31's real goal is to solve the Indian Problem once and for all, and it may very well succeed in doing so in just a few more generations (NWAC 3–4).

Despite the abuses and tragedies that continue today, First Nations cultures continue to thrive. And, almost unbelievably, there still exists within First Nations people some measure of hopeful persistence and a constant affirmation of the willingness to share. This was always the message that came down from the older generations, those that trusted a great deal in ideals of tolerance, patience, and justice. Today, however, the younger generation often states that they will no longer be as polite as their grandparents once were.

a path through forest is
contradictory:
timber-stands deny mere
wanderers,

devil's club and deadfall intruding, space con-
stricting, eye-dark and adderbright: moss hanging
    —W.H. New (2004)

plot D2

devil's club:
mental arrest
and healthy respect.

THE FIRST TIME I ENCOUNTERED DEVIL'S CLUB, I WAS REPELLED AS MUCH as I was captivated. This was out in the patchwork denudations of late-1980s clearcuts, plantations, and predominantly intact forest lands of the Morice River district, at the easternmost edge of the CWH zone. Together with the seemingly hostile characteristics of its prime habitat, devil's club (*Oplopanax horridus*) easily overwhelms all human thought and activity, whether with its sprawling spiny octopus limbs or the hidden water-filled holes and tangles of blowdown where it thrives. When you are in its company, you cannot help but be captivated, and this state of mind and being is a non-negotiable condition of this relationship. Literally, it will grasp you and alert you, often quite painfully, to its presence—which should best be interpreted as your personal intrusion into its home. At my first introduction, my self-absorbed greenhorn reaction was to categorize it as being overly aggressive. I felt as if I had stumbled accidentally into some drunken thug who was looking for a fight. But I soon began to think differently, realizing that there is no other plant quite like it in BC or all of temperate North America. Even now, after so many years, when I must flounder, duck, and dodge through its leaves and limbs, the only way I can approach devil's club is with respect.

This species does not allow people to rush about from place to place, and for good reason. Devil's club prefers to grow overtop, around, and amongst the toughest obstacle courses the forest has to offer. It entangles itself over the slipperiest rocks, obscures the mire of extensive sinkholes with its massive leaves, and provides a thick screen overtop of half-rotten crash courses of crisscrossing fallen logs. As *Oplopanax horridus* snakes its limbs up through the most inhospitable terrain, its giant leaves grow in such a way as to spread and interlock horizontally to form a closed canopy, raising up an impenetrable, spiny green ceiling that is often nearly impossible to see or move through. Despite the hazards of the terrain below, this horizontal, puzzle-form barrier will most often present itself either right in your face or down between your shoulders and knees, and, in some dizzying locations on the steepest ground, the unseen limbs of this interlocking green ceiling loop down for three to four metres and then climb back up for two or three metres, often blocking out the light, far above your head. When you reach to push one prickly limb out of the way or step upon one by mistake, three others swing in out of the periphery, and their painful spines penetrate your clothing and break off in the skin of your knees, thighs, arms, forehead, and, as many find out, often up between your legs. As you struggle to be free, the giant leaves rake back and forth across your face, sparking across your knuckles and elbows, your forearms, knees, and calves, giving repeated warnings of your stupidity in entering their realm. Quite often, devil's club will even splash you all the way awake with the cold water that has been collecting upon the broad platters of its upturned leaves, which can be thirty to fifty centimetres wide.

In the wilderness one's vision is enriched by abundant
curvilinear forms, but it is also threatened by them. There is
a genuine relief and assurance in the taut lines of the tent,
the crisp angles of a bridge, a road, even—if mildly lost—a
powerline cut.

—Don McKay (2001)

Devil's Club: *Oplopanax horridus* (J.E. Sm.) Miq. (view 1

ALONG THE ENTIRETY OF CASCADIA, FROM THE OREGON COAST TO THE
Gulf of Alaska, Indigenous peoples have as many different names for
devil's club as they do reasons to give this plant tremendous respect.
Where it grows, starting from flat estuary splays cropped with kneeling
angelica (*Angelica genuflexa*), northern rice root lily (*Fritillaria cams-
chatcensis*), and Lyngby's sedge (*Carex lyngbyei*), ts'iihllnjaaw (as it is
called by the Skidegate X̲aaydaa) entangles trees and fallen logs as it
grows, coiling its long arms downslope and ravelling its broad leaves
up and outward, forming dense communities near sea level that can
muster themselves all the way up to the harsh fringes of the subalpine (Turner *Plants* 153). At all elevations, *S'áxt'* (as it is called by the
Sitka Tlingit) dominates wet ground, rolling its prickly ginger hoses
over the roots of hemlock, alder, redcedar, black cottonwood (*Populus balsamifera*), spruce, and trembling aspen (*Populus tremuloides*),
coiling itself out basically anywhere a steady supply of water perco-
lates through acid soils, whether spilling down steep gorges of predominantly bare stone or crawling in slow, boggy percolations across
nearly level seepage lanes (Thornton 208). Over ephemeral drainages
choked with windthrow, *cukilanarpak* (as it is called by the *Alutiiq* of
Kodiak, one of the most northern peoples of the subpolar rainforest)

tends to crowd within a diverse community of thimbleberry (*Rubus parviflorus*), cow parsnip (*Heracleum lanatum*), goat's-beard (*Aruncus dioicus*), and fireweed (*Epilobium angustifolium*), where it still stands head and shoulders above the rest, where its leaves, stems, and roots perform the bulk of the heavy work, dispersing much of the otherwise erosive force of the torrential rainfall that comes down on the coast of Turtle Island (Alutiiq Museum). Along with the voracious colonizer red alder, *wa'umst* (as it is called by the Gitxsan) is one of the few plants strong enough to revegetate and stabilize the torn rubble of north-aspect avalanche chutes (Daly 148). And, strangely enough, in the summer of 2007, *qwa:pulhp* (as it is called by the Central Salish) brought me to a dead stop in my city sneakers when I found it in a neglected sidewalk garden at the unlikely urban debris slide of Fourteenth and St. George, growing as a renegade stray in the middle of the concrete sprawl of Metro Vancouver (SFU).

The City dreams of a balance.
Of finding land under its feet.
Of exchanging commodities that are not on fire.

—Tom Wayman (1973)

transect 6

wild triads,
the ecology of bad ideas,
water, and ancestral time.

STANDING WITH MY PARTNER LISA OUTSIDE THE SKEENA BAKERY IN New Hazelton, right beside Highway 16, we strain to hear the sounds of the Land over the drone of traffic. Heading toward Rupert, we are well past *Gyolugyet* of *Kyas Yax*, the House of *Woos*, one of the heritable territories of the Witsuwit'en, which is a beautiful landscape made up of broad valleys and sharp mountainous pitches, an area now occupied by the town of Smithers (Glavin *Death* 27). Today, from the highway, what you can see of this part of the House of *Woos* looks very Swiss-German and is as stereotypically Canadian as it gets.

But here, biogeoclimatically, about an hour and more northwest along the highway from Smithers, we have arrived on the brink of the warm-wet coastal influence and all that it reveals. Biogeopersonally, I have spent forty-plus years mentally and physically heading in this direction, with more than twenty-three of these years spent walking for a living in northern and coastal forests. In the much larger scheme of things, this is just a tiny bit of time, and yet a much smaller portion of my life has been spent within the hard-earned thoughtfulness of any kind of useful learning; like it or not, we all must put our heads down for part of each day and just do our jobs. But in this big, wet, green place, I did eventually find the means to unlearn many old, irrelevant ideas and learn a few Other, new-old things worth knowing. Along the way, I might imagine myself having become a bit of a devotee of the Northwest, and I might also presume that I am now ready for a Kaien Island winter, with all the weather that the Alaskan Gyre can bash out of Hecate Strait. We shall see.

Here at the tipping point of the Babine and Hazelton mountains, two strong climate systems are always surging against one another to see how much each might give: First, the coastal warm-wet streams in from the Pacific, overlapping and transforming the cold-dry of the interior system that is always pushing in from the northeast. Here, where the maritime and the continental meet, and, as many people will tell you as they shudder before the prospect of yet another winter "trapped" within this no-man's torrent of denigrating climate—wringing their hands, threatening to abandon the spouses who dragged them here— winter can be gloomy and oppressive, dreary and miserable, destructive and much worse. No matter how the complaint manifests itself, there's too much cloud and too much rain and not enough of whatever else is potentially happening everywhere else. Even the knowledge that another, less-drenched reality exists somewhere else can induce a complex of debilitating anxiety. I have also heard that the tourist zones of Mexico where many northern residents flee to are a lovely place this time of year (if you don't mind the heightened possibility of murder).

On any given day within the larger-than-human realm of the North Coast, tensions run from surly to giddy: saplings of high elevation conifers barely survive under the dense understory, and a young Sitka blacktail deer feeds on the plentiful blossoms of commercial ornamental shrubs in residential Prince Rupert. When we want to, we can impose our perception of duality upon both the Wild and ourselves: it's what humans do best. But both of the seemingly disparate realities are brought together into a whole within the study of *landscape ethnoecology*, which is a perspective that engages in qualitative surveys within the overlapping complex of the human influence upon the larger-than-human and the influence of the larger-than-human upon the human. Landscape ethnoecology is an investigative sphere within academic geography that can be described as the process of taking the geopolitical temperature of a particular place and all that it constitutes, influences, and affects. This is quite different from studying a place from an anthropocentric or utilitarian perspective, where there is the Western, enlightened human being and the rest of the world always far beneath, in one way or another.

Under the draconian vision of recent governments in both BC and Canada at large, a dualistic, utilitarian view has become the preferred device for gauging outcomes and legislating new policies, leading to an increase in underscrutinized and unregulated practices, whereby industrial activities seek the quickest, most "efficient" means for accelerating intense transformations of wild and human communities. With the federal government's omnibus bills and the large-scale dismissal of over two thousand scientists over the last few years—most of whom were employed in the sphere of the environment—the dearth of critical oversight increases as the potential for future problems expands, exponentially.

If we consider the world we will be leaving behind, not just for future generations of human beings but for the larger-than-human systems that sustain life, we must embrace the challenge of accepting a deeper vision and consider the depth of theoretic practices like landscape ethnoecology, and then find the political will and social courage to adopt management policies that do not address the immediate bottom line. As geographer Monica Turner tells us, landscape ecology undertakes critical investigations of relationships that occur in a place within a comprehensive, interdisciplinary frame (173). Ideally, landscape ethnoecology gathers together the fullest possible breadth of perspectives—it intends to be a system of forensic consideration, sensitive to the influences and interfaces of the diversity of both wild and human structures and their overlapping functions.

What this means for an individual living here on the North Coast is that, despite the frustration that salal, devil's club, and many other plants create for us with the nearly impenetrable barriers of their tangled communities, the will and courage we require to respect their vital necessity must not be as short as our ability to stagger across the rainforest floor in an to attempt to meet and understand them where they grow. These are both human tasks on the order of the superorganic.

Positivist psychology would lead us to imagine that the colonialists, immigrants, and nomadic job seekers of BC's history have all done their best to build a new life for themselves in the New World. And for some, this is indeed true. But if most of the newcomers had actually tried to fit in, perhaps we'd all be living in some technologically updated version or another of a longhouse or a pithouse, and perhaps we'd be working through the seasonal routines, harvesting in the berry fields, attending the salmon rivers, sharing these tasks along with our Aboriginal sisters and brothers, as well as potlatching and feasting through the winter. Instead of complaining about the terrible weather, we might have learned to rejoice as well as endure. But history and our own open-eyed experience reveal that most of the newcomers actually chose instead to reconstruct as much of their old ways of life as possible. Understandably, these reactions were undertaken mostly in order to combat symptoms of homesickness, alienation, fear, harsh environmental resistance, and various other conditions that are generated within cycles of intense culture shock.

All of the various problems of cultural collision can become contaminants, not just within local human cultures but within the larger-than-human communities. These resonances of interspecies damage and their downstream effect are investigated by social theorist Gregory Bateson within what he calls the "ecology of bad ideas" (484). As heedless consumerism continues to disrupt so many Indigenous and larger-than-human ways of being, it becomes ever more important that we come to understand the diverse and subtle ways in which our mainstream habits of consumption and living the good life negatively affect the diversity and integrity of both local and global systems.

As industrialization continues to expand, its trickle-down effects continue to disperse and compound, not just over time with various detectable signs (such as water pollution, deforestation, and decreasing biodiversity) but with the exacerbation of landscape, plant, and animal equivalents of "psychological" problems. In response, Indigenous communities of people and the Wild must work harder to compensate, in addition to the Real Work they already perform in order to maintain the delicate balance of their lives. Often, Indigenous communities must find new methods to re-emplace themselves within their disrupted environments while they attempt to repair damages that are psychic as much as material. As the participatory components of an ongoing, regenerative, reciprocal forum that Bateson calls the "wider eco-mental system," even here, within the wild complexity of the North Coast relationship, many Indigenous systems have been working and continue to work intensely and usually wholly unnoticed within the assimilatory forces of Canadian culture and its mechanisms of industrialization (ibid.).

Briefly, the eco-mental system is made up of all of the deeply connected communities of the Indigenous Wild and the means by which they communicate and regulate their health and well-being; it also includes the activities and effects of the human concept and practice of interbeing. As well, the wider eco-mental system also includes quantifiable material processes, such as the biologic integrity of biotic systems. Importantly, the wider eco-mental system includes all of the introduced forces that negatively influence it, such as the disruptive human activity, perceptions, and values we hold that allow such activities to occur. In its way, the wider eco-mental system is like a Western, academic vision of kincentric philosophy. At the very least, its scope, its acceptance of interconnectivity, and its long-term view bring us as close to thinking about the trees, streams, soils, and skies as beloved and respected members of our families as any concept we have on hand.

Within such a vast, wild, and powerful place as the North Coast, it might be difficult to accept that a great many wild communities experience struggle. When we grasp that the wider eco-mental system does not operate with the same short-term intentions, quick exit strategies, and transformative capabilities as our own lives that are geared to operate by the forces of heavy industry—forces that work *against* the natural revolution of the earth itself—we begin to see that only those processes that are truly wild and Indigenous, in both theory and practice, work fluidly in the same direction, intention, and revolution of the earth. This is, as we already know, the direction that seeks to grow and thrive by means that are healthy, civilized, and true. And, as we shall find out, to be "true" is, both etymologically and literally, to behave like a tree.

If we set up our new home on the brunt tear of a wild coastline, or if we go snowmobiling in the alpine at the peak of avalanche season (as many do), and if we support large-scale industrial transformations of watersheds and landscapes by living lifestyles that encourage these activities, more and more of this ecological destruction is due to our choices and should become our own personal responsibility. As some of the most devastating effects of industrialization and our own lifestyle choices reach beyond our lives in both the short and the long term, these ecological stresses can be considered the "psychological problems" of the wider eco-mental system; and when we grasp and accept this concept, we diminish the distinction between larger-than-human and human systems.

Considering the ecology of bad ideas, the largest human tragedies we can point to on BC's North Coast are those that have been experienced by First Nations peoples. In some cases more than 80 percent of the population was killed by smallpox and other introduced diseases. This alien biological destruction swept up and down the coast and into the interior with mysterious waves of death that, at the time, were blamed upon numerous spiritual, social, and psychological failures. The majority of all First Nations villages were emptied, up and down the coast, and the ruins of many of them remain, crumbling and rotting, being slowly reclaimed by the rainforest. At the time, the few who survived were forced to either consolidate into the few remaining cultural centres that could find and shelter them, or else assimilate within the expansion and boom of the many new Euro-Canadian towns. Considering the wider eco-mental system, Bateson reveals a detail that turns out to be a rather luminous, new-old concept: that the environment itself is a layer or parallel entity of conscious mind, that it is a presence of intelligence, decision, and activity, one that exists in resistance to the conceptual duality we impose within the human and the larger-than-human world. In our case, this is a conflict between the short-term goals of a noxious alien invasive and the long-term presence of a diversity of sustainable Indigenous communities.

Bateson tells us that, just as human individuals can be "driven insane," this same "insanity is incorporated in the larger eco-mental system of thought and experience," which is represented in concrete terms within the functional systems of biotic life that link the human and the larger-than-human together (ibid.). As people live out the intense, seemingly crazed tempos of their lives, mental and material pollutions spread. Wild communities, human families, and various individuals become poisoned in body and spirit. People are estranged from one another, humans become estranged from the Wild, and, although we often fail to recognize it, the Wild becomes fragmented and estranged from itself.

The means by which complex natural processes can be negatively affected are often roundabout in material sequence but are often readily discernible in concept and practical detail. Currently, here on the North Coast, there are fewer scientists employed to provide objective oversight and assessment of the impact of human activities, while many who remain serve the federal mandate of accelerating and streamlining industrial development. Within a situation where increasing deregulation privileges the expediency of resource development at the expense of assessing environmental health, and, with the future possibility of pipelines, supertankers, and liquefied natural gas plants coming into the region, the ecology of bad ideas may increase substantially, rippling like a disease brought in by a noxious alien invasive species.

In the coming years, the wider eco-mental system of the Storied Lands of the X̱aaydaa, the Tsimshian, the Gitx̱san, the Nisga'a, the Heiltsuk, the Haisla, the Tahltan, the Tlingit, and all of the other groups face an increasing risk of further neglect, abuse, and environmental degradation—which will, undoubtedly, harm us all.

≈

Near Highway 16, Lisa and I stand and listen in front of the Skeena Bakery in New Hazelton, watching reflections of traffic flash by upon the surfaces of rain-filled potholes. We wait with anticipation, curiosity, and more questions. Do we have much more than an illusion of what we are doing here, and why, and of how we should behave? Do we realize that there are so many local laws and protocols tied to aspects of life that are thousands and thousands of years old? Are we capable of adapting to a new-old set of foreign variables, principles, and paradigms, all of which add up to a strange system that may make very little sense for quite some time? Are we capable of considering what we are getting ourselves into? Or, is it good enough to just wing it and let the chips fall where they may? Can we proceed with a new life as we lived our old one? What about an ecology of good ideas?

Of course, such a thing has always existed, as healthy life is the avocation of the world. From the perspective of ecological science, the region around New Hazelton is a unique intersection of three major biogeoclimactic zones: the Coast, the Interior, and the North (or Boreal). All three converge up *Xsitxemsem* (the Nass River) somewhere in the vicinity of Meziadin. For Indigenous peoples, there are many other important and well-known conjunctions that highlight the fact that this region has long been a valuable and diverse locus for personal, community, larger-than-human, and numerous geographic values—all of which are retained in trust and safekeeping within the traditional territories of many groups. And the Canadian entitlement of Highway 16 cuts across it all. The asphalt follows the riverbanks wherever possible, climbing mountains as it must. As much as we all live here, fundamentally, Highway 16 is the access route for a multitude of Canadian and international industries and the transport system for the workers and raw materials required to operate them. Finished in the fall of 1944, the "Hirohito Highway" was originally a US military venture that meant to provide an alternate route along the Skeena if extreme weather events (or an imagined Japanese invasion) cut off the rail line to the coast.

In the crosshairs of the Hazeltons, Highway 16 is also the propulsion system for an expanding variety of foreign cultures and religions, all of which channel into the already swollen cultural seams of a wild geography where three distinct First Nations cultures have long been triangulated in a relative and sometimes strained cohesion. Having lived at much higher population levels in the past than they do today and yet with much less transformative impact upon the larger-than-human realm, First Nations cultures survived and thrived within the pragmatic bounds of sustainable subsistence economies under the cultural guidance of TEKW. These complex systems of local science utilized as much of the wild landscape and its gifts as was feasible within the capacity and capability of the rainforest, coastline, and ocean, always considering only the seasonal requirements of village populations. Over time, Russian fur traders, European explorers, British colonists, and eventually contemporary Canadians arrived, and the earlier balanced equation of Indigenous supply and Indigenous demand has quickly become overcomplicated and overburdened by the large-scale global export of local products.

Although I admit to having been about as much of a greenhorn as is possible, under the shadow of *Stikyoo'denhl*, Mount Rocher de Boule, I must be fooling myself when I imagine that we can stop and comprehend the depth of our impact as we live out our daily lives. I can only crouch at the roadside and wonder, observe, and listen, hoping for the boldest of North Coast stereotypes to reveal themselves out of the understory of their overstory, here at the cut edge of what I presume is an Indigenous forest, sprawling off in every direction through dripping green. While the Hazeltons possess a milder and moister climate than the drier and much colder sub-boreal zone just a few highway hours east, they still receive half as much rain and twice as much frost as the outer coast. One small and amazing thing I learned recently is that the forest lands of the Hazeltons gather together all three complexes of different species that live elsewhere in their more distinct communities: those from the warm, wet outer coast; those from the colder, drier sub-boreal of the interior; and those from up in the even colder boreal zone of the north. Although it isn't obvious to most people when they drive by, the Hazeltons and surrounding area are an important meeting place for numerous cultures, climates, and biologies.

Back in 2008, just west of *Kitwanga*, not far from *Wii Sg'anist*, "Big Mountain" (one of the Seven Sisters), I was excited to find that I could walk into the edge of the forest and pick not just black huckleberries but also Alaskan blueberries *and* red huckleberries, all from the same site, which was just some random point where I had stumbled in off the highway (34). Here they were: the Three Sisters of North Coast berries, one example of so many triads that do not occur in the north, the west, or the east. But here, all I had to do was kneel, crouch, stand, and always reach, as all three of these related but usually geographically distinct plants were growing together in stratified layers. The black huckleberries were lowest down, growing right above the moss and up to knee high. The blueberries were next, from knee to breast height, and the red huckleberries stretched above, from shoulder height to higher than you could reach, stopping just under the lowest branches of the hemlock and cedar. And, of course, all of this wild bounty hung with droplets from a recent August rain, and all were delicious.

Later: crouching, sitting, and sometimes standing at my desk, I see that we are often met with expressions of seemingly impossible possibilities. For me, one is the personal choice to find ways to start and continue thinking by dissident means, to find energy and the way to keep writing, and to somehow find a way to keep a roof over our heads.

Although it is just one method, thinking and writing is one small means by which we can all begin to revise our sense of community and actually build a new culture of experience and lifelong learning, one where we can all engage with processes that can eradicate the ecology of bad ideas.

Social theorists Deleuze and Guattari investigate this possibility as practice, urging us to create a new-old community and societal assemblage as part of the cultural process and activity of *rhizomatics*. This idea comes straight from the ground. In some varieties of plants, the rhizome is not just a kind of root and is also not just a vegetative outgrowth; as well, the rhizome is not only an energy sink for periods of dormancy; a rhizome is all of these things, depending on what conditions demand of it by season or the moment. As root, stem, and vegetation all at once, a rhizome is the structural and mechanical form of plant physiology that does what is biotically necessary and knows what makes the most ecologic sense, not only at the moment but for the long term. A rhizome works in this way to best fulfill the individual thriving of the plant within the often wildly fluctuating circumstances of the habitat within which it grows.

Deleuze and Guattari take the biological processes of the rhizome and bring these as ideas to transform human thought and action. Considering the accumulated knowledge formations of sustainable eco-logic we have access to from science and the energy potential of individual creativity, there is the potential to reform both our cultural and industrial systems. This can start with the thoughts and activities of just one person as they undertake new and equitable partnerships. On the North Coast, we can draw this together with what we know about wild ecology and Real Work, along with a large degree of personal sensitivity, and thus bridge our thoughts and activities with lessons provided by the TEKW experiences of First Nations and their land-embedded concepts of *being* and *dwelling* (ideas that will be explained soon), also utilizing the sustainable, health-giving elements of knowledge and experience that Western society already has to share (of which there are many).

The broadly interdisciplinary engagement of rhizomatics that Deleuze and Guattari refer to is a cultural assemblage, one where human acts of thinking, writing, and activity reflect and practise the health-giving principles within the tripartite relationships outlined at the beginning. Again, these are the three most distinct communities of the North Coast: the Indigenous Wild, First Nations peoples and their experience, and the cultural complex of both assimilated and immigrant Canadians. And it is important to remember that these communities are as materially permeable as they are conceptually distinct: We have the conservative and the restrictive, those who are considerably well interconnected, and those who are always ready at the drop of a leaf or a phrase to get busy and start anew. All of the players of the North Coast triad are spectral expressions and influential elements of landscape ethnoecology and they all represent the eco-mental system as a whole. All of these individuals, whether they be Steller's jays, school children, mill workers, drops of water, moss-covered stones, conifer trees, mink, or salmon, are also, unfortunately, equally subject to negative influences from the nearly ubiquitous ecology of bad ideas.

Rhizomatic assemblage is first a local activity; it is a personal means for taking responsibility within the larger community, however broad the perception. What follows can be any degree of communal and individual engagement, with potential rippling beyond through any number of activities. Within the plant world, the rhizome can thrive only because of various conditions and influences within its interconnected community, just as any real change or growth in human life and community requires personal activities that have impact beyond themselves. Even though strong-rooted, institutional forms like old-growth conifer trees or federal governments play important roles in directing and managing the economies of communities, the existence of the many smaller and often largely unnoticed elements of daily life are key to the health of the whole.

Important effects can even be initiated by the simplest act that provokes thought, which can lead to others taking an active participation.

One example for us is the compulsion to become involved with the various philosophical, mystical, political, ethical, and moral systems of Canadian life, and, more importantly, our desire to engage with the many new systems that are created, day by day—through friendships, work relationships, technological ideas, and education—all of which contain potential to open the seeds of eyes and minds.

Although it may seem a strange comparison, I propose that the thoughtful and emotional threads of human life all find their representations within the Wild, most particularly within the complex, interconnected societies of fungal mycelia. Just as human communication, understanding, belief, and duty in conceptual spheres of religion, politics, philosophy, and love are vital to the health of human society, the highly connective and incredibly subtle activities of fungal mycelia are as important to the "psychological" health of the forest as they are key to its biological integrity.

Within the Indigenous rainforest, the ideas of "sensitivity" and "connectivity" do not mean that a spawning salmon is not also dragged out of a stream by its head and eaten alive by a bear that is hungry for marine-derived lipids. We must retain a pragmatic understanding of life and death within the interconnectedness of the Real Work of the Wild: these are qualities that are necessarily red, visceral, and messy. The fact is that the seeming random violence of the night-fishing bear, as it drags its way in and out of the salmon stream, with its chaotic dispersal of mainly uneaten carcasses throughout the riparian zone, works as an important nutrient input for the long-term health of the zone. Similarly, any human process of rhizomatic assemblage must discern, realize, and accept what does and does *not* make eco-logical sense, and our intuition is not the only magnet we need to follow as we discern what *is* and what *is not* ethically sound. Hopefully we can also knuckle down and perform the difficult math equations and take the time to consider the many unpalatable concepts, giving them as much of our unflinching conviction as the Sitka blacktail deer who must sleep outside in the driving sleet of winter and then, in the morning, get up and pick through the roadside garbage for the windblown food of torn old-growth lichens. While the deer must concern itself with survival on a daily basis, this is hardly a daily problem for human beings. Instead, we have ethical choices to make about the survival of so many others. We have to discover what it takes to truly live.

Human participants in the philosophy of cultural rhizomatics must engage more knowledgeably, weighing conflicting values about needs and wants with a critical eye, acting appropriately in consideration of so many potentially unforeseeable outcomes. Moment to moment, participation in Real Work requires a fundamental baseline of eco-logic, with appropriate shifts in our values and lifestyle choices as both local and global natural systems require; then, we work to maintain these habits until they become new patterns in our life, where we hold fast to certain and sometimes uncomfortable duties as required for long-term benefits. The human player who is conscious of the wider eco-mental system and who lives responsively to a rhizomatic means of cultural assemblage is always keeping the protection of evolutive processes in the front and centre of thought, activity, and consequence.

Considering these ideas of sensitivity, knowledge, and participatism while we stand here in the parking lot of the Skeena Bakery, Lisa and I are entirely surrounded by what seem to be more rain puddles than gravel across the surface of the road. This obvious but easily overlooked detail reveals what gives, changes, and yet what always stays the same on the North Coast. A great deal of knowledge and wealth moves in and around this quiet, seemingly impoverished, isolated, and sparsely populated land, and water is the dominant catalyst. Water slides in so many directions around and through the relatively open structure of the Babine and Hazelton Mountains. As more than just the essence of life, water tumbles and rushes at the behest of gravity around so many massive upright structures, each of which warps and folds and opens again with heights of almost immoveable stone, objects that are open gates as much as solid barriers. As they contain and release so much of the biotic, climatic, and physical variations of wealth and knowledge within communities like *Kitwancool,* Moricetown, *Kitwanga,* the Hazeltons, *Gitlaxt'aamiks, Gitanyo,* Fort Babine and *Anspayaxw,* the waters that move through these Gitx̱san, Nisga'a, and Witsuwit'en Storied Lands drench the region into one long transition zone of interior, coastal, and northern ecosystems. The mountains themselves are the zigzagging thought troughs through which all things of relevance divide, tipping either westward down 'Ksan within what Roy Henry Vickers calls "the juice of the clouds," the Skeena River, or else trickling eastward into and eventually down the Fraser River, winding all the way east and south to Metro Vancouver (8).

Grasping these wettest handfuls of ground-truth, ecoforester Herb Hammond tells us that "water connects all aspects of a forest" and that "plants use water from the atmosphere and soil for cooling, for photosynthesis, and for other growth processes" (104). Water transports minerals and nutrients from the soil for all aspects of life, while "the forest acts as a sponge and filter that slowly releases pure water through the soil, into creeks, and into the atmosphere" (ibid.). Hammond tells us that during storms, millions of litres of water descend upon the landscape in a great multitude of energy, force, and essence, most of which the forest deflects, absorbs, and transforms, dispersing it more slowly within itself and into streams and rivers, where most of it drains by roundabout means down to the Pacific (ibid.). Here in the Hazeltons, standing by the highway amidst so much coming and going of life essence, it is bewildering in and of itself to just stand and adventitiously drip and dream, as so many others have done before—the trees and the birds, the plants and the lichen, the people and the fish, the mountains and the clouds.

This might be a very wild and perhumid place, yet this is also a place where so many people hold their own new-old ideas for much-needed change, where so many ancient communities and families still stand, remembering that water is wealth and life, that water is an elusive power always moving quickly away and yet always present, just as poet Lisa Robertson glimpses and blinks: "There as well as here streams sifts chops up spits out twists passes and too remains" (5). While I am transported in my own flimsy, culturally misguided, immigrant Canadian version of recognition—standing here in rubber boots beside a highway above a river in Gitxsan territory—there are always more and more opportunities to recognize the value of wild processes and the cyclical time that gives and gives as it shows itself everywhere, right now, within every kind and through each body of water.

This takes us to the concept of ancestral time, which can be found anywhere in the simple witness of water itself: always flowing away and yet always returning to its distant upland headwaters—water reforming from the ether of sky to drip down small green branches and percolate over and through depths of soil and stone—water regathering and flowing away again and again, covering everything everywhere, all the time. This is how Sherman Alexie writes about time—existing as cyclically as water: "See, it is always now. That's what Indian time is. The past, the future, all of it is wrapped up in the now" (22). Just as water reappears to disappear, anadromous salmon also migrate upstream to die every year amidst great flows that, like themselves, start as single trickles wriggling in the shallows upstream. It's the same concept as a giant conifer tree starting out as a tiny, single-winged seed that floats in a spiral down from the canopy, sprouts, grows for hundreds of years, is knocked down by a wind, dies, and slowly changes its wood back into soil, initiating this process all over again. If only we saw ourselves the same way. These ideas as concrete actualities are another living principle within the North Coast's version of ancestral time—that which is always leaving and yet miraculously returning—here, there, and somehow ever present, perhumid, green, ancient, and ephemeral, and always *now*. Holding these ideas as firm ideals is a good way to think about an ecology of good ideas.

Back on Highway 16, as we head west on and on through the transition zones that stretch to Rupert, Lisa and I bewilder over more sky, road, and riverside observations. And, as we go, we grasp for more tree-root, rhizomatic, and mycelial notions out of the biologic, geologic, and climatic transformations of the rainforests that continue to alter their structures along our route. To the south: more and more dangling of serpentine tops. To the north: the drooping wings of elegant, fine-leaved branches. Now the hemlock and redcedar have begun to rise and crowd in amongst the lodgepole pine, aspen, and hybrid spruce. The species composition and the very forms of the trees themselves bend and sway in adaptive response as more and more moderate climate meets more and more immoderate terrain. Blunt, sturdy, and spare, interior species are exactly as they must be in order to survive and thrive. The short-limbed pine and hybrid spruce of the east receive ample sun in the summer and have evolved to bear consistent levels of dry snow, finding optimal patterns of growth in wide-open stands within the much colder, drier lands of the interior. By contrast, coastal species sweep and curve long limbs to flex and shed heavy downpours under quick accumulations of rain-heavy snow. With their flexible whip tops and long, drooping branches, both redcedar and hemlock have developed small, pliant needles or reptilian scales that do not grasp onto snow as a potential future water source, as do interior species. And, within the dense, long-lasting cloud and fog they experience, their branches reach out to touch one another and spread wide, as they live within a strong competition for light. Drought and heat. Dry and moderate. Dry cold. Cold and dry, thin and frozen. Wetter, warmer, wetter. Moderate, warmer, wetter. Wettest. Warmest. Wet.

If only I could suss the story
of every patchy soil or soul
and beyond belief, not be
another brain-born stem
buttressed up on roots, but
be better, and come up
with some sort of way out
of competition. I'd agree
to disagree and become
an individual and evolve,
and give ground and place,
and fade away to shade.

—Ken Belford (2012)

Blue Chanterelle: *Polyozellus multiplex* (Under.) Murr. (view 1

BLUE CHANTERELLES ARE NOT ALWAYS BLUE AND ARE ALSO NOT NECESsarily chanterelles. *Polyozellus multiplex* has a nomadic taxonomical history and has been shuffled from fungal group to fungal group since it was first documented in North America (in Maine) by Lucien M. Underwood in 1899 (Imazeki 555). As a recently adopted member of the larger *Thelephoraceae* family (the leathery earthfans), *Polyozellus* is unique with its single species, one that still doesn't quite fit anywhere.

Mycologist Alexander Smith describes *Polyozellus* as I have stumbled upon them: frosted (glaucous) blue to deep blue, with crowded, veinlike gills (30). Duane Sept gives his own view of their appearance, which I have also seen, here and there, hidden in the moss: on the dorsal side, a deep violet to bluish black, smooth, with a wavy margin; on the ventral side, purple, with a "bloom" (55). This bloom is a powderlike covering, similar to that which you see on a plum or a grape. In the case of blue chanterelles it is partly a dusting of spores and partly the stuff of forest magick. Gary Lincoff tells us that the fruiting bodies of blue chanterelles form into many dull purple to purplish grey caps with veined undersides that are usually fan- to spoon-shaped (444). David Arora writes that blue chanterelles have primitive, very shallow, blunt gills running down the stalk, and that in coastal Alaska they are jet black, with a dark grey underside, while in the Rocky Mountains they are most often deep blue or violet tinged (22). Over the years I have observed that if the fruiting process (which may take many weeks with this species) occurs during a period without rain, the mushrooms will start out bright blue and become more complex and vivid in their coloration over time, eventually changing to bright violet and taking on elements of silvery or brassy gold (which is partly due to the heavy accumulation of spores). But if blue chanterelles fruit in a period of constant or even intermittent rain (as is most often the case in the fall for southeast Alaska and the North Coast of BC), the sporocarps will appear dark blackish blue or blackish purple. The reason for this different appearance is that rainfall washes away all of the brightly coloured flock, thus removing the silvery blue or purple-gold layers, revealing the unadorned, normally dark quality of their flesh. There certainly are distinct variations within the species—some are bright blue and some are black, while in Korea they are even a leaden grey—but unlike most other mushrooms, blue chanterelles are dramatically transformed by their own spore accumulation and the different effects of dry and wet weather.

But there is one detail that is accepted as true—that blue chanterelles are universally scarce. Alexander H. Smith writes that they are found only in the Pacific Northwest, but in this case his myopic observations reveal a neglect of Imazeki's much earlier text (30). In fact, *Polyozellus* have been found hiding out in the moss under old-growth spruce and true fir in Quebec forests as far back as 1937; they have been documented in Newfoundland and Colorado, and they will likely keep bursting from rain-soaked Septembers in many more remote, ideal, high-elevation habitats throughout the temperate world. But my Swedish field guide—Olof Andersson's *Lömskt och Läckert*— does not include the species, which is not a surprise if we consider the limitations dictated by the fragmented land masses of Europe. But it is hardly surprising to discover that blue chanterelles are spiralling up in tiny, purple-black hyperbolic planes out of the coniferous undermosses of remote forests in northern Korea and China, where they are still every bit as secretive as they are on the North Coast, but where they are also quite well known to researchers. Of course, blue chanterelles are also found in Japan, where they are called *Karasu-take* or *Kara-su-maitake*, named after the location where they were first documented by mycologist Tashiro in 1910, high within the misty temperate rain-forests of Crow Mountain (Imazeki 555).

Languages mould themselves to a particular place; their
vocabulary and cadences harmonize with the surrounding
landscapes, often embodying unique nuances and reflecting
meanings incapable of translation.
　　　—Nancy J. Turner (2005)

transect 7

rainforest magic:
blue trees, the Purkinje effect,
and the social network of fungi.

A CRISP DAY IN LATE SEPTEMBER, TIMBER CRUISING NORTHWEST OF
Babine Lake in a very old stand dominated by late-succession hybrid
spruce and subalpine fir. This was the closest I had been to the tran-
sition/conjunction zone of coastal and interior climates all year, and
this forest was the greenest I had seen in some time. As late after-
noon approached, the heavily diffused light under the humidity of the
north-facing slope had transformed to illuminate the otherwise normal
brownish grey tone of the conifer boles so that they glowed with an
extraordinarily rich blue-grey cast—a striking phenomenon that I
have witnessed to this degree only a handful of times. Known as the
Purkinje effect or *Purkinje shift,* this arresting optical curiosity was first
investigated in 1819 by the Czech anatomist Jan Evangelista Purkyně.
Up here, in this forest at this time of day, just as Purkyně described in
his study, the blue-green light-sensitive rods of my eyes had taken over
visual duties from the yellow light-sensitive cones, those that require
more intense light (Wade and Brožek 13). In actuality, this wet, dark,
north-facing forest was so green it was blue.

　　Well before this visual trick revealed itself, I had been making mental notes about the startling variety of fungi: *Russula, Cortinarius, Tricholoma, Hydnellum, Agaricus, Clavariadelphus, Sarcodon, Thelephora, Lactarius, Chlorociboria,* and more, everywhere underfoot. As he hauled away on the one-hundred-metre tight chain, Kasper (my young Swiss jakeyman) had compassed ahead and in typical Swiss fashion was using his hatchet to clear out the branches for a nice and neat plot centre. This was a low-light stand and not just because of the variety of thick-limbed conifers overhead. These spruce, true fir, and pine comprised a broad range of ages, yet there was something else that the average forester wouldn't have paid much attention to, something underground that showed itself with various small clues above ground. I was still a distance behind Kaspar, walking up the tight chain, taking stand composition notes along the traverse line. But everything stopped when I saw *them* down in the damp forest floor. Blue chanterelles. I gave a whoop, shucked off my cruiser's vest, and genuflected with joy. Kaspar stood back with hatchet in hand and smirked at yet another eccentricity.

Whether they are true chanterelles or not, *Polyozellus multiplex* are also mycorrhizals (myco = mushroom; rhizal = roots), a variety of fungi that forms mutually beneficial underground relationships in its communities with particular associate tree and plant species. As mycologist Nicholas P. Money tells us, these associates are often phylogenetically linked to one another's biotic requirements—this means that they have evolved in association with one another, in some cases for many thousands or even millions of years (59). Here, just under moss, the electrical communication systems of mycorrhizal fungi support an intense barter economy as well as serving to manage thousands of reciprocal exchanges within the communities that exist within the topmost layers of forest soils. Within this arrangement of thriving, fungal mycelia maintain complex systems that stretch over great distances from tree to plant to shrub to bacteria to microbe to water to rotting wood and back, and all through a tiny physical relay network of roots, microbes, bacteria, and hyphae that is one cell thick.

Hyphae are both the largest masses and the smallest components of fungal growth: they are composed of fine white hairs that stretch in vast colonies of streaming filaments to connect with one another and other organisms at the level of the single cell. Hyphae branch and spread like river deltas and organize themselves into the parallel threads of fence- and railway-line patterns, creating dense mazes that crisscross above and below other streams of hyphae. Although most of these hyphae networks are hidden within the decomposing matter of the forest floor, you can also find hyphae streaming vertically up and down under the bark of dead standing trees or even within thick moss on the largest of the uppermost branches of old-growth trees. The unbelievably long web and lace structures of mycelia engage with trees in two ways: by creating tiny sheath connections around the outer surface of the growing roots of *partners*, or by invading the interior root cells of *hosts* (Stamets 24). In both of these mutualistic relation-ships, where "neither partner can thrive without the other," there are large and fundamental increases in both water transpiration and the ingestion of essential nutrients and elements like phosphorus, copper, and zinc (Money, Stamets 19). On the North Coast, in order to thrive, fungi must create long-term, sustainable relationships with a diverse range of tree, plant, insect, bacterial, and microbial partners across the breadth of a field of highly acidic, nutrient-poor soils. Fungi can extract otherwise unobtainable inorganic compounds such as calcium and magnesium for use by their plant associates by using their minute hyphae to slowly penetrate and break apart rocks; and, after they have transported the nutrients, they extract and transfer carbohydrates they need for their own food from their plant partners (Money). In this kind of relationship, survival of the fittest reaches out with communi-cation, barter exchange, and cooperation—resulting in the health of the entire community.

The transport systems of water and minerals that fungi create also function as regulatory mechanisms of balance and supply to numer-ous species simultaneously over large distances. In ideal situations, the hyphae of mycorrhizal fungi envelop hundreds and even thousands of hectares together in continuous, broad-ranging networks of cells that share biotic information along white matrices that are extremely fragile yet extraordinarily adaptive. The hyphae of mycorrhizal fungi stitch themselves together throughout the forest floor in order to associate and exchange with hundreds of species throughout the greater community (Stamets 24–26). Importantly, these vital activities happen at much higher rates than would occur without these associations, and these connections themselves also extend over greater distances along the length of a multitude of healthier root systems within a multitude of healthier species. The increased root growth of associate species also enables fungi to access a greater breadth of woody debris for decomposition, as a cooperative system enables fungi to access and infiltrate a broader range of elements within the matrix of the forest floor. All of this Real Work of the Wild is happening actively, everywhere, all the time, mostly hidden under moss, at least until conditions are right for fruiting bodies to burst into air, which happens for only a few weeks or even a few days of the year (Stamets 24).

To give an indication of their profusion and propensity for infiltrating soil, in a typical forest habitat, fungi outnumber plants at a ratio of six to one. While a casual glance may reveal almost no trace of their presence, fungi are so pervasive that the average human footstep in a perhumid rainforest ecosystem impacts upon up to 480 kilometres of mycelium, if the individual hyphae were separated out into a single strand (10). As they operate at the scale of the single cell, the absorptive capability of mycorrhizae can reach to stratify themselves not only horizontally but also vertically with intricately layered patterns throughout the litter, fermentation, and humus horizons of forest soils. This creates a fungus-soil-forest-floor community that functions similarly to the means by which information is stratified within the pages of a book. In this way, the layered area of activity may be ten to one hundred times greater than the measurable distance (or mycelial page size) that stretches between trees and plants over the forest floor

(Stamets 24, 10). Throughout this intricately woven process, plant and fungal growth accelerate and substantially extend the capability of their communities and their physical ranges. More robust tree and plant growth creates healthier forests overall and increases the strength of the many associate species' resistance to attacks by insect pests, diseases, as well as diminishing invasive stresses like the physical damage created by weather, humans, or attacks by other animals.

Numerous insects play important associative roles in the broad mycorrhizal community. Drawn by the scent of spore activity during the fruiting season, insects lay their eggs directly within developing mushrooms. The field of mushrooms is a high-activity zone, where the adults congregate and mate and hatched larvae feed upon the seasonal bounty. As a benefit to the fungi, the movements of both larvae and adults disturb the microscopic spores that then adhere to their body surfaces, which they then transport to other parts of the forest, where new fungal communities begin.

In addition to the benefits of so much cross-cultural cooperation, mycorrhizal fungi also work to stabilize and aerate forest soils. This happens first as they establish the far-reaching structure and patterns of their associative connections, which increases both the strength and growth of roots and serves to tie the soil together with a fine hyphaeic net. Secondly, wherever they grow, fungal activity acts like minute garden forks that are always at work plying and bulging the soil. This is especially true during the fruiting season, when thousands upon thousands of often very large mushrooms are expanding rapidly upwards and outwards, rupturing and aerating the forest floor as they quickly and quite literally explode out of the ground, sometimes taking a few weeks to unfold but sometimes tearing out of the ground within a matter of a few days (Stamets 11). Soil scientist Kenneth A. Armson explains how hyphae also create beneficial aggregate and binding structures between organic and mineral compounds in soil through the mechanical "net" effects of hyphae as they expand and create resins and gums as by-products, as well as through the soil-melting effect of gases that are created through the activities of decomposition that mycelia both support and perform themselves (25).

Despite the incredibly diverse capabilities and functions of mycorrhizal fungi, their ability to thrive depends on a particular balance of ideal conditions. And, unfortunately, each chemical-laden stretch of asphalt, every scrape of a road-building machine, and every industrial transformation of a wild landscape bifurcates and interrupts this critical aspect of Real Work. Ordinary gravel roads for either industry or residential development are the most common of many man-made barriers that fungi cannot cross, as their mycelia need the moisture that the forest floor holds onto. As well, fungi require the food sources provided by decomposing matter and the cooperative life processes of microbes and bacteria that thrive within soil in order to create the far-reaching, interconnected communities that benefit the forest.

Mycologist Paul Stamets also tells us that human disturbances such as deforestation cause "a rise in saprophytes [wood decomposers] and a decline in mycorrhizal [plant associate or partnership] mushrooms," which creates an imbalance in species and shifts fungal activity from aiding forest plant and tree growth to mostly engaging with the vast decomposing debris fields left behind after logging or other industrial activities (19). Even though saprophytes play essential roles in forest health and are always present in the incremental rise and fall of coastal rainforests, conventional logging practices tip the scales wide in favour of the decomposers, reducing the more fragile mycorrhizals to fade and even disappear until such a time as their mycelia can find an appropriate supply of mature, living plant- and tree-root networks that can allow them to reestablish the balance. After clearcut logging, this can take many decades, and, depending upon the species, even half a century or much longer.

"Mushrooms," as Stamets writes, "are forest guardians. And a forest ecosystem cannot be defined without its fungi because they govern the transition between life and death and the building of soils, all the while fuelling numerous life cycles" (35). Despite the dearth of scholarly and scientific attention given to fungi, studies are slowly accumulating and uncovering important contributions to the knowledge of how old forests work. For example, K.A. Vogt, C.C. Grier, and others found that while mycorrhizal fungi make up only about 1 percent of total ecosystem biomass, their organic productivity is between 14 and 15 percent, which, when combined with the cooperative benefits they give to conifer fine roots, contributes between 45 and 75 percent of organic productivity in both young and mature forests (39). The lowly, mostly unseen fungi, working at the level of the single cell, contribute the lion's share of both health and wealth to the forest. Thankfully, as Stamets admits, "more foresters are coming to realize that a rotting tree in the midst of a canopied forest is, in fact, more supportive of biodiversity than a living tree" and that parasitic fungi, while earlier stigmatized as blights, "may be nature's way of selecting the strongest plants and repairing damaged habitats" (23).

It is hardly enough to say that fungi are the fundamental transport systems, media divisions, management teams, recycling agents, and labour force of the forest floor. Forest biologists Randy Molina, Thomas O'Dell, and others write that besides their interactions with numerous plants, fungi also perform roles as "critical links in the complex food web," as they parasitize other organisms, decompose woody debris, and interconnect and associate with "many soil organisms, including bacteria, other fungi, nematodes, microarthropods, and insects" (11). All of this—invisibly, indifferently, or perhaps with a certain degree of biotic sentience—establishes that fungi are the most profound elements of grammar in the living lexicon of forest ecosystems.

Northwest of Babine Lake, back at our timber cruising plot, I had begun, with ritual reverence, to pluck soft blue out of wet green, my work neglected for the moment. As timber cruising is "piece work" and time is quite literally money, Kasper wouldn't be happy to have me stall out for long. But the blue chanterelles were all within easy reach of where I was kneeling in bryophytes, having burst up in three broccoli-sized masses that just barely breached the surface of the red-stemmed feathermoss. I collected and packed them into my vest as quickly and as carefully as possible. Back at the logging camp in the evening, while most of the loggers and equipment operators drank beer, smoked cigarettes, worked on crossword puzzles, talked shop, and mostly slumped to watch TV in the ugly couch room, I was in my small room in C bunk, brushing conifer needles and shreds of moss out from between the clustered layers of the blue chanterelles. I admired them as I cleaned and separated them into smaller clusters and singles, packing them carefully away into brown paper bags. Disconnected from the culture of the logging camp, where most everyone else either laughed or sneered at my excitement over such things as wild mushrooms, my thoughts and my presence were back up in the subalpine old growth, kneeling in the moss, where they most usually always are.

True: (etymology) from the Greek treu *or the Indo-European* derew, *(*deru *or* drue*), which derives from "tree." In Old English, "tree" was* trēow *and "true" was* trēowe. *Both refer to wood—firmness—rootedness. Truth is a tree: etymologically, literally, figuratively.*

—adapted from Webster's Dictionary (1939)

transect 8

hemlock surprise,
traditional ecological knowledge and wisdom,
earth's mind, interbeing, and dwelling.

As we look out the windows of our apartment here in Prince Rupert, most often all we can see are diagonal washes of grey, and, a couple times a day, if we look at the rooftop that stands just below ours, we may see at least two or three eagles hunched in the drizzle. Perfect. Truly, these are some of the reasons Lisa and I live here. We're not allergic to sunshine or heat but it does overwhelm us and beat us down; I always start to fall apart both mentally and physically any time the mercury heads past twenty degrees Celsius. No one else I know besides Lisa shares this predicament, but way out here the constant combination of cool rain, the blessing of cloud cover, and the added bonus of eagles circling the rainforest make for our ideal habitat.

Around town, as is true for most small centres across the rural north, nothing much of consequence seems to be happening. Here in Prince Rupert, on a normal day, the fog builds up and once in a while it steams off, revealing shreds of rainfall here and there on the horizon—"distant precipitation" spiralling down in silver cones onto the dark ocean. Sometimes, there's even direct sunshine, which so many locals yearn for but start to complain about if it carries on for more than a few days. A great many stores sit empty along Prince Rupert's main streets, as do many of the canneries, mills, and moth-balled shops that hide along its dense hemlock and redcedar fringes. Poor people and working people, lots of teenagers, many representatives of local and distant First Nations groups—all kinds of human beings walk here and there around town, while the more affluent and time-pressed residents drive everywhere in newer automobiles that cram the parking spaces. To me, for the most part, the constant presence of so many vehicles in town makes little sense, as there is nowhere that is not accessible by what would be at most a ten- or fifteen-minute walk. But I guess it can rain at any given moment, and who wants to get wet?

Whether out on the distant periphery of green tangles near the BC Ferries terminal or right down in the Safeway parking lot, blacktail deer wander from one end of town to the other, strolling from forest strip to forest strip as they feed on the town's ornamental flowers or the foliage in people's front yards. A great many eagles and ravens form their own cultural strata all over town, acting as if they own the place, which they plainly do. Even members of the Kaien Island coastal wolf pack appear frequently on city streets—darting off a path, crossing a road, watching everything: grey-brown, long-limbed, snub-eared, peering from their hiding spots behind veils of red huckleberry and lady fern or creeping from out of the darkness of conifer branches. Not only are there blacktail deer to feed on but a large population of stray cats that have just as many thick green places to hide as deer and wolves. And, with its bewildering, overwhelming perhumid omniscience, a dense rainforest stands above everything on the steep mountainside, trickling water down and down as it grows ever thicker and thicker upward. Here and there, every autumn and winter, parts of the rainforest blow down, one to twenty trees at a time. This is the main means by which the oldest inhabitants of the rainforest make room for the youngest, creating an ever-shifting balance between the push and pull of decay and renewal. Just as new things grow taller and thicker within the light, their forebears are falling apart and disintegrating within shifting zones of shade.

From an industrial forester's perspective, the rainforest above town is mostly junk wood—hemlock surprise: half-rotten, badly deformed by mistletoe, most either inaccessible across looping muskegs and a zillion creeks, or strutted up a network of abrupt cliffs that no machine can climb and certainly no road can be built through. From an Other perspective, these inaccessible, mostly useless hemlock forests highlight the difference between their own intrinsic and pragmatic necessity for long-term integrity and health, and the extrinsic capitalist drive for constant market growth and immediate shareholder profits. For industry, equity is transformed into the abstract form of monetary wealth and is most often completely removed from its place of origin. For the rainforest, the majority of its wealth is retained, where it slowly and quickly transforms into nutrients that are reused locally and at key locations downstream. In economic theory, these are examples of *hard* and *soft* values. Both are similar and yet dissimilar by perspective, just as are some of the reasons for the differences that exist between poor and affluent human beings in town.

Urban planning writer and activist Jane Jacobs writes about hard and soft values in her scrutiny of the ecological parameters of economic activity. Jacobs argues that "nature affords foundations for human life and sets its possibilities and limits" and that economic life itself "is for teaching our species it has responsibilities to the planet and the rest of nature" (10). The naturally established biotic limits for healthy productivity are some of the most direct organic evidence of the existence of any economic truth. While trees, fungal mycelia, blacktail deer, salmon, and other larger-than-human entities live out Indigenous economies of wild autonomy within their interdependent communities, humans can decide whether or not to reperpetuate and thrive with similar modes of non-participation with the forces of post-globalization. We can chose to act ethically, perhaps with a refusal to accept or allow what anthropologists Charles R. Menzies and Caroline Butler call "the limited vision of those who see value only in activities that generate immediate profits" (3).

But every day, all kinds of decisions happen, whether or not we realize their consequences or feel their effects rippling through our relationships. If a cook at a floating logging camp north of Kincolith pauses to scan the outline of conifer crowns above the inlet, she may or may not recognize a solitary mountain hemlock tree on the ridge. Standing dead and fully lemon-grey with its trailing coat of old man's beard and witch's hair (*Alectoria sarmentosa*), this tree, to a timber-cruiser, is an age class 4 snag, with conk in 1 and a crook in 4; it has a sap-rotten butt and a broken top—and, of course, it's *hemlock surprise*—just another dead tree with no *merch* value. For the logging-camp cook, this tree might or might not be something else: perhaps just a quaint, even poignant story of persistence and endurance, reminding her that all lives are gestures of taking and giving, where, as anthropologist Paul E. Minnis and biologist Wayne J. Elisens tell us, "the relationships between culture and nature are, not surprisingly, reciprocal and ever changing in a variety of ways" (8). Perhaps the logging-camp cook may receive a glimpse of what Indigenous literature scholar Roger Dunsmore calls, "the pervasive experience and concept of the primal value of relatedness" (13). After a brief pause and reflection, the cook may, as usual, just look away and continue burning the camp trash in the incinerator, then have another cigarette and watch reality TV off the big satellite dish. But she may also think further—perhaps of her father or her littlest sister; maybe this lichen-hanging pole of mostly rotten wood will remind her of her grandmother: holding fast, accepting a mostly unnoticed, seemingly quiet place in the larger scheme of things, persevering against injustices and still continuing to give. Perhaps this will be just another goddamn dead tree and *by Gawd I can't wait until November when I can get the fuck outta dodge...*

Not at all trivial along the arch of this lateral branch of thought, there are still other perspectives. A female American mink (*Mustela vison*) may view this same hemlock snag as safety, home, nest, food cache, a perfect hiding spot and a prime lookout for hunting, also, perhaps as a shelter from the wildly inclement weather, and even, on rare occasions, as a fine sun deck—all of which are the reasons that her ancestors have lived here for generations. This tree, after all, has stood for seven hundred years, maybe more, standing dead for the last two hundred.

At face value, both the mink and the snag may appear to be useless from the purely utilitarian perspective of their negligible economic value. But Paul M. Wood and Laurel Waterman explain that "each species is a component of a collectivity which spawns the emergent property that is biodiversity—the essential environmental condition" (168). Within ecological science, both the mink and the tree are seen as important niche species that perform necessary, if highly nuanced, roles. And within recent investigations in economics, previously ignored species have been found to have hidden but quantifiable values, revealing their long-term, downstream contribution to ecosystems and human life. As ecocriticism, science, and economics work together to incrementally revolutionize Western perceptions of subtle, soft values in "deep accounting," and, while so many of us as Canadians are caught up in the technological fury of globalization and the increasing industrialization of the environment, often against our better judgement, there are many elements within First Nations cultures—especially traditional ecological knowledge and wisdom—that have been working to seek the values of a deeper, ecologically sensitive economic system, and have been doing so for thousands of years. As proponents of sensible, long-term land use strategies, many First Nations groups in recent memory have been waiting, albeit less and less patiently, for Western society and our government in particular to slow down and recognize the many benefits and qualities of life that can be found by shifting our perspective and thinking in different directions.

Still, for some members of First Nations communities living up-coast, there does exist the perception that to identify with images of tradition is to do nothing more than adopt a shallow sentimentalism that is used as a convenient crutch for political opportunism. The truth is that First Nations peoples are subject to the same pressures of consumerism and conformity to negative habits as any other Canadian. Anyone can make poor lifestyle choices—whether to buy potato chips and soda pop instead of real food, or to speak of an ethical outlook while practising something entirely different. Values can become skewed within any culture or background, but when we consider the multigenerational repression that First Nations peoples have been subjected to here on the North Coast, we must resist judging others as we would judge ourselves. Of course, for so many First Nations peoples there does exist the very real intention to maintain contemporary forms and rituals that give life to some version of tradition, rising from the base of ethical consideration where personal convictions are backed up by a context of thoughtful and practical understanding.

The *Nuu-chah-nulth* of the west coast of Vancouver Island have an idiomatic phrase, "*heshook-ish tsawalk,*" which means "everything is one"; this is an important concept that educator and *Nuu-chah-nulth* hereditary chief *Umeek* (E. Richard Atleo) describes as a living consideration of the fact that all things are related and interconnected, that all things are sacred and must be respected (quoted in Turner, *Earth's* 72–73). *Umeek* tells us that the Creator brought the physical world out of the spiritual world but that the two realms remain, for the most part, experientially distinct (10). Anthropologist Fikret Berkes tells us that a major part of this traditional perspective of connection with the Wild centres upon a "community-of-beings worldview," an outlook that remains a potent social force, one that many Indigenous peoples insist continues to hold a vital and palpable connection within their contemporary lives (92).

Viewing it now, through a circular lens of branching inclusivity, the Indigenous rainforest appears as much more than a tangled barrier of inhuman growth—it has become much more than a wild force that means to stifle human potential with millions of rotting barricades of wood and endless walls of mossy stone. For traditionally-minded peoples, the Indigenous rainforest is wild and sometimes dangerous, but it also contains the living persistence of a loving family—it is part of a larger community, one that participates within the personal thoughts, activities, and consequences of the individual. This is another aspect of Real Work: observing, regulating, and challenging human beings within the timeless inevitability of the many truths that may be invisible to the naked eye but are obvious to alternate perceptions of the heart and mind. Considering our recent look at mycelial interconnectivity and the many ways that science has revealed the interdependencies of life in the rainforest floor, it is no surprise to find that science itself confirms a great many of the perspectives that hold age-old representations in kincentric philosophy.

Still other alternate methods for investigating Western ideas of social and natural values appear within the seemingly romantic and sentimental imaginings of the cook at the floating logging camp near Kincolith. As we look at the hemlock snag that stands on the ridge across the bay, enveloped by vivid beards of lichen, riddled with the excavation holes of birds, mammals, insects, fungi, and smaller organisms, we might envision Roger Dunsmore's description of "the pervasive experience and concept of the primal value of relatedness" that traditional First Nations people have historically embodied and practised with their ancient land-based knowledges. This is a larger, highly nuanced conception of the Land, a concept which should give the land a more respectful capital L and signify it as more than a generic object. Berkes tells us that the Indigenous sense of Land provides more than obvious physical descriptions of geography, focussing instead upon the Land as a seamless complex of story, community, culture, and industry (6). The Land is defined as much by its soft values (its mental and emotional qualities) as it is by its hard values (its material qualities), both of which are influenced by the intentions, emotions, and activities of its human residents as much as they are by those of the larger-than-human realm (6). On the one hand, the hemlock snag on the ridge is a quantity of rotting wood fibre that never made it to the pulp mill; it could also be a memory trigger (a mnemonic peg) for the story lessons of an influential elder; it is also a complex living and industrial space for a multitude of organisms within the rainforest community; and, potentially, the hemlock snag is perhaps much more than all of these things combined.

Thinking beyond the history of Land-based lessons accumulated through traditional ecological knowledge and wisdom (TEKW), kin-centrism is hardly a concept exclusive to First Nations people but can be important to all who respect Indigeneity in mind, spirit, and action. In Europe, where many Canadians find their origin, various forms of kincentrism exist in the pre-Christian myths of their own ancient cultures. Caitlin Matthews tells us that the old Celts believed that "where human memory ran out then the memory of animals, plants, and rocks was available to be drawn upon" (108). If we could look back far enough, we would find that most of our ancestors lived this close to the Land. The closest familial ties we held with animals, plants, water, mountains, and all of the ground-truths they share disappeared only over the last three to four hundred years, when the Age of Enlightenment and the scientific revolution began to spread the absolutist, reductivist ideas of rational thinkers like Bacon, Diderot, Locke, Newton, Spinoza, and others.

As it is for Indigenous peoples the world over, on the west coast of Turtle Island the depth and complexity of TEKW has arisen out of many millennia of careful observation, synthesis, and experimentation within the changing climatic and biologic conditions within which they have lived. The importance that is placed upon reciprocity and respecting the value of the small and the intangible as much as the powerful is evident in the grounded cultural clan symbols of raven, redcedar, vole, whale, fireweed, eagle, spider, salmon, hummingbird, and so many others, all of which were once related to humans, held the ability to take human form, and played a crucial role in the people's survival, if not their origin. Within the myths where people married or had close communication with animals, there were many situations of struggle for survival that led to an understanding of how their linked societies shared the necessity for mutual respect and fair treatment. These ideas are relevant today, not just as quaint morality tales for children but as vital reminders for anyone who has yet to grasp the primary ethical concept that entities as small as insects and small plants have as much intrinsic value and right to life as their own mothers, grandfathers, and themselves.

Even if we overlook the fact that science affirms what kincentrism and TEKW teaches—that we must maintain the greatest possible natural breadth and balance of healthy diversity—the myths of human and larger-than-human relations still reveal a studied and intimate understanding of how people can thrive in a place where the most extreme combination of climate, mountains, forests, and coastlines on the planet can provide a long-term, prosperous, and welcoming home for people.

TEKW has been both fundamental and critical to the Indigenous means of thriving on the North Coast. The state of interbeing that arises from such a long experience of realization, reflection, location, and industry in this place is a fundamental precondition for creating such a biogeocultural system as TEKW. As they performed Real Work within the ancestral complex of intensely managed Storied Lands and fringe zones of truly wild territory over a series of multigenerational eras, Indigenous peoples in turn created a variety of bountiful cultures of unique beauty and lasting power, and, importantly, an incredible amount of local knowledge. Telling the historical truth, most of the earliest European explorers, fur traders, and settlers owe their lives to the knowledge and skills of the First Nations peoples who helped them, in one way or another, to survive in this land of wild extremes. None of this would have been possible without the key ground-truth understanding that people are just one small part of a larger complex of interbeing and that we are dependent upon the Wild for our health and well-being as much as the Wild is dependent upon us to understand and practise this principle.

The means for the thriving and surviving of TEKW can be partly understood when we consider three of its most obvious modes: 1) the ancient, institutional *root-forms* of traditional practice, industry, culture, and belief; 2) its spontaneous and adaptive *rhizomatic* engagement and adaptation within the flux of day-to-day reality; and 3) its engagement with a deeper ontological mysticism and cosmology—a sensitivity to the deeper cycles of transspecies reciprocity, those that are not bound by linear time but ancestral time—or, as we can also envision it, TEKW's *mycorrhizal*-like connectivity and direct yet abstract intellection within the wild superorganic.

To understand kincentrism, TEKW, and the power of Storied Land with less theory, ethnobotanist Nancy J. Turner tells us that its practitioners are those who instinctively "seek to discover a richness in understanding and wisdom, as well as gaining an immense satisfaction in knowing and living in their home places" (3). Anthropologist Basso reveals the results of partaking in Real Work immersions in Storied Land, explaining that "with symbolic reference points for the moral imagination and its practical bearing on the actualities of their lives— the landscape in which the people dwell can be said to dwell in them" (102). The spiritual and practical elaborations that Indigenous peoples "impose upon their landscapes have been fashioned from the same cultural materials they impose upon themselves as members of society. Both give expression to the same set of values, standards and ideals" (ibid.). The distinctions that make Real Lives out of the Real Ideas that lead to the Real Work that creates Real Things in the Real World are what make TEKW such a culturally integrated, holistic, and inter-disciplinary worldview. Day by day, as many of us slip further within the ubiquity of the imaginary within the distractions of contemporary media, swept up by technological forces that keep us separated from and ignorant of the workings of the Real World, the lessons of TEKW will also slip further into the static of the antiquarian and perhaps toward the realm of the extinct.

Revealing a deeper connection within an Indigenous worldview and the nature of its embeddedness within Storied Land, anthropologist Julie Cruikshank describes the interaction of the Tlingit of Southeast Alaska as they exist within their very real and very wild homelands. Not only does Cruikshank tell us that the land, the glacier, and the river "hear" the people, but through the *at.óow* (their historical oral narratives) and various less formal means, the Tlingit themselves "hear" the Storied Land transmit its wisdom, which they interpret and obey with duties that transform both personal behaviour and cultural norms (11, 25, 40, 69). Anthropologist John Swanton relates one interspecies perspective of how Storied Land reveals its purposes, meanings, and knowledges: "The world and all it contained were the products of mind and bore everywhere the marks of mind. Matter was not something which had given birth to mind, but something which had formerly been mind" (quoted in Snyder *Proceedings* 37). Swanton adds: "This mind was visibly manifested in the so-called 'living things' as plants, and…animals," which reminds us not only that body, mind, and spirit are never distinct from one another but that "human beings must not isolate themselves from the mind residing in [the larger-than-human realm], lest the human mind so isolated become impoverished and imbalanced" (ibid.).

Swanton's retelling of this older perspective takes us to what anthropologists Tim Ingold, Thomas F. Thornton, Keith H. Basso, and others understand of the Indigenous sense of *being* and *dwelling*, which finds its bearing as deeper phases of interbeing. Being and dwelling are what traditionally minded peoples lived, intuitively and intimately, as part of the fluidity of experience they enact as part of the practical experiences of cultural production and industry they undertake in an embedded way within Storied Land.

Even though modern science has made legitimate skeptics of many of us, kincentrism is also a cosmology—a belief system. Being, dwelling, and interbeing are made up of unique perspectives for "feeling, hearing, knowing what else is there," as Indigenous author Linda Hogan tells us: "that which is around us daily but too often unacknowledged, a larger life than our own" (38). Whatever truths science may reveal about our world, there are still many things it cannot and may never answer. But a belief system can also be a theory or even a philosophy, whether taken spiritually in the subjective sense or as metaphorical examples that mean to be literal and objective. Ethnoecologist Leslie Main Johnson describes the Gitxsan sense of mind and memory as held within Storied Land: "The world itself is aware, and people exist in a dynamic and interactive relationship with all of its aspects, threading a careful path across the landscape, alert to all possibilities... rooted in experiential engagement" (148). Tim Ingold also reveals how the Tlingit do not "approach their environment as an external world of nature that has to be 'grasped' conceptually and appropriated symbolically within the terms of an imposed cultural design...indeed, the separation of mind and nature has no place in their thought and practice" (*Perception* 42). Although we may come to grasp a sense of traditional kincentrism, interbeing, and dwelling, the hard part may be what we can do with this little bit of information. Today, even though things are more complicated, this need not overwhelm to the point of futility or inaction.

Interbeing is found in daily practice within the material world, where people accept that *everything* in their lives has origins in the Storied Land: food, stories, building materials, thoughts and emotions, clothing, creativity and knowledge, spirits, and all of the aspects of interiority and humanity that cannot be seen or touched. *Everything* is not so much the general materiality of things like tools, rocks, animals, and rainfall but their meaningful presence as influential memory in ancestral time, especially as they help to decide our thoughts and intentions.

For the Tlingit, as with other First Nations groups along the North Coast, dwelling is second nature, a normal state they have cultivated on the wild northern reaches of the outer coast for millennia. To the Tlingit, dwelling is not philosophically abstract but plainly practical. As Ingold tells us, *everything* simply becomes "constituted in life, not just in thought, [as] it is only because [the Tlingit] live in an environment that [they] can think" (60). This is the most direct and clear vision of ground-truth, as Sitka elder Herman Kitka explains to Thornton, "if we didn't put up our foods, we wouldn't have a culture" (119). Here, the focus is always *within* the outside world (which negates the very idea of the external), centring the individual or culture upon the ordinary work and social activities that create and direct everything that nourishes and provides for their existence.

Ingold describes dwelling as a complex, embedded perspective, one "that involves substantial knowledge-in-practice," and this is the sense of purpose and activity that evolves and changes with people's seasonal work routines (*Hunting* 32). Perhaps it starts with a trip to the spring fishing camps for eulachon and then to tidal areas for the herring roe harvest, followed afterwards by routine travels up ancestral trails for marmot and goat hunting on the mountainside. Weeks are spent embedded in the summer and fall within the subalpine berry patches and then there is a movement down to the river camps for the salmon fisheries. Then there is even more time spent outside, drying and smoking meat and engaging in various storage preparations before an eventual return to the winter village.

Traditional dwelling includes both personal and group emotional integration within all experiences of life. Ideally, these activities also cohere within spiritual and community connections that occur with ceremonies and institutional rituals. Essentially, dwelling occurs within any activity and every event that resonates within the memory-laden, permeable depths of Storied Land. By contrast, as most Canadians move from place to place in order to live out their lives within a series of industrially manufactured offices and buildings, utilizing industrially manufactured tools and implements for their work, a similarly deep connection to the Land, its memories, and its lessons is neither experienced nor expressed. We do develop our own æsthetic and emotional connections to the material things in our life and admire handmade tools, clothes, and furniture for their uniqueness or their association with the outside world, but we are still usually shocked into an altered state of being when we come out of our workplace and enter into the outdoor space filled with birdsong, fresh air, the sound of a breeze moving through leaves, and various larger-scale expressions of geography and weather.

Dwelling is dependent upon day-to-day practicality as much as it is dependent upon the deeper nuances of experiencing and participating in ancestral ceremonies. People who dwell in this sense cannot exist as human beings except with their retention of the importance of being immersed within the larger-than-human component of Storied Land. In this sense, the Land does not simply fulfill a set of sufficient conditions for human survival. Stories, rituals, and deeper relationships with larger-than-human entities are as important as seafood, water, and wood. Just as mathematics can only answer so many questions in our Western lives, it is our emotions and our ability to reflect, and our gut reaction to the intangible and tangible things we connect this information to, that help to answer so many other questions and urges we cannot avoid in life.

Interbeing and dwelling require that the continuity of a dynamic process of principles and cultural habits be kept *alive* and *wild* in the routines of everyday. In this way they can become automatic, like the regularity of breathing. If we in the West can breathe, hopefully we can also retrace a path back to some new-old patterns of interbeing and dwelling. Meanwhile, the lichen-draped hemlock snag continues its stand on the ridge near Kincolith, overlooking the thoughts, intentions, and activities of the cook at the floating logging camp, just as it also provides a hiding space for the mink and so many other organisms, all of which call this slowly crumbling symbol of persistence *home*.

the repetition of grammar:

Luxury, River, Outdoors, Budget,
Fishing, Mountains, Nature.
  —Richard Ibghy and Marilou Lemmons (2012)

plot D3

high-elevation hemlock,
high-lead lay-out,
coastal heli-logging.

BACK IN 1997, I WORKED FOR A SMALL FORESTRY CONSULTANT COM-
pany on the outer coast. We spent the early winter chasing wood on
a northwest-aspect, mid-elevation slope, about 450–600 metres above
sea level. This week, my job was running deflection lines up and
down from the edge of the redcedar flats to the steep hembal crests,
all to the drone of an Erickson skycrane running circuits from the
heli show up top. Each day, all day, fresh bundles of large mountain
hemlock, yellow-cypress, and silver fir came roaring down the mountainside at the end of cables and plunged with an explosion into the
inlet. Every time I reached the crest where our proposed block ran out,
I would finish my notes and wait a few minutes before heading back
down, watching for the skycrane to arc into view, sometimes catching
a glimpse of two or three giant black logs diving into water. Wednesday
morning of the second week, the sound of the Erickson abruptly disappeared. Curious about the silence but freed from distraction, I continued to work in the comparative quiet of intermittent fierce downpours
and winds that pushed forcefully in gusts above the crown ridge of this
winterdark forest.

Hemlock trees are known for having the highest moisture content of any tree in BC, at around 60 percent, and often higher. Yet these hemlock up top were inordinately dense and supersaturated. This was not just due to their local habitat conditions but also because of the immediate influence of heavy rain and snow. These trees up top were so dense that, after two weeks of the heli show, not one bundle that had been dropped had risen back up to the surface of the bay. Admitting the worst, the company stopped work and sent the loggers home. It was an early Christmas holiday for the fallers and a lost gamble for the company. But for the mountain hemlock community, four hundred to eight hundred years of individual growth and thousands of years of deep succession were lost for nothing more than an empty bald patch of stumps on the mountaintop, a place where any kind of regeneration, natural or manual, would be protracted and precarious, and all without the legacy of the hundreds of years of rotting wood contained in the lost trunks, which would ordinarily have fallen to replenish the high-elevation soils.

Forest biologist R.D. Boone and others tell us that, after harvest, mountain hemlock forests are unusual compared to other stands because very little regeneration occurs (4). High summer temperatures in the clearcut zone and the extreme nutrient deficiency of these high-elevation soils are blamed for long delays in seedling regeneration (5). As forest biologist K.W. Seidel found, "mountain hemlock seedlings [are] very sensitive to microclimate extremes. Seedling survival [is] very low" (34). With these details in mind, apart from the immediate input of nutrients from the bleeding roots and limbs left behind after the heli-show, the majority of the long-term release of carbon, minerals, and nutrients of the mountain stand was sunk somewhere in the saltwater bay. These bundles of fresh logs were likely drifting out on the tides to intimidate all manner of fish and whales, lunging like a series of giant battering rams as they roamed with their slow, obtuse plunge and cannon across the Pacific shelf.

MasGaak (Don Ryan) of *Wilps Ha'naamuxw*, who worked for the

Gitxsan treaty office, told Richard Daly that the Gitxsan look "at the forests in a completely different way from what the province's standard view is. All the province wants is to take the best logs off our territories" (301). UBC political philosopher and forest biologist Paul M. Wood states that forest science and applied science, as regulated into policy by the Ministry of Forests, Lands and Natural Resource Operations (MFL-NRO), serve merely supportive roles in land-use decisions, with ethical enforcement being their primary function (7). In actual practice, these important principles are warped by the forces of dollars earned and lost through the micromanagement strategies of licensees, where changes trickle down through the profit-driven ideologies of the shareholders of these large international corporations. Most of these actions are organized through a much larger conglomerate power structure, the Coalition of Forest Industries (COFI), a corporate body that dictates most of the government policy and practices for the lumber and pulp mills that own the forest licences across the province.

For example, although the prescriptions of ecological science in relation to the problem of clearcutting and restocking late-succes-sional stands of mountain hemlock are not vague, immense pressures come down from capital interests in Vancouver, Seattle, and numerous national and international offices, compelling managers at head offices and local mills to continue denuding stands that ecological science warns are extremely difficult, if not impossible, to regenerate. From the perspective of a small community where work is scarce, the actual logging season brings big dollars for a very short time, which is hardly vague. And even though most mountain hemlock trees cut in log-ging are designated as unavoidable "bycatch," these sensitive stands of high-elevation hemlock are being selected more often for inclusion in development plans. For licensees and workers, it's nothing but a num-bers game. For the political boosters of mills and small communities, it's a case of *Jus' giv' er! Balls deep 'n git 'er done!*

Although a math equation leads to an answer for a very specific question, the industrial transformation of ecological systems leads to questions that business accountants lack the authority to answer. What about all of the many questions asked in various green, grey, and brown lan(d)guages, questions that are mostly neither understood nor heard?

As he comments about so many long-term values squandered and wasted for short-term gain, former World Bank economist Raj Patel tells us that our "market society is embedded in the natural world, which the myth of the self-regulating market equally tries to deny. Human civilization depends on Earth's ecology, even though we're literally exploiting it to death" (20). This prognosis links up with what economist Herman Daly has uncovered, that "current economic growth has uncoupled itself from the world and become irrelevant. Worse, it has become a blind guide" (950–51). While the bulk of the monetary wealth generated with the industrial transformation of the natural capital of local forests is displaced and transferred into bank accounts thousands of kilometres away, what is left behind are the majority of the negative outcomes from which the wealth itself originated. There may be seasonal work for a few manual labourers and a great deal of paperwork for a handful of trained technicians, but after this we are left with many generations and hundreds of years of waiting for a new forest, as it attempts to reestablish itself upon a denuded landscape that has been stripped of the most essential components it actually requires in order to renew itself.

All of this is a loss, not just for those people connected to industrial forestry work, people who attempt to build lives for themselves and their children, but for the ecological systems and the Real Work they perform as crucial components of local and global health. The clearcuts receive the window dressing of a sprightly plantation of seedlings: spruce, redcedar, hemlock, pine—row upon row of laboratory-enhanced stock, none of which have their genetic origins in the local forest or even the geographic region, as their DNA is usually extracted from industry-selected "superstands" located in the southern part of the province. Here is the way this process works: Technicians use rifles to shoot branches down from the upper crown of the choicest trees.

They collect, root, and cultivate these cuttings in a laboratory and grow them to size in outdoor research plots. When they are mature, technicians blast a series of explosive charges in their vicinity to shock the young trees into creating overproductions of cones. Technicians collect this oversupply of cloned seed for distribution to the regional nurseries, facilities that produce the millions of seedlings necessary for treeplanters who will work, one or more years later, mostly in the spring and summer months, to plant them, one by one, over the breadth of the hundreds of clearcuts that are felled across the province every year.

Just one of many alternatives to the unsustainable practice of clearcutting hemlock stands is to make use of the medicinal mushrooms that grow upon them, most notably the varnish shelf (*Gandomera oregonense*), a close relation or local variant of the *reishi* (Japanese for "divine") or *lingzhi* (Chinese for "tree of life mushroom") (Stamets 231). This saprophytic polypore grows annually on dead and dying trees and is revered as a panacea in Traditional Chinese Medicine. Its recognized therapeutic effects are as an antibacterial, anticandida, anti-inflammatory, antitumor, and antiviral; as a blood-pressure and blood-sugar moderator, a cholesterol reducer, a cardiovascular and immune system enhancer; it is known as a nerve, kidney, liver, respiratory, and lung tonic, as a sexual potentiator, and as a stress reducer. Reishi is used to treat specific cancers, such as leukemia, liver, lung, prostate, and sarcoma (41).

The Plants are for healing, not for profit.

—*K'ii7lljuus*, Barbara Wilson, X̲aaydaa Elder (2004)

Devil's Club (view 2

AFTER LOOPING ITS SPINY BRANCHES ABOVE THE CRISSCROSSED TRUNKS of dead windthrow, devil's club stretches its giant palmate leaves into the puzzle-form of a light table punctuated with interlocking maple-leaf shapes. Often reaching three or more metres high in tangled complexes that have to be seen to be believed, the tall stems position themselves so that each fan of four to six leaves meets in a formation that maximizes the dimmest light of the duskiest ecosystems on Turtle Island.

Ethnobotanist Nancy J. Turner shows the welts and scratches of her acquired knowledge, telling us that some people are deeply allergic to its spines (*Plants* 153). Biologists Rita M. O'Clair and Robert H. Armstrong tell us that the leaves are rich in proteins sought by many animals, which is one reason why it has evolved to carry such a heavy armament of spines (221).

All parts of the plant, especially the roots, stream with human and ecological medicine. Many special songs are still sung today when gathering, preparing, and using *wa'ums*, as the Nisg̱a'a call this plant (FPCF). As much as it is revered as a medicinal, many practitioners of traditional knowledge also acknowledge its spiritual powers. *Wooms* (as it is called by the Tsimshian) is an important component in carving rituals, and the plant (which, quite literally, can only be handled with respect) gives shamans supernatural protection against evil spirits (*Sm'algyax̲*, Turner). As Turner writes, devil's club bestows its strength and power only upon individuals who treat it with appropriate respect. Combined with bear grease by the X̲aaydaa, *ts'iihllnjaaw* was also inserted under the skin with thorns to create a blue tattoo. Dancers wore devil's club charcoal on their faces to protect themselves while vulnerable to evil influences and while participating in ceremonies and rituals. Travellers and hunters carried sections of the stem as amulets; as I've seen myself, bundled lengths of the cut stem are placed above a doorway, under a mattress, and in the four corners of a room for household protection and family safety (ibid.).

Dr. Robert Fortuine points to the central importance of the species: "Among all the Native groups, devil's club was preeminent—almost a panacea" (201). Berries were rubbed in the hair and scalp by the Xaaydaa to treat lice and dandruff and to make the hair shiny (Turner *Plants* 153). Today, the plant is used to cure ailments of the digestive tract, ulcers, arthritis, measles, pneumonia, diabetes, and infections from conditions such as broken limbs; it was used as a cleansing emetic, a purgative, and was put in steam baths to reduce fever, pains, and stomach troubles, and to relieve rheumatism. Devil's club was made into a poultice for swollen glands, boils, and other infections; the bark was pulverized for a deodorant and for tea; it was combined with prince's pine and cascara for fighting tuberculosis, to re-establish regular menstruation after childbirth, and to stop the flow of milk from a woman's breast when weaning her child; it was used by the Tsimshian as a laxative, to improve vision, and to treat blindness (Pojar and MacKinnon 82). For the Tlingit, Alutiiq, Tahltan, Eyak, and other northern groups, the fresh inner bark of the stem was mixed with seal oil to induce vomiting; it was used to soothe black eyes, constipation, and gallstones. The dried inner bark was mixed with cedar pitch to heal sores and cuts. Concoctions were used to treat venereal disease and even insanity, as Fortuine describes: "the patient's head was beaten gently but repeatedly with the plant until blood was drawn" (202).

Do I keep moving north
beyond object or
direction? Is distance
measured by
confusion?

　　　　　—Susan Musgrave (1976)

plot D4

snowflakes the size of Steller's jays.

Q-8.

THIS WAS THE NAME OF A PROJECTED BLOCK WE WERE LAYING OUT within clear view of the Pacific Ocean. It wasn't called *sbaayt sginist ts'imts'uu'lixs* (pine stand in the gulley), *lumks tsee gantx sbagaytgan* (all the timber going up again amongst the trees), or *la̱xsga usim ges* (forest area in a narrow place on the mountain) (Johnson *Trail* 45, 48). No, this beautiful expanse of forest-covered mountain was simply Q-8. Back at the mill, I know that the pressure to get things done as quickly as possibly runs high, and names like Q-8 reinforce the fact that the whole endeavour is about numbers running black down a ledger sheet. But imagine a young, university-trained forester who works for a coastal licensee calling up the local First Nations band office and saying something along the lines of: *Hello, we're going to be clearcutting more of your traditional territory this winter and we need an official label in our logging plans for this particular area, and we were just wondering what your traditional name is for this patch of timber?*—Yeah, it's not likely to happen, and so, Q-8 it is.

　　Cursing louder than usual above the roar of the engine, the Jet Ranger pilot who was taking us in and out of the mountains was now using his elbow to clear the windshield. Needing both hands to maintain control in the heavy winds, every two or three minutes he would swear and twist around to rub out a spot just big enough to see through. As if this wasn't alarming enough, once we got to the mountainside "helipad," as usual, we had to just step right out into open space off the thin landing skid that was scraping on and off the edge of a wet cliff. All the while, the helicopter hovered over an expanse of endless mist being sucked away in curling spirals, and below, all there was to step out onto was flailing branches and rocks that launched spatters of cold water in every direction. Wild-eyed, day after day I scrambled with my gear out onto the face of one small muskeg or another and hunkered down on top of some throbbing pond, mesmerized by whipping leaves and flailing sedges. Once, I watched as the powerful rotor blast froze the surface of the water right before my eyes.

While we attempted to complete our tasks over the course of a week, the pilot soon started to radio us earlier and earlier in order to get us out before turbulent weather closed in. On Tuesday he insisted on picking us up by 2:00 p.m., and then earlier by half-hour intervals to the end of the week. Helicopters are expensive at the best of times, and as our window of productivity shrank to a few hours a day, productive time in the field diminished to the point that the whole endeavour became pointless.

On December 18, our last day of winter work that year, snowflakes the size of songbirds were clapping down into my face. They looked fluffy enough as they tumbled down out of the sky, but they were as wet and heavy as snowballs when they hit, and just as aggravating. I was brought to an amazed standstill when I saw a snowflake conglomeration the size of a crow plummet down amongst many slower, smaller snowflakes and rattle a four-metre hemlock sapling. A-Ma-Zing. Not surprisingly, within minutes the radio was making noise. It was 11:30 a.m. and our pilot was coming to get us, immediately. Rushing back to our helipad from a few hundred metres across the side of a steep mountain that was being quickly buried under heavy snow, I was jostled down and down through a cold, wet rush of branches, each of which dumped shovelful after shovelful of snow upon me with every step. I pushed myself as fast as I could, just planning my movements from step to step, reaching an interior and exterior place that squeezed me into the aperture between intense misery and ecstatic relief. More than anything I was awestruck, silenced, and once back in town, I walked dazed but wide-eyed for days on end.

It was dark. The water was below, or was it water? It might be mud flats. It might be rocks. It might be Alaska, it could even be BC. What it looked like was a black hole, probably the entrance to a parallel universe, with guys on the other side just as stupid as us.

—Les Watmough (2008)

winter weather on the North Coast:

(single event catalogue for the week of October 8–14, 1991

RECORD RAINFALL IN THE TERRACE AREA: 242.4 MILLIMETRES BETWEEN October 6 and 14, over half the mean precipitation (ppt) for the wettest winter month. Kitimat: 221.2 millimetres between October 8 and 10, a record for a forty-eight-hour period. Sudden erosion at the Deep Creek dam cut off the Terrace water supply and the rising Skeena backed up its side rivers, flooding neighbouring communities. Burdick Creek flooded near *Kitwanga*, cutting a new channel across the backroad. Flooding and washouts closed Highway 37 between Terrace and Kitimat, with a 150-metre-long section disappearing into the river. Hirsch Creek registered a record maximum instantaneous discharge, and the Kitimat River moved itself to the east, rising more than five metres in just over thirty hours—another record. The highway near Lakelse was closed. Williams Creek flooded Blackwater Creek, as the road culverts could not handle the excess capacity, which resulted in heavy erosion damage.

The Copper River Forest Service Road (FSR) sustained damages requiring seven hundred thousand dollars in repairs. Many bridges were damaged along the Nass-*Kinskuchl Kwinatahl* and on the Nass FSR, the *Ginmiltkun*, and the *Telkwa* FSRs. PNG reported pipeline damages along the Copper River, most notably a massive rock slide near *Tauw* Lake in the *Telkwa* Pass. One slide near Middle Lake blocked the road and filled the gas line with water for six and a half kilometres; the same slide exposed sixty metres of line at the junction of Limonite Creek and Copper River, the force being so strong that the bed of Limonite Creek was obliterated, which led to 270 metres of the creek being rechanneled. In the Nass Valley, approximately 360 millimetres of rain fell in seven days—which is about the usual monthly average. Many roads were overrun with more than a metre of water. Flooding along the *Kitsumkalum* River and Lava Lake closed the route from Dover to *Laxgalts'ap* (Greenvile); nearly three thousand residents of Nass Camp, *Laxgalts'ap*, Canyon City and New Aiyansh were isolated by extensive flood damage. Fresh food, mail, and ballots for the provincial election were airlifted to trapped residents through the Provincial Emergency Program (PEP), resulting in the largest airlift in PEP's history, totalling fourteen flights. *Laxgalts'ap* residents were isolated for fourteen days, while 80 percent of the twenty-two-kilometre road was completely under water, resulting in numerous washouts and damage to bridge structures and approaches. At one point, the Cedar River rose ninety centimetres in fifteen minutes (Septer and Schwab 168–71).

The value of respect is one discernible theme or thread in a complex web of life and existence. In the modern world, this theme has been completely replaced by science and technology. At the moment, the themes of respect and the applications of science appear to be at odds. They are at odds when one or the other is denied. They can be balanced and harmonized if both themes are accepted as part of one whole within the human.

—*Umeek*, E. Richard Atleo, *Nuu-chah-nulth* hereditary chief (1999)

transect 9

corporate greenwashing and traditional knowledge, the claws of a grizzly bear, clearcutting Hoonah heritage.

IN HIS 2002 CONTRIBUTION TO THE BC GOVERNMENT *FORESTS FOR THE Future* project, anthropologist John Corsiglia analyzes research and public education strategies within the traditional territories of the Tsimshian Nation, with the hope of bringing TEKW together with objectives of industrial forestry. Within this paradox, Corsiglia presents the Nisga'a legend of *Txeemsim*, where an impressionable and uneducated neophyte figure is "afflicted by a netherworld demon and becomes consumed by ravenous hunger, lust, and continuous cravings for stimulation and advantage" (222). After a long journey filled with mishaps, the comic supernatural hero finds maturity and enlightenment, learns the value of respect and reciprocity, and turns to a life of selfless devotion to community (ibid.). The story of *Txeemsim* illustrates how youthful ignorance and short-term ambitions can lead to an accumulation of mistakes, even tragedies that we must first admit to before they can be fixed, but which lead us to gain the strength and wisdom necessary to benefit others after adopting values and teachings that are much larger than ourselves.

As we live today in an increasingly fragile world where industrial activities have consequences that ripple for centuries, the casual decisions we all make each day can have repercussions on a global scale. With this in mind, how can a local traditional story such as *Txeemsim* be useful to anyone outside of the Tsimshian Nation? Anthropologist Nancy J. Turner explains that the "traditional approaches of Indigenous societies provide models to follow—models that recognize the interconnectedness of everything," and that these are "models of relationships to foster within our communities, between past, present and future generations" (212). Corsiglia also considers that lessons borne out of traditional knowledge systems are "an important key to re-establishing workable relations between human communities and the environment" (234).

Anthropologist Berkes describes this idea of hybridity, stressing that the "interest in traditional ecological knowledge in recent years reflects the need for ecological insights from Indigenous practices of resource use, and the need to develop a new ecological ethic based in part on Indigenous wisdom" (179). Menzies also confirms his own personal "operational optimism" for the industrial and cultural usefulness of TEKW, his optimism having arisen from "observing the many times that [his] colleagues in the natural sciences simply 'get it all wrong,'" describing as well how, "in spite of everything that might suggest problems and difficulties with TEKW and in implementing or deploying it, [he] can recognize the clear value in actually listening to the people closest to the resource, the people who live there, work there, and know the resource in an intimate and profound fashion" (240). Yet within developing strategies that include sharing knowledges, it is important to understand, as anthropologists Menzies and Butler warn, that Western utilizations of TEKW must also be viewed with a degree of skepticism and be subject to intense critical analysis, considering the often empty "green salvation" that misappropriated knowledges reveal when they are utilized as sly, idealized, and functionally empty smokescreens (17). This important point gives validation to the hesitancy that most First Nations have in sharing their knowledge beyond the Aboriginal sphere. Here, Menzies and Butler mean to point to the growing problem of corporations who incorporate veneers of TEKW into their media communications and working practices, which is just another version of corporate greenwashing (ibid.). After seeking out and establishing a relationship with an economically fragile group (one that has been under more than a century and a half of colonial oppression), some corporations mean to dupe both consumers and the First Nations group themselves with complex legalese and a glowing media campaign that misrepresents their real activities. Besides disrespecting all of the parties involved, this also goes against a set of principles that were never been meant to be co-opted by a system that is best known for changing its stripes along with the exchange of money.

This system also works at the level of an individual being acculturated or assimilated into Canadian culture. In the summer of 1996, while out in the remote mountain forests of northern BC, I had an encounter with a young person from a local First Nations group who was also a graduate from a university forestry program. In the typical morning habit of forestry workers, a small crowd of field workers was gathered around the tailgates of numerous pickup trucks in preparation for a day in the bush. While studying maps, waving off mosquitoes, drinking coffee, and organizing field gear, there are always those who have a bush story to tell, which can often become a way of delaying the inevitable start of the hours of isolation and physical struggle that lie ahead. First, one macho blowhard (of Euro-Canadian background) was explaining how he had once encountered a young grizzly bear on the road and had beaten it to death with a stick. A few of us with many years of experience rolled our eyes and made louder gravel-crunching noises with our boots. I imagined this story was just a purposefully offensive tall tale. But the young forester I mentioned earlier, who was working alone on a road layout task for a new cutting permit, boasted with a wide grin of how, the previous summer, she had shot and killed a grizzly bear at pointblank range with her defender (a snub-barrelled shotgun that fires slugs at close range, manufactured especially for forestry workers). It is important to note that she had not shot the bear because it had threatened her life but had done so just to possess its claws, which, she explained, were powerful symbols that were sacred to her culture. She had cut the claws from the dead animal's paws and pocketed them, walked away, and carried on with her workday. This incident happened while she was an employee for one of the big licensees in the area, perhaps getting paid, like she was this day, to lay out a road that now (as was the common practice) bears her name.

Reflecting upon this over the years, I find Stó:lō author Lee Maracle holds a partial answer to the surprise and confusion that has stayed with me. Maracle states "that Europeans cannot define our societies with any accuracy or draw connections between our society and their own" (*I am Woman* 39). Admitting the legitimacy of Maracle's statement, my attempt to seek understanding may very well be futile. I am left in the complex place of living here in BC while not being able to make a connection, and thus, find no understanding. Of course this doesn't even begin to compare to the experiences that First Nations peoples have endured for centuries—being overwhelmed as they have been, in terms of population, language, culture, power, and perhaps insanity. Although my personal knowledge of local First Nations cultures and protocols is extremely limited, I have been taught that animals and all aspects of the Land are to be treated the way you would treat a member of your own family. But with this incident we enter into a strange zone where the means by which an animal is killed—either for food or for its material value—cannot be judged by contemporary utopian value systems of right and wrong.

Even though Maracle tells me that I cannot understand, I still try, and in my reading I discover that Koyukon elder Grandpa Williams once told anthropologist Richard Nelson that grizzly and brown bears have incredible strength, a volatile temperament, and a potent spirit—that they are so powerful that every hair on a bear's hide has a life of its own, and that any bear that is killed must be carefully honoured and placated (62, 63). Williams also states that no one should either brag about killing a bear or show it any disrespect (ibid.). Academic and ecosocialist activist Joel Kovel writes that people from all walks of life are often unconsciously transforming life-communities and unwittingly taking on the ideology of alien forms of reason (17). My relentless questioning may very well be more of the same old colonial routine of white, male, patronizing control. Perhaps the young, university-trained forester I met did honour and placate the spirit of the bear she had killed for its claws; maybe this is all part of a contemporary vision of the *Txeemsim* legend. Yet the story of the young forester killing the bear in the way that she did, while working as an employee for a major forestry licensee, and told the way it was before the tailgate of a pickup truck, still leaves me blinking. Nonetheless, I tell myself that I cannot possibly understand—and, more importantly, I tell myself that I have no right to question the actions of someone who comes from a First Nations cultural background. Perhaps all I can do is blink respectfully and carry on.

In 1968, the educational philosopher Robert Hutchins wrote a book called *The Learning Society*, in which he describes how the educational system is not meant to produce hands for industry but to create responsible citizens, and states that continuous lifelong learning should be a core principle of active citizenship for any society or culture (3). Nonetheless, assimilation and conformity can manifest themselves in numerous ways and can affect anyone, and my own experience of the courses I took within the UBC forestry department were, for the most part, very Old School. Whether people make mistakes as agents of large industrial corporations or as ordinary consumers, people cannot help but also exist as individual human beings, whether they are immigrant Canadians or Indigenous peoples. People are grandparents, aunts, uncles, mothers, and fathers, often with their own children, nieces, nephews, and siblings. And all of their decisions have consequences beyond themselves.

The Hoonah Tlingit are a cultural group who, in addition to professing and practising a great deal of respect for their Storied Land, are mostly a small group of people living in a very remote place. They have also been subject, without much recourse, to large political forces from the federal government of the United States of America. In 1991, the leadership of the Hoonah Tlingit was pressured to take on government-sponsored capital and make significant, damaging decisions within the management of forest resources within their traditional territory. As Indigenous activist Jerry Mander writes, in its twinned attempt to facilitate maximum development of Alaska's resources and fully assimilate Indigenous peoples into the market economy, in 1971 the US government passed the Alaska Native Claims Settlement Act (ANCSA) (295). This sweeping legislation resulted in bringing an unprecedented influx of cash and transformative power shifts within many small Alaskan communities. As Canadian Justice Thomas R. Berger describes in his official report for the Alaska Native Review Commission, one of the chief architects of the act, congressional staff assistant William Van Ness, wrote himself that the act was "a very radical effort at social engineering, [which] was done on a very calculated basis" (quoted in Mander 295). Berger goes on to describe that the intention of the act was to impose an immediate and thorough corporate structure upon Native life, which was fully achieved without the US Congress holding any field hearings, wherein the government purposefully excluded all local Indigenous communities from having any part in ether consultation or implementation. Berger also argues in his report that the overriding goal of the US Congress was to provide the most direct means for rapid industrial development of these state lands (ibid.).

With the abrupt creation of the act, the federal government received 60 percent of the land, the state received 30 percent, and Indigenous peoples received 10 percent (ibid., Mander 290–91). Indigenous peoples were given only three dollars per acre for 90 percent of the land base that was taken from them, yet Mander details how all of this money was placed in the control of twelve Indigenous-owned corporations, while the people received shares that could only be put to day-to-day use *after* the protracted process of profit taking could trickle down to reach them, which would be after all industrial activities had concluded (291). Then, after 1991, twenty years after the act was implemented, with the provision of 50 percent approval by Indigenous shareholders, these shares could also be opened for transfer (sale) to non-Indigenous peoples (292).

As journalist Larry Pynn describes, one of the twelve new Indigenous corporations was Huna Totem, which was based out of Chichagof Island's community of Hoonah—a small, predominantly Tlingit town of about one thousand people. Through their federal settlement, Huna Totem received control of about 23,000 acres (9,307 hectares) of land covered in old-growth perhumid rainforest. In 1994 and 1995, after a decade of negotiations and with the realization that they were not capable of managing land in the corporate realm on their own, the community sold their stumpage rights to the regional mother corporation, Sealaska (60). Taking advantage of the exemptions and loose regulations that many of the Indigenous corporations were given within the Tongass National Forest (as opposed to the otherwise tough regulations that had been recently set for non-Indigenous loggers), Sealaska quickly liquidated the breadth of Hoonah's Indigenous heritage—that is, it clearcut the entirety of the mountains of rainforest that rose in plain sight of the village (60).

As Pynn writes, Sealaska shipped the entirety of these raw logs on giant international barges like the *Pan Leader* from South Korea (57). For the people of Hoonah, all proceeds from these transactions were directed into investments, stocks, bonds, and various other outside initiatives. Berger notes in his report that the ANCSA "is a domestic application of theories of economic development that had been applied to the Third World," by which Berger means that the rules of Bankers' Row from the urban south were forced into the business administration vacuum of a small-scale, mostly traditional, subsistence economy, all with the express purpose of displacing and eradicating the traditional Indigenous way of life (quoted in Mander 295–96). Forced into an alien corporate realm, various village corporations were pitted against the twelve regional corporations across the entire state of Alaska. As Mander describes, village corporations found their backs against the wall under pressures to fulfill various legal obligations that included paying state and federal taxes and to avoid bankruptcy and losing their lands altogether; and so many were compelled to hire lawyers and accountants for which they needed to produce income in order to pay more incoming bills from lawyers and accountants, bills that often amounted to between sixty thousand and eighty thousand dollars annually; this meant being forced to develop their lands quickly, far beyond the limits and means and the ethics of their traditional subsistence economies (293–94).

As Berger's report details, giving an overall picture of the consequences of the act, the "ANCSA has affected everything: family relations, traditional patterns of leadership and decision making, customs of sharing, subsistence activities, the entire native way of life. The village has lost its political and social autonomy" (quoted in Mander 295).

Soon after the logging wrapped up, Pynn asked the mayor of Hoonah, Albert Dick (also the chair of Huna Totem), if the whole process was good or bad for his people: "Probably bad. We seem to be getting away from our culture. Our traditional values are disappearing. In the old days, our families were closer" (63). Not surprisingly, Dick exhibits the same characteristics as any politician—he must deal in his community with the same issues found in the white industry towns or the larger multicultural cities of the south: he is worried about succeeding in the following election and about improving the immediate lives of people who are also voters.

"There is pressure," Dick told Pynn: "Our job is to make money. The nature of people is they always want more" (ibid.). Not surprisingly,

Rick Harris, then senior vice president of resources for Sealaska, told Pynn: "If someone else had bought [the timber rights to West Port], they would have gone through it as quickly as possible to recover their investment" (61). Closer to home, UBC historian Richard A. Rajala points to this same general working pattern as he summarizes the routine of abrupt failures experienced by industrial forestry on BC's North Coast: "Its structures of technological and managerial control served only to pursue profitability in world markets at the expense of social and ecological sustainability" (245).

With much of their stumpage revenue tied up in outside investments, the Hoonah Tlingit must wait for future dividends and the rise of second-growth plantations while the clearcut mountain in plain view of the community has disrupted, among other things, most tourism opportunities for generations to come. Alternately, if the logging had been done on a small scale within the considerations of ecosystem-based management, there could have been long-term employment for the Tlingit as well as protection for the biodiversity of West Port. Instead, the 9,307 hectares of clearcuts on Chichagof Island have become yet another consequence of the leading priority of industrial forestry: to maximize activity toward the most immediate profit. For the Hoonah Tlingit, the clearcuts that surround their village are also a forced removal from "the place of sacred thought" that their Storied Lands are meant to actualize within their daily lives; this is all part of what Stó:lō author Maracle characterizes as the ongoing "drought of thought" that infects so many remote communities (23). As the demands of government and industry combine to force Indigenous peoples to "manage" and "develop" their local "resources," this usually means one or another means of liquidating the heritage of their traditional Storied Lands (23).

Change is serious business—gut-wrenching, really. With
humans it is important to approach it with great intensity.
Great storms alter earth, mature life, rid the world of the old,
ushering in the new. Humans call it catastrophe. Just birth,
Raven crowed.

— Lee Maracle, Stó:lō author (1993)

transect 10

human garbage versus rainforest damage,
windthrow and dwarf mistletoe,
fungi and coarse woody debris.

HERE ON THE NORTH COAST, THE THANKSGIVING WEEKEND STORM OF
2010 was one of those increasingly frequent "once-in-a-century"
events. From about 10:00 p.m. on October 9, winds gusted up to
126 kilometres an hour (68 knots) across *Xaaydaa Gwaay*, reaching the
mainland in the small hours of the morning, with one source declar-
ing that the winds rose to 150 kilometres an hour (Luba, Armstrong
Thanksgiving). Captain Pawel Urbanski at the container port in Rupert
told Bruce Wishart that his gauges hit 160 km an hour (about 86 knots).
Urbanski believes that many gusts exceeded the capacity of the gauges:
"That's far into Beaufort force 12, the top of the scale. A hurricane."

On the North Coast, exaggerations about climate and geography
are mostly just distracting redundancies that serve no helpful purpose.
At worst, ornate tales of spectacular incidents can sting those with
unsettling memories into reliving their own experiences of discomfort,
which often stretch beyond awe to psychological harm. Just as no true
local ever bothers with an umbrella, personal facts about the weather
are usually stranger than fiction, to the point where it appears rude or

just inane to add superfluous details. Mostly, it's embarrassing. As far as winter weather goes, most locals wish the superfluity would ease off for a few minutes. It would all be laughable were it not that the often unwelcome outcome of extreme weather events can become serious problems for people who have to make a living and keep a roof locked down over their heads.

Both the *Muskeg News* and the *Northern View* wrote that Saturday night's storm left significant damage, throwing trees and roof materials onto numerous streets throughout Prince Rupert (Armstrong *Thanksgiving*). A number of freestanding transport trailers were flipped over in industrial parks, sometimes onto other vehicles; one house lost its roof—not just the shingles, but the joists and beams. The funeral home down by the RCMP station lost part of its roof, as did the camera shop across from the museum, and many mobile homes were dragged from their supports, with the front end of one being ripped entirely open (Armstrong *Thanksgiving*, Luba). North of Terrace, the Nisga'a highway was closed due to downed trees, and the storm knocked out hydro service for every district west of Smithers in the entire North Coast area (*A Town Called Podunk*). The *Haida Gwaii Observer* reports that within a few hours the wind had knocked out four hundred BC Hydro power stations, while sheet lightning and exploding transformers gave most communities an unwelcome fireworks display. By Sunday, fifty thousand residents had lost their electricity (Wishart). At dozens of sites, telephone lines and infrastructure for cell and internet service were taken down by falling trees. For those who did not lose their power, the TV, cable, and radio had nothing to broadcast except static.

Not surprisingly, Pacific Northern Gas (PNG) was impacted, as winds and heavy rain combined to initiate a debris flow that severed the natural gas line, twenty kilometres east of Prince Rupert (Armstrong *Gas*). Greg Weeres of PNG told the *Muskeg Press* that the severed line was in a remote valley that had to be accessed with helicopter crews. During the interval of repairs, the gas flow ran dry and PNG workers had to go door to door in order to reactivate household service (*Gas*).

The *Province* wrote that the windstorm swept all the way to Chetwynd and Fort St. John in the Peace District (Luba).

Out in the woods, it's always a different story.

From downtown Prince Rupert, a fifteen-minute walk south or west is all that is required to put anyone with cooperative feet up and inside of an old-growth rainforest. You just step off the gravel, and, if you can muster it, penetrate the seemingly impenetrable biotic band-aid of salmonberry, alder, and elderberry that is always at work in the sprinkling light to repair and refill the disruption zone.

Gary Snyder describes how "the whole phenomenal world and the mathematics that might be said to underlie it are all creatively and freely orderly" and how "in the non-human universe, not a single leaf that falls from a tree is ever out of place" (*Ecology* 6). This idea leads me to follow intuition and find out whether or not there is coherence, purpose, and even a human lesson lurking in the aftermath of the Thanksgiving storm of 2010. I prepare myself with rain gear and the right boots in order to plunge up into the shaded slope of living conifers and crisscrossing windthrow. I have an inherent understanding that there is knowledge to be gained up here, of a kind useful for considering the haphazard grid of streets and buildings below—those that, as Chris Armstrong writes, the town's wealthy founder, Charles Hays, created with destruction, "blowing most of the muskeg and rocks to bits at the waterfront, levelling the land for trains," as Hays envisioned that Rupert would one day rival Vancouver as a port and commercial centre (*Dwelling* 1).

Curious as I am for inferences to be drawn from storm wind-throw damage, I have hiked a long ways up Wantage, the gravel road that runs behind the golf course and eventually arcs up to the top of Mount Hays. After a short distance I am surrounded by rainforest—it struts up a very steep slope that steps back and forth from jutting rock bluffs to slightly gentler terrain, every bit of it wrangled by big trees, deadfalls, mosses, and ferns, all reaching up as trickling water streams down. At this point I have found a young hemlock tree whose broken top, thoroughly overgrown with moss, looks like the head and antlers of a shaggy green caribou. Commonly referred to as witch's broom, this example of "disorganized growth" is caused by a parasitic plant, western dwarf mistletoe *(Arceuthobium tsugense)*, which often leads to structural weaknesses and breaks in the trunk at points directly above the abnormal growth (Pojar and MacKinnon 308). Windstorms of the kind experienced in October 2010 are perfect for taking down the malformed tops of hemlock and other trees such as this, which diminishes the spread of the parasite. Dwarf mistletoe must renew itself by explosively ejecting seeds from the tiny berries that form upon its tiny, primitive, leafless stalks where they grow high up in the canopy (ibid.). Seed dispersal occurs with a buildup of hydraulic pressure after cold weather; the sticky seeds fly from the branch and rain down within a radius of a few metres, rarely landing upon the branches and trunks of younger, smaller trees. As University of Alaska biologists Rita M. O'Clair and Robert H. Armstrong describe, most of the projected seeds land uselessly upon the forest floor or fall onto hemlock needles, where they are loosened by the rain, fall to the moss, and die (214). Still, some are caught within the feathers of Steller's jays and the fur of flying squirrels and are then carried to new parts of the forest; here, the transport species preens free the sticky seed, which then can bond to the branches of a new host tree and start a new process of infection (ibid.).

As a strident supporter of clearcut logging, resource ecologist and industry advocate Patrick Moore writes that western dwarf mistletoe will eventually infect each tree in an older stand, "resulting in stagnation of growth and deformity to the stem as well as the branches" (72). "The only effective way to remove the infection," Moore writes, "is by killing their hosts" (ibid.). Moore proposes that all hemlock stands of this kind be clearcut, as a selective cut will leave both younger trees and the planted stock "subjected to a rain of mistletoe seeds from the big trees growing over them" (74). By Moore's estimation, the spreading infection would "produce a forest of deformed, slow-growing trees," and, as he adds his own socio-political tone to the supposed disaster, he tells us that "this is not good for the trees or for the owners trying to make a living and pay their taxes" (ibid.). While it is true that the activity of tops breaking off in windstorms is not as efficient a kill of mistletoe as clearcut logging, there are many forest biologists who have alternate perspectives on mistletoe management.

Forester Barry R. Noon writes that "structures such as cavities, broken tops, epicormic growths, and mistletoe brooms…provide nest sites for old-growth-associated species such as spotted owls, goshawks, flying squirrels, tree voles, and bats" (46). From the microcosm of the pro-clearcut perspective, the parasitic aspect of the destructive activity of mistletoe is the only one selected for examination, as the pest apparently does nothing but destroy quality sawlogs and keep the working man from performing his civic duty. In this view, the only thing that the forest is good for is the timber it supplies, which must be harvested as quickly as possible, before the forest destroys itself, leaving in its place a rotting rubble field of no value. For Moore, it's all death and taxes, and the forest is its own worst enemy. From Moore's perspective, western mistletoe is a plague, and it's a wonder that there are any hemlock-dominated rainforests left anywhere on the North Coast. From this clearly anthropocentric view of pure utility, stand liquidation is the only option.

By contrast, Noon reveals a more complex picture of balanced self-management within the ecological breadth of the rainforest macrocosm. Taking a longer and a deeper look, dwarf mistletoe is one of many "plants" within the community and plays an important role in the regulation of rainforest health and biodiversity. Not only does the rainforest have its own substantial evolutionary experience to properly and adequately develop the most productive breadth of interconnected species and communities, as human beings, we would do better to mimic its natural strategies with more respectful harvest practices, those that promote long-term health and diversity more than liquidation for the sake of a few winters' work of profit taking.

Drawn onward by the abstract æsthetic pull of the witch's broom that has warped the top of the young hemlock, I walk further up the gravel to a spot where the weave of salmonberry canes does not appear completely non-negotiable. Once I've scraped myself past them, I head straight up the rainforest slope as much as the steepness of the terrain, the intermittence of devil's club, and the water rushing over everything allows. The pitch varies from 40 to 100 percent, which means I'm switching back and forth from crawling uphill on all fours to climbing haphazardly over the crumbling rungs of mossy ladders collapsing with each step. Still, within 150 metres of heading up the dark slope I come upon the tall, jagged stump of what I consider to be a fairly significant spruce. Having fallen uphill on the diagonal, its shattered remains lie in giant pieces, some thrown up on the other side of a small but loud gully where January snowmelt rushes down the mountain.

After slithering into the gully, stumbling over the stream and crawling up the other side in a haphazard line, I meet the first and then the second of the drenched chunks of shattered tree. Each is the size of a living-room sofa and covered with thick moss that links with the forest floor. The pieces are in different stages of decay, depending upon how much of their mass is in direct contact with the shaded and always wet (perhumid) ground or, conversely, how much is either suspended or caught along the tracking path of sunfleck openings that receive more sunlight.

Here I see a number of healthy examples of a common polypore fungus known as artist's conk (*Ganoderma applanatum*). Their large fruiting bodies jut in numerous grey-brown and cream-striped brackets, each the size of a hubcap or larger, all thriving in cool shadow upon their stations along rotting wood. One conk in particular is over forty centimetres wide, with typical form—a half-moon-shaped bracket, brilliant white on the underside and arranged in brown, black, and grey zones above. It has been growing on a quartered-off piece of trunk that has been jostled about once more, upended by an even more recent tumble, perhaps twenty-five or thirty years ago. Since then, the section with the large polypore growth has turned partway around and is no longer on its side, yet the fungus has continued to thrive within the decaying wood. Having been moved from the horizontal to the vertical and taken one half of a turn in relation to gravity, the large fruiting body became dormant but has erupted with six smaller brackets, each flaring out horizontally along the older, now vertical, half-moon spine. The fungus has merely reorganized its growth to realign with its physiological requirements. Each of the six new brackets, mere outgrowths of the older one turned on its side, is slowly expanding and enveloping the upright structure of the now dormant original.

Adaptive. Persistent. Beautiful. Here is an organism that not only did not mind one bit being tossed about in a windstorm but actually responded favourably to being knocked sideways into next week. This polypore also reveals to the critical observer the fact that some disturbances are not just acceptable but are welcome, perhaps even necessary and crucial, for encouraging and renewing health. The windthrow and death of the mature Sitka spruce does not mean its end, but only marks the halfway point of its life within deeper stages of rainforest succession. While the fungus growing on the downed trunk consumes and transforms the biomass present in the rotting trunk, it also creates a snapshot time-lapse image of the incidents that made it change from the horizontal to the vertical and back to the horizontal, all of which is revealed in the Now.

Of course, this creates more questions: Was the Sitka spruce infected beforehand by a parasitic fungus, one that killed off part of the roots or butt of the live tree, or did this weakening effect cause the live, standing tree to break in the wind and fall? If the *Ganoderma* species had been growing on the weakened but standing tree, what role did the substantial weight and structural decay created by its developing mycelia and its crop of fruiting bodies play in hastening the rotting snag's fall in a windstorm? What might this say about the function of wood-composing polypores? Perhaps they are not only the chief decomposers of the rainforest but are also its own strategically and purposefully positioned fulcrums of destruction. Either way, as sledge-hammers of forest decay, fungi pound away at the cellular level to drag these older trees down, laying them low one crumbling snag at a time, actively regulating the efficiency of energy infusion and discharge, doing their part to release useful nutrients within the dead wood for the benefit of ecosystem renewal.

Although some of us know that seemingly lowly organisms like fungi play crucial roles in forest health and the maintenance of bio-diversity, we rarely imagine they possess the power to tear a giant tree down from the canopy and lay it in pieces upon the protruding ribs of the mountainside. Yet this is evidently true as we consider western mistletoe and many other microscopic organisms, most notably *Armillaria* fungi. Unlike the decomposing polypore *Ganoderma*, which invades the tissues of already dead wood, *Armillaria* is a parasitic or predatory fungus that works to kill its host outright, similar to the Real Work that a grizzly bear performs as it drags a salmon out of a stream, tears its living brains out in one bite, then drops the twitching fish to go after another.

Most commonly, *Armillaria* encourages a rot that invades the ground base and roots of a tree and begins to decompose them while the tree stands upright and still very much alive. After a period of perhaps dozens of years, a windstorm will come along and the weakened tree either shatters at the base or tears within its roots, and down it comes. Next, the downed tree quickly dies and is transformed into a *nurse log*, which is another new-old stage of life, one in which its wood fibres slowly disintegrate into essential nutrients that nourish a broad variety of other fungi, bacteria, insects, and a multitude of microorganisms (Stamets 23). Importantly, the fresh opening in the forest canopy also allows younger trees that have been waiting in the shadows the opportunity to launch themselves skyward, where they soon take their places as dominant trees in the ever-changing rainforest.

In looking at the stolid, business-as-usual "common sense" of normative human behaviour, sociologist Sennett warns us that submission to conformity lulls people and groups into the "anonymous kind of respect" we receive from and reciprocate with the strangers who have become neighbours in our increasingly detached communities; an example of this is the typical window-dressing mode of "doing what everyone else did, keeping home and garden neat, living without incident"—at least so long as it appears this way on the surface (17). Yet these tidy scenarios and neat gestures of seeming safety are not necessarily any healthier for human lives than they are for lives in the Wild. Although it may appear that organisms in wild systems are held within regimes of stress and restriction that allow small windows of opportunity, and while there is a need to maintain the integrity of wild systems with human activities that most closely mimic wild processes, we know that ecosystems are perpetually shifting within continuums of change: rainforests move forward through cycles of renewal and decay, revolution and evolution, at once affected by and yet also creating large-scale, dramatic events that are always gestures of creative destruction.

One historic example of the conundrum whereby people make seemingly obvious decisions that inadvertently disrupt Wild necessity can be seen throughout the intensely managed forests of Europe. Here, earlier generations of loggers and rural people "tidied up" their forests and their fringes by removing all of the forest litter and fallen logs from the forest floor. Their purpose was not just to tidy up the landscape but to salvage every last bit of useful wood, yet these habits are responsible for part of the forest health problems that persist here today. The removal of every stick, twig, log, and branch from the forest floor has robbed European ecosystems of their own long-term investments of natural capital (in the form of decaying wood), which is needed for maintaining the overall health of all of the forest's organisms and processes.

Forest biologist Victoria Stevens writes that there is now a lack of naturally occurring fungi in Finland and Sweden and many other countries where this "clean logging" has occurred (95). At both the small and the large scale, these practices have led to a depleted and sterile environment, one that can no longer support the growth of trees with the same qualities as the old-growth forests that existed before the arrival of large human populations, never mind the even more recent "efficient" philosophy and technology of industrial logging. While humans often want things to stay the same in order to make our lives easier, if things must change, it must always be to our own personal benefit. Along this line of thinking, we create institutions that are immoveable and static, frozen in concept and time. We also want our normative ideas to be adopted by others—we imagine this makes things smoother for everyone. Most especially, we alter the larger-than-human world to suit our ideas and purposes, hardly considering that most of this leads to negative consequences in the long term, not just for the voiceless Others of the Wild but also for ourselves.

As readers, writers, and active communicators of the eco-logic that we find in the natural forms of fungi decomposers and rotting nurse logs, philosophers Deleuze and Guattari also invite us to re-participate with similarly intense processes of change within our own communities, as it is our responsibility to imagine and react both ethically and creatively and to engage to the fullest of our ability when disturbance and change gift us with their potential for new opportunities (11). True enough, many larger-than-human organisms and people are injured and die from the powerful forces of disturbance such as windstorms, interpersonal conflicts, and political upheavals, yet both rainforest ecosystems and people are inherently charged with a unique evolutionary adaptability. We all share the same essential will as well as the biotic instinct to reclaim, recycle, and repropel ourselves, even, if we must, beyond the psychological husks of our former selves.

In the Wild, some trees, especially willows (*Salix* species), often have all of their main stems sheared off and yet can rebound in a coppice form with ten times as many shoots, each of which can become more robust than the original. Here on the North Coast, we can find many varieties of this regenerative force at work, such as in the common candelabra forms of some mature western redcedar: A top shears off in a windstorm and three or five or more branches alter their supporting roles and transform into new leaders. If there are a dozen heavy wind-storms over a few hundred years, some trees may develop forty or more heads along the upper half of their trunk. Often, the rainforest harnesses what human beings call destructive power and turns it to its immediate and long-term advantage. The redcedar may be ruined for high-quality sawlogs, but it will still perform a great deal of Real Work in the ecosystem for decades or centuries to come, work that is likely more important than providing building materials for a fence built by a wealthy homeowner who is motivated to present an outward social image of prestige and status. For the larger-than-human realm, there are no questions of why, if, or how to live, just a matter of the degree of intensity realized within each brief opportunity. As we often choose to make a competitive display of dominance, for people these objectives are not quite so clear. We are often more interested in demonstrating our ability to win than we are in expressing some form of participation in our community. This generates a palpable division, one that we force between ourselves and the larger-than-human realm. And it is from this realization that we either choose to participate with Real Work in the Real World or else continue upon more and more imaginary, futile escapes into the unreal.

creatures creatures and creatures the faces of leaves the
shoulders of mountains the movement of ideas in the
tributaries of the Skeena—what is it that I need to say to
transcend that plane, cross over, think like a thicket, move
like lichen ages and ages across my face and nutrients sifting
into the text the spore your eye
—Rob Budde (2008)

Blue Chanterelle (view 2

ALONG WITH THOUSANDS OF OTHER SPECIES OF FUNGI, HERE ON THE
North Coast the mycelia of *Polyozellus* are almost always present within
the forest floor. While they all perform their own biotic duties as para-
sites, saprophytes, or mycorrhizals, only a handful of fungi species will
go on to reveal a fruiting of mushrooms that is visible to the human
eye. Many of these are beautiful to behold, but for some reason, few
are as cherished to me as blue chanterelles. Within the late-successional
forests of spruce, hemlock, and true fir where *Polyozellus* are found, the
appearance of their fruit is much rarer than with other species. Forest
biologist E.J.H. Corner writes in his *Monograph of Cantharelloid Fungi*
that blue chanterelles occur only in association with the roots of *Abies*
(true fir) within mid-elevation, montane coniferous forests, but this is
not true, as *Polyozellus* has also been found hundreds of kilometres
away from the nearest true fir (96). They are even locally plentiful on
the isolated islands of X̱aaydaa Gwaay, where there is not one Indigenous true fir to be found.

The reason for this and other local discrepancies is mostly due to
the fact that no comprehensive study of the species (or any other fungi)
has been conducted in northern BC. Fruiting as they do for just a few
select weeks of the year in the hidden heights of very wild forests—

places where visits by humans are even rarer than blue chanterelles—it is no surprise that they are seldom found, or even reported when they are. Northern BC is also a place where science dollars for non-timber values are almost non-existent. These days, research funds are funnelled into the most lucrative profit-generators possible, activities such as mining, gas-plant development, the clearcutting of beetle-killed pine, and the promotion of bitumen transport across some of the most fragile and rugged lands of clean water and wild salmon habitat on the planet. It's calculator logic: if an inscrutable, unprofitable species cannot be man-handled into the crib of a transport truck and transformed into some kind of immediate dollar value, it will receive little or no attention beyond a bit of lip service, even though it may be critical for the build-ing, communication, and maintenance of the last healthy, productive rainforests on Turtle Island.

Walking as I do in the trees, trying to see beyond the blind spots of science and culture in Canada, I have found the inspiration of outlier dissidence and blue chanterelles in nearly every forest I have worked in. I have even found these items down in the driest, pine-dominated stands of the Cariboo, in south-central BC, and, again, with not a true fir in sight, and amidst the furthest thing from temperate, perhumid conditions.

When I am very lucky, I find small clusters of semigloss, often sparkling, bright purple, black, or vivid blue sporocarps, most usually spreading their blue mouths just above the moss. Here and there and there, circling under the trees in sparse, interrupted arcs, these small mushrooms burst to air like folded hands as bright and pure as cobalt, marking out an outer perimeter with broad mycelial rings that have been creeping wider and wider under the moss and through the roots of conifers for generations upon generations. I have wandered in slow pursuit of small pocketfuls of purple and gold, silver and blue, and sometimes jet black mushrooms, spying them out where they hide under suspended logs, within shaded nooks at the fluted bases of trees, obscured within other shady spots covered by branches, hidden within leaves and the thick foliage of herbs. Often, they unfold into loosely fragmented rings over the moss in collections of only a few mushrooms, taking up a space no wider than the breadth of a hand, or they can grow in fragmented rings of clusters that stretch around in a circle thirty metres across, containing hundreds of mushrooms. Usually, the route for finding and collecting these punctuated clusters of fruit takes me around in a loop through the tangled forest, right back to where I started.

Morphologically, the dorsal caps of blue chanterelles usually rise only two to four centimetres above the moss, but there will often be five to twenty or more half-funnel-shaped or partly spoon-shaped mushrooms joined or fused together to one long central stem, with each individual "spoon" being six to eighteen centimetres high, swimming intertwined as they are, deep within the local complex of bryophytes and a thick sprinkling of conifer needles. Sometimes, after stumbling along in the forest for weeks without a discovery, I stumble over a blue outcrop the size of a truck tire, with a hundred or more mushrooms crammed and overlapped together in a dense glomeration. Amazingly, between early September and early November of 2011, after a summer when my co-workers complained about the endless rain and fierce mosquitoes, I brought home boxes and boxes of blue chanterelles. I even found a place near the north shore of West Francois Lake where they were dappled like dark blue cow-pies for a hundred metres along the edge of a logging road.

Polyozellus has also recently become known for its medicinal properties. Besides the fact that the species has been neglected by Western science and that the Occident itself is generally fungiphobic, views in the Orient are quite different. Korean research has uncovered chemopreventive effects within *Polyozellus* when used in combination with other cancer-fighting treatments, having particularly positive affects for the treatment of leukemia and hepatoma (Hyun-Jeong Kim and Jung Han). A number of cancer inhibitors have been isolated in polyozellin (as the extract compound is called), which may prove important in the fight against Alzheimer's disease (H-J. Lee and I-K. Rhee;

Hwang, Song, Kim and others). Polyozellin and its associate agents also inhibit the growth of many cancer-cell growth lines and have been found to protect a key tumour suppressor against DNA damage (ibid.). Polyozellin has also been found to provide significant reductions in proliferating cancer-cell growth in combination with other drugs (Hyun-Jeong Kim and Jung Han). This early-stage research affirms that polyozellin deserves more study in order to establish its potential as a cancer-preventive agent (Kim, Lee, Song et al.). Much more than a culinary delight, a rare element of ecological æsthetics, and an important agent of forest health, blue chanterelles also represent a precious gift of potential medicine for human beings. For me, this "new" information is no surprise.

Here in Prince Rupert, hanging on the wall above my writing desk, there is a photo of my partner, Lisa, standing small and beautiful in her dark blue raincoat underneath a large and equally beautiful mountain near the shore of the *Khyex* River. Beside this photo is a large map of *Xaaydaa Gwaay* and a small coloured-pencil drawing I did a few years ago of three blue chanterelles. As a raven might fly, southeast to northwest, the islands of *Xaaydaa Gwaay* are approximately 270 kilometres long and comparatively rich with rarified communities of *Polyozellus*. Although it is always a singular experience to pluck even one handful of purple-blue winged fruit out of moss, I see another aspect of wonder that I hadn't considered. More recently, I was back out on my knees in the wet neckera under a fat, resinous subalpine fir, stripping away one *Polyozellus* sporocarp from its purple-blue cluster, not just to admire it but to pack it away with the rest for my supper. Laying it upon my hand, I was struck by the sight of a nearly exact imprint of the islands of *Xaaydaa Gwaay*, resting small and blue upon the palm of my hand, which told me that much more exists under the surface of things than we ordinarily pause to consider, understand, or imagine.

People are challenged to understand, to be able to relate to the time and space of forest landscapes. Forests operate on cycles of 200 to 2,000 years. If we are lucky, our lives may last 100. If our governments are lucky, they last four years. Our corporate institutions function on one-year profit and loss statements...A moderate-sized watershed (e.g., 500 hectares or 1,235 acres) would require months for two people to explore, to map, and to begin to understand the relationships within this landscape.

—Herb Hammond (1997)

transect 11

perhumid rainforest succession,
small-scale patch events,
snags, deadfalls, and nurse logs.

TO USE MORE THAN THREE WORDS, THE STRUCTURES AND DYNAMICS OF a perhumid rainforest contain a multiplicity of interrelationships, all of which reflect the community histories of numerous species in the process of adapting to small-scale changes in weather, climate, and stand composition. Within perhumid rainforest succession, the daily mosaic of interconnectivity cycles within the push-pull of growth, decay, and renewal, and the long-term pace is set by the species composition, structure, and age of the canopy of very old trees, those that rise above the foundation of even much older legacies of dead wood upon which the whole system stands and expands.

As for the common myth that old-growth rainforests are so ancient as to be unhinged from time, forester Thomas A. Spies writes that "no single scale is sufficient to understand these natural systems. Forest patterns and dynamics are always varying (although not uniformly) across time and space" (36). BC government forest researchers Roberta Parish and Joseph A. Antos describe how these perhumid rainforests have been changing in their development over the last seven thousand years (and in some cases much longer), almost always through the system of mosaic complexes of small-scale patch dynamics (573). Change is rarely the result of major, stand-level disturbances such as fire (which is the commonest form of succession in the interior) and stand-levelling episodes of disease are just as rare in coastal old growth, because the broad diversity of species and ages creates a biological fail-safe against the heterogeneity that encourages infestation within single-species dominance (562).

The kind of small-scale patch events that are typical of North Coast rainforests are usually the result of *gatgyeda uksbaask* (heavy winds), *maadmgyeks beega aks* (snowstorms), *gaddziks* (rains) and other intermittent seasonal and climate-related events (572). Incidents like these affect only a few trees in close proximity. One tree will break and part or all of it may fall to the forest floor, often taking a few smaller trees with it, likely damaging a few more on the way down. While a great many of these damaged trees remain standing, some will die as a result of injury and will fall over in the intervening years, repeating the process and perpetuating a slow-motion domino effect of self-thinning across the breadth of the rainforest (573). Either way, there is now a break, with a one- to ten-tree opening in the dense canopy, which introduces an increase of *gyemgm dziiws* (sunlight), which means the opportunity for seed germination and an episode of relatively rapid growth for conifer seedlings over the next few years. A foliar eruption begins with the *here* and *there* of this small, sagging tree group of decomposition, which is also a starting point for the consumption and redistribution of the unravelling story volumes of the giant that has recently fallen.

Although the small-scale patch dynamic is the primary method of succession for perhumid rainforests of the North Coast, the germination of new conifer seedlings by this method occurs very infrequently. Sometimes these small-scale patch events are separated by decades, but in most cases the interval is many centuries (ibid.). In addition to the growth of new seedlings, there is often the regenerative release of many nearby *k'yiin* (saplings). In many cases these small, shade-restricted trees will have gained less than a centimetre of diameter stem growth in thirty, fifty, or even one hundred years and will be no taller than a *wan* (blacktail deer) (571). Regenerative release is the rare moment in temperate rainforest time when the many smaller trees that have been waiting in the shaded understory for decades are given their first real opportunity to experience enough direct light to be able to grow (573).

In order to comprehend the perspective of the perhumid rainforest, we must disengage from the relatively rapid pace and focus of human life. With its moderate climate, extreme rainfall, and complex biological conditions, the perhumid rainforest has the biotic propensity for the extremely slow yet profoundly long growth of conifer trees, while the development of some of their smaller associate communities, like lichens and fungi, can take nearly as long (572). For a *gyiik* (hemlock tree), the fate of spending decades or even a century down in the understory is common. But even though a tree is unable to change position and move a few metres over to a better microsite, windstorms and snowstorms achieve this effect when they tear other, larger trees out of the way and create an opening.

Even as human-observed details of ecological science expand our understanding of the functions and processes of perhumid rainforests, as forest biologist Victoria Stevens tells us, "there are many more species and interactions than we currently know of," which should caution us to carefully consider any large-scale transformations of forest lands (93). Even while it might seem obvious at first glance that the life of a giant tree ends when it dies and meets with the forest floor, there are hundreds of other individual life forms and small communities whose lives depend upon the relatively brief moment of opportunity that a tree's death represents. Various mammals, birds, and amphibians, networks of minute plants; miniscule insects, countless varieties of microbes, and bacteria all move in to perform their own *Hałels Gyilhawli*

(Real Work) as they quickly transform the mass of the tree upon the ground and slowly fill the scrap of grey sky that blinks from above. With the arrival of the gift of *lu galam spagaytgangan* (an opening in the forest), many creatures and plants that are dependent upon the presence of a dead tree will fly, crawl, scurry, sprout, and convene to both compete and collaborate for various means of access to its riches (Bartemucci, Coates et al. 685). Within the dynamic scenario of the small-scale patch event, the rainforest is always in the process of picking itself back up right from the moment it falls down, sending up sprightly new revisions of itself, either upon or near the crumbling biomass gift of this large dead tree.

Considering that many species here will grow for millennia (as do trees and fungi) or that some species may take a century or more to establish their communities (as do some lichen, birds, and other terrestrial and non-terrestrial vertebrates), a few hundred years or more between this patch and that patch represents only a moment in *biogeochronic* time. The biogeochron is a term that is valuable to consider, as it signifies both the biotic complexity and breadth of the perhumid rainforest. Combining elements of life (bios), physical setting (geos), and time (chronos), this deeper concept was created in 1965 by Vladimir Joseph Krajina, the UBC forest scientist who also developed BC's biogeoclimatic ecosystem classification system, a research and management model that is regarded highly and utilized to protect Real Work in ecosystems across the globe (Hebda and Whitlock 228). Yet, to think of our own coastal perhumid rainforests in terms of their various life-giving properties, the dynamism of their varied geographies and weather patterns, and the scale of their overlapping time frames, a consideration of such a thing as biogeochronic time is still one small part in coming to understand the ground-truth importance of the Real Work they perform.

When viewed as a whole within such an old-growth forest system as this, a mosaic of the various patch ages in the process of long-term succession will often include the fullest possible breadth of species found in the local region. And more. Within what can be called a zone of exceptional quality, diverse communities of interconnected species survive and thrive in response to innumerable influences and features that are all likely present in the habitat or that exist within close proximity (Parish and Antos 573). In turn, many small-scale local (microsite) features have a considerable affect upon *yugyetk* (the health) of any number of overlapping rainforest communities. These features may be the elevation, the hydrology, the position and frequency of streams, the relative presence of slopes of differing aspect (facing north, south, east, or west), the influence of areas of open rock and standing water, and, importantly, any interface with *dzoga'aks* (the terrestrial/marine ecotone—the rich intertidal zone where salt water and land overlap) (Simenstad, Dethier et al. 149).

If we imagine the composite elements of the small-scale patch disturbance model, the *lagangan* (oldest trees) consist not only of the overarching living matrix, with individuals up to one thousand years old, they also include the underlying dead matrix of much older trees, those that have remained intact and in various stages of *lox haaya* (decay) for many more hundreds of years. As research biologist Lori Daniels and others tell us, a variety of snags may stand for more than 250 years within numerous stages of decline, while decaying redcedar logs on the rainforest floor may persist for as long as 550 to 1,200 years after they have died (1132).

A comprehensive look at this dead matrix reveals a breadth of age and size classes of woody decay elements (WDE). These WDEs are made up of standing dead trees (snags), horizontal dead trees (with those that lie fully integrated in the ground often categorized as nurse logs), and ever smaller pieces of coarse woody debris (CWD). These smallest elements are all of the branches, splinters, chips, twigs, and conifer needles that make up the decomposing base of the rainforest floor (commonly called "litter"). Considering the often immense piece sizes of dead wood present in the perhumid rainforest, CWD is found not only embedded within and resting upon the forest floor but vast quantities of it remain lodged at various layers within the canopy for years, where they slowly decompose upon large branches and jammed between the boles of crisscrossing trees.

Throughout the CWD/forest floor matrix, there are untold numbers of organisms engaged in thousands of symbiotic, parasitic, and hunter-prey relationships (Marcot 4). In terms of species, all of these smaller organisms profoundly outnumber the limited but essential number of larger plants and trees that we can see as we walk along (or, as is so often the case, as we crawl or stagger from place to place). As well, interpenetrating and "clinging" to the rainforest floor and whatever might be embedded within it are thousands of large and small varieties of *microflora*. These are the common fungi and lichen we can see, as well as so many more that are microscopic, most of which remain unidentified and whose greater value in forest health can only be imagined.

There is also a vast community of competing and symbiotic *microfauna*, mainly taking the form of bacteria, microbes, and various other tiny organisms, most of which live in the *rhizosphere* (the zone of plant-root activity) and within the fibres of CWD. In both living and dead trees, whether upright or down on the forest floor, communities of large and small vertebrates and multitudes of smaller invertebrates make up the *macrofauna* and *mesofauna*. These are the *laalt* and *gyiik* (worms, insects, mites, and many smaller creatures), most of which are tiny to the point of being invisible. These tiny communities live generation after generation in vast colonies within the stage depths of decomposition and all are essential for the productive capability of everything that is good, healthy, and rotting (Armson 90–108).

Stepping back, when we look up the dead standing length of an otherwordly "living," dead tree—perhaps a conifer snag bearded with flags of *nagaganaw ada demtii* (lichen and epiphytic fern), we know that it teems with numerous microbes, slime moulds, bacteria, insects, and worms; and we must take as much care when we step as when we look up or down, knowing that everywhere under our feet live the largest and most crucial components of the living matrix of creatures and communities within the perhumid rainforest. Considering the productive value within a forest, a tree is actually *amwaal* (worth) much more dead than alive. This makes sense, as biologist Stevens tells us that half the time a mature tree persists in a forest is time spent giving back as decomposing wood (89). Whether standing upright or jackstraw, living and thriving for the sake of its own growth, playing supporting roles for so many other life forms, or slowly rotting down within the forest floor, the life model presented by a tree presents a wholly equitable eco-logic. Both alive *and* dead, trees represent an upstanding principle: that at least half the lives and half the energies of all living things should be spent in *gaxk'eeyła* (giving back) to their communities, and with the same intensity with which they received their life and growth in the first place. Practitioners of traditional First Nations customs perform this ritual act with every *xmas* (ceremonial death feast) they hold; as *xmas* itself means, quite literally, "to experience/consume red."

Describing its roles in rainforest productivity, Stevens reveals that CWD "adds a significant amount of organic matter to the soil" and, as coarse woody debris degrades, it becomes more porous, thus holding onto moisture, not only for times of drought but in order to create damp refuges for mycorrhizae, plant roots, salamanders, insects, and many other smaller organisms (90). Forest biologist Stevens tells us that CWD also provides an active site for asymbiotic and associative nitrogen-fixing bacteria and that CWD also represents "a capital pool of nutrients for the ecosystem" (ibid.). What this all means is that dead, rotting wood is one of the crucial exchange sites for the activities of the microorganisms that manufacture chemical nutrients for the establishment, survival, and growth of so many of the newly germinated plants that help create the rainforest in the first place.

Stevens also tells us that CWD provides "a site for the regeneration of conifers" (ibid.). And it's true, as so many new green things require the aid of a nurse log, even the giant trees themselves. For a seedling, a nurse log is a hummock that gets them out of standing water; it is a perch for reaching sunlight and to help in climbing above the thick green throng; a nurse log is also a rich nutrient source, as its fibres are constantly changing into useable food. Almost any crumbling stump you find on the North Coast may have a variety of plants and small conifer trees growing upon it from wherever there is room for roots, stems, and leaves to grow. Eventually, the sprawling roots of new conifers will enlarge and swell to hold on like a clenched fist, and after a century or more of slowly consuming the nutrients in the decomposing wood, most often nothing will remain but an immense cage of mature roots surrounding an empty cavity.

As BC forest biologist Les W. Gyug tells us, CWD in the form of nurse logs and nurse stumps is valuable due to the fact that in wet riparian forests and coastal floodplains, the germination and early development of conifers can often occur only upon the hummocks that they provide, as these are often the only locations that persist above the water table long enough for seedling survival (17). And what is this dark wet lint that rainforest trees find within the hummocky god-pockets upon which they grow? Cellulose (polyglucuronics); hemicelluloses (xylans); lignins; water-soluble fractions (simple sugars, amino acids, and other compounds); ether and alcohol-soluble compounds (fats and oils, waxes, resins and pigments, proteins, and mineral constituents)—all of which are the very stuff of life (Armson 68–69). Lastly, any nurse log you can find upon the rainforest floor does not *ksi niits dabn* (discriminate) about who or what shall receive its gifts: perhaps it will be another young hemlock tree, or the asphodel lily (*Tofieldia glutinosa*), red huckleberry, golden thread moss (*Leptobryum pyriforme*), turkey tail polypore (*Trametes versicolor*), nitrogen-fixing pink wintergreen (*Pyrola asarifolia*), false azalea, as well as so many varieties of lichen, and on and on and on—all are simply *gyiwilanool* (welcome).

In addition to the maintenance of forest health and productivity, another benefit of CWD is the crucial role it plays in maintaining *łagayt txa'nii goo diduuls* (biodiversity), as CWD provides ideal habitat structures for the wide variety of organisms that crawl, wriggle, or squirm through the rainforest (Stevens 93). While upright snags (or wildlife trees, as the more generous forester might call them) provide unique habitats for species such as bats, insects, and birds, the dwelling spaces provided by downed logs are even more dynamic due to their essential connection to the forest floor. On the North Coast, while it may take up to 1,200 years for a large log to fully decay, the variability of size, species, and placement of such a wealth of snags, logs, and large fallen branches makes sure that the fullest possible breadth of structure are available for an immense number of organisms to build their communities and live out their lives, which benefits us all (Daniels et al. 1132).

Looking closer still, as they perform the most essential kind of Real Work, the first invertebrates to arrive at a dead log or dying tree serve double duty, as the entrance tunnels they make with their feeding activities become inoculated with fungi, bacteria, mites, nematodes, and protozoans, some of which are the phylogenetic partners they carry along with them upon their bodies or leave behind within their frass deposits. As the log decays over time, more varieties of organisms make their way through these initial entry points, feeding, making homes, and burrowing deeper and deeper within the decaying sapwood, and, perhaps after centuries, penetrating and decaying the heartwood.

As we look at the whole picture from afar, CWD provides a beneficial infrastructure for the entire mountainside, playing an important support role in the geomorphology of streams and steep slopes. Besides the fact that its water-retaining fibres absorb rainfall and runoff, the overall strength and ubiquity of CWD across the slope creates a physical matrix that slows and diverts the many trickles, flows, and powerful deluges that sometimes rush with overwhelming force down the mountain. Lastly and importantly within our current situation of industrial pollution, CWD are vessels for long-term carbon storage (Stevens 94). And while there is much more to be learned about the functional relations of decaying wood and the various colonizers and decomposers that live within their influence, the contribution of CWD to the health and maintenance of forest systems cannot be overstated.

While the greenhorn human might come to see that there is much more cracking and squishing underfoot than they first imagined, what else is there that eyes cannot see but that the mind might grasp? What is there to be read out of so much piling and compiling debris? What does the rainforest say, if it can be said to "speak" at all with its many tree, moss, forb, and fungal voices? To borrow from poet Ken Belford, what lan(d)guages does the Indigenous rainforest speak? And, going further, do these lan(d)guages speak in ways that human beings can hear or even perhaps understand?

For local First Nations peoples, this subject is hardly new, and this is what makes up the eternal object of *Earth's Mind*, a concept that many traditional thinkers have believed and experienced over extended generations spent dwelling in the Now of reciprocal interbeing within their Storied Lands. While we now know that downed logs, limbs, branches, and litterfall are all part of the health, function, and structural systems of these local perhumid rainforests, these elements can also be seen as vital components of the communication network of their larger-than-human communities. Woody decay elements are the tables of contents, bibliographies, and indexes for the ongoing recomposition of every story that has ever been told in the life and death and influence of a tree. The simmering floors of the rainforest are wood-fibre filing cabinets arranged by minute degrees of redrot, with new files of leaves and branches being added, with everything always in the process of crumbling apart into new episodic plotlines—these red to green to red stories cross-referencing themselves within innumerable foreshadows of the next season's as well as the next millennium's events.

Linguist and poet Robert Bringhurst tells us that every living thing is a story: "spruce trees and toads and timber wolves and dog salmon," all of which are composed of the carbon, nitrogen, and phosphorus that eventually make their way back into a rainforest tree and back into the body of yet another organism (Tree 167, 168). Sociologist Sennett explains things similarly, describing how human "narratives are more than simple chronicles of events; they give shape to the forward movement of time" (30). And it's the same when we consider a young hemlock tree waiting for decades in the shade and being finally able to penetrate the canopy after a storm takes down just one mature spruce tree from the canopy.

The upward growth of rainforest time is written with more than just the tearing of roots, the pungent uncovering of soil and stone, and the obvious mark of a long resinous scrape down the mountainside. For every monoecious leviathan gymnosperm that goes down, a million microscopic mouths of macrofauna and mesofauna are opened and filled. In the larger narrative of the smallest forest activities, there are far more productive revisions and renewals than destructions and losses.

After the fungi-infected, butt-rotten tree is laid down as a crumbling log to collapse and re-merge with the mountainside, its grey-brown mast becomes an even larger moss-wood-fungi-insect-microbe community—it becomes a complex of minute biotic cities that swell and slowly shatter within the rain-dissolving broadcast of redrot fibres across a cascading series of decades of rainy seasons. Darkening and softening, eventually expressing and consuming red, writing new life stories in smaller and smaller lexical units, these crumbling components will all eventually be overwritten with a steady, white fungal cursive. And these new stories of decay and dispersal only extend the narrative, pushing it even deeper into finer and more intimate layers of community life, just as they physically separate and expose all of the knowledges that have previously been bonded within sapwood and heartwood, tearing them all into smaller, wetter, darker specks of tree-spoken ink.

Eventually, perhaps after one thousand years, there will be a full return of the ecosystem's initial upward investment into a scattered group of new, small young sapling trees. This is Real Work: the loosing of elemental Indigenous phrases in rain percolations from branch to stream to sea, and back again. *Ła dm yaayu dm gooyu wap ha'iliitsx a spagaytgangan* (Tsimshian terms from *Sm'algyax Living Legacy Dictionary*).

Prosperity, of course, was the name of the game; the Bible
decreed it, and the government encouraged it. If not for profit,
advancement, or adventure, why else would one leave all that
was safe and familiar to do battle with giants?

—John Vaillant (2005)

Mountain Hemlock (view 2

WILD ÆSTHETICS/TROPES OF BRANCHES: EAGLES WITH OUTSTRETCHED wings—dark, bluish-green, drooping—spread for landing, pitched for take-off. Scrappy foliage spreads outward excurrently in mossy green beards, in diagonal layers, often holding itself in thick patches against the bole—twisting and turning within shreds of dark green, always with a bright upward sweep where the shiniest young tips burst in spring.

Wild pragmatics: Unlike the broad flat sprays of western hemlock, mountain hemlock needles are short, equally stomatized, curved, smaller, and cover the branches in dense, variable sprays. Pojar and MacKinnon give us a heads up, pointing out that "mountain hemlock do not provide good shelter from the rain because some of its branches slope upwards" (31). And it's true: rainwater is directed toward the trunk and drips down through the entire depth of the tree, often running in waves down the bark.

Mountain hemlock prefer the loose, coarsely textured, well-drained soils of the kind found on the North Coast, where steep mountains are subject to often relentless rainfall (Dahms and Franklin 32). Root production is higher in the subalpine than in the lowlands, and so mountain hemlock create more active root material than is required for water uptake, yet this investment in fine roots and mycorrhizal associations has a purpose, due to the scarcity of mineral nutrients in these extreme upland sites (Grier, Vogt et al. 17).

As essential icons of the hypermaritime subalpine snowforest, mountain hemlock can still thrive after spending eight or nine months of the year encased in a snowbank, but, oddly enough, they cannot grow where soil freezes. Having evolved mainly on community sites where their roots are well-insulated throughout the coldest part of the year, *Tsuga mertensiana* can grow only where snowpacks are established in the warm fringes of early fall and late spring, at the highest elevations (Pojar and MacKinnon 31). Although their foliage can sustain episodes of harsh frost better than either western hemlock or redcedar, the North Coast retains a great deal of open ground at sea level throughout the winter. This keeps roots exposed and in repeated contact with frost, which restricts mountain hemlock to staying just above the snowline (ibid.). Holding this unique and strangely counterintuitive requirement of climate and geography, the species demands that a person must climb quite high to see them.

Mountain hemlock exemplify the paradox of transitionality, as they thrive both within the more competitive subalpine and yet high into the fairly inhospitable alpine. Their niche strategy has been to endure and tolerate where other species cannot, as well as to remain patient down in the deepest shade and wait while their competition outgrows, then dwindles and expires around them. As they are subject to high stress, mountain hemlock carry with them only what will survive the violence of high-elevation winter storms, adapting a form of foliage that can sustain hurricane-force gusts as well as the metre-deep slushfalls that often occur overnight at the snowline. As well, they have adapted to contort-transform their branches to seek out and utilize the smallest patches of sunlight—latching onto those small, gleaming bits that arch in intermittent, elusive circuits through the darkest layers of the fiercely competitive lower elevation understory.

Mountain hemlock form patch communities along the rock crests that reach above all the river systems that collect and drain out of the North Coast: *Xsitxemsem, Shtax' Héen, Gitnadoix, Exstew, Zymagotitz, Babine, Wedeene, Exchamsiks, Xaaydziks, Ecstall, Quaal, Dala, Atna,*

Thautil, Ishkheenickh, Ensheshese, 'Ksan, Kisumkalum, Kincolith, Kateen, Kiteen, Kitamaat, Ktsʹmatʹiin, Kitnayakwa, Khyex, Kitsault, Kwinatahl, Kinskuck, Kemano, Kitwanga, Kehlchoa, Klastine, Klappan, Shelagyote, Nilkitwa, Chutine, Iskut, Spatsizi, Chukachida, Chilkat, Taku, Telsequah, Nakina, Zymoetz, Inklin, Sutlahine, Siltakanay, Anspayaks, and *Stoko.*

Despite the fact that global climate change is increasing both the high-elevation boundaries and the productive capabilities of the species, this "step up" the mountainside also proportionately and substantially decreases the zone they used to dominate at lower elevations. As they are led further up the mountain, western hemlock, yellow-cypress, Pacific silver and subalpine fir also press up at their heels. As lower-elevation species encroach upon them, they displace mountain hemlock from the broadest limits of their lower elevation habitats, forcing them into substantially smaller areas within the almost inhospitable transitional zones of heath and rockland (Franklin, Swanson et al. 15). Thus, every year, mountain hemlock come a bit closer to truly actualizing their name.

Underground: Importantly, mountain hemlock engage in beneficial exchange and growth relationships with more than one hundred fungi and with nearly as many plants. They have important associations with one of their main habitat competitors, Pacific silver fir. Both trees interact with black huckleberry (*Vaccinium membranaceum*), false azalea (*Menziesia ferruginea*), and white-flowered rhododendron (*Rhododendron albiflorum*), three of the most common shrubs of the zone (Brockway, Topik et al. 14). One way that these associations benefit the community is expressed where vegetation influences "microenvironmental dynamics by hastening snowmelt and extending length of the growing season over short distances" (Brooke 14). The cooperation of mycorrhizal fungi, shrubs, and trees creates more hospitable conditions and more robust growth. Increased branch structure of individual shrubs breaks up snow faster and in turn provides a longer growing season for the nearby tree associates. But due to the harsher conditions that exist at the highest elevations, these poorest stands may have as few as eight floristic species to associate with for beneficial exchanges, and the lack of even one associate can make all the difference for survival (Douglas 9). As mountain hemlock are pressed farther and farther up the mountainside, it is unknown whether the associations they hold with their shrub and floristic partners will continue, as these smaller, frailer plants may not survive at higher elevations.

When Rose lived up the coast, her mother sent her new books once or twice a year. "So you won't get too out of touch with reality," her note might say. Or, "So you'll know what's really happening." Exclamation mark. "Love mother."

—Joan Skogan (1994)

transect 12

the moss compass, needs versus wants,
certainty, outliers, and dissidence,
being Xaaydaa and being human.

IN APRIL 2011, WHILE TRYING TO STAY UPRIGHT ON A MOSTLY DIAGONAL Kaien Island mountainside, I found the fresh spring explosion of a tree-ruffle liverwort (*Porella navicularis*) growing upon the stub of a dead branch. Small enough to cup within the palm of one hand, this new addition had sent out between thirty and fifty tiny green compass needles in a radiating spray that completely denied the otherwise standard theory of *negative geotropism* (the typical upward growth of a plant, *against* the force of gravity). What the "anything goes" growth spray of this moss tells me is that when living green bursts out of the rhizoid, all directions are viable, even down. In a place where the sun can rarely be detected in the sky, where light must diffuse at odd angles under thick branches, and where just about any object that juts into the air can become a flower pot, the sky is the ground is the limit.

As an aggregate of entities with a wild logic of their own, the forest "has no beginning and no end because it isn't a linear structure," as Bringhurst describes: "it simply starts where you enter it and ends wherever you come out" (*Tree* 171). The simply dizzying impact of the forest is hardly directionless, although it may not take you where you imagine you want to go and perhaps you will never return the same to what you thought was your home. Within the flapping spectrum of green leaves, as it reconstructs so many repeating signs of *here, here, here, here, here, here, here, here,* and *here* with its endless varieties of leaves, limbs, lichens and mosses, the Indigenous rainforest speaks and writes its own story with its composite of enduring and ephemeral expressions within seemingly unlimited volumes of information— whether crawling, flitting, tumbling, unfurling, or disappearing with a flash into salal. If we take the time to learn even a few of the interconnected stories of green that surround us, we might find that the leaves, the flowers, the muskegs, and the rivers, everything that wriggles and runs and flies, all are signs with specific instructions of where to stop, how to yield, when to turn aside, why to welcome, and who to handle, always, with respect and care.

As a professional investigator of interior human wayfinding, psychologist Tim Kasser works to reveal the complex mechanisms that interfere with our biotic and emotional needs and disrupt our own inherent sense of eco-logic. Although we might assume otherwise, today most human signs, decisions, wants, and needs make very little Real sense. According to Kasser, a need "is not just something a person desires or wants, but is something that is necessary to his or her survival, growth, and optimal functioning" (24). Ideally, needs are the cues humans should respond to for building sustainable, healthy communities, yet the reason why people often feel lost, disoriented, scared, or pointlessly bored is due to perceptions that transform superficial wants into essential needs.

Kasser describes how most of us are inundated by "messages glorifying the path of consumption and wealth [and]…all of us to some extent take on or internalize materialistic values" (26). Providing a similar synthesis of their clinical work, psychologists N.T. Feather and R.A. Emmons tell us that the values and perspectives we hold that arise from our obsession with materialism both transform our lives and influence our goals, disrupting healthful attitudes that we could otherwise construct about people and material objects, which transforms our behaviour and the way we live our lives (118, 98).

Stó:lō author Lee Maracle reveals the importance of maintaining healthy, life-affirming goals when she reflects upon the struggles experienced by wild salmon as they perform the Real Work of migrating inland to spawn in their natal waters. Maracle believes that human beings who witness this activity may reclaim a clear sense of duty and might find their way back to *the Teachings*. In her novel *Ravensong*, Maracle's character Stacey wonders if "maybe some white people had no roots in the creative process, so could not imagine being that devoted to being alive. If you have only yourself as a start and end point, life becomes a pretense of continuum...a kind of frantic desperation" (61). The truth is that most salmon return as mature adults to the exact place where they themselves hatched, fulfill their duty to their species' survival by spawning, then give the entirety of their life essence back to their natal streambed, where they die, rot, and disintegrate. Through this process, essential marine-derived nitrogen isotopes of their remains stay to become part of the trophic system of the local groundwater, adhering within sediment layers below the streambed (the area of activity called the hyporheic zone) which then feeds communities of microorganisms over the winter, chiefly zooplankton, which then nourish the newly hatched salmon in their fry stage through the early spring (Kline 229). Besides returning at the peak of their lives to give themselves back to nourish the greater riparian community of bears, eagles, ravens, insects, crustaceans, and other organisms, Pacific salmon feed their very own young with the transformed wealth of their own bodies.

Synthesizing decades of research and theory into human health, Kasser explains that there are at least four sets of needs basic to human motivation, functioning, and well-being: 1) *safety, security,* and *sustenance*; 2) *competence, efficacy,* and *self-esteem*; 3) *connectedness*; and, 4) *autonomy* and *authenticity* (24). As "psychological nutriments," these are as important to us as water, air, light, and soil chemistry are to the health of plants (ibid.). Kasser tells us that "each of these sets of needs has been empirically associated with humans' quality of life," and that each "appears to be relatively unfulfilled when people hold materialistic pursuits as central in their value system" (ibid.). Kasser and colleague Richard Ryan find that the most prominent materialistic values are: 1) *striving for financial success and possessions*, 2) *conforming to the right image of social acceptability*, 3) *being well-known socially*, or, more keenly stated, *dreaming or striving for fame*, and 4) *having a desire for a great sex life*, or *seeking a variety sensual pleasures* (6–9). Looking closely, we see that these are *extrinsic* in nature: that is, they are mainly found outside of ourselves and are not things we search for, find, or inspire within our minds—they are things that must be attained in their material form.

By contrast, Abraham Maslow, the father of humanistic psychology, characterizes well-being with the concept of *self-actualization*, which defines health as a state where people are motivated by *intrinsic*, interior ideas of growth, meaning, and æsthetics (quoted in Kasser 7). What is missing from Western clinical investigations into well-being are elements akin to the more complex Indigenous sense of interbeing and dwelling, those that nurture thoughts and perceptions that value human health in connection to the larger-than-human world and how the larger-than-human world finds its health within our own. Even though these ideas have been largely vacant from our lives for many generations, the Wild remains as our place of origin and exerts the largest influence upon our strengths and capabilities. In order to maintain our own health it is paramount that we return to a functional understanding and respect of the processes of the world we live in. This is important whether we live in the big city or way out in the who-in-the-middle-of-maybe-nobody-knows-where.

As she underlines the essential value of community cohesion in traditional Stó:lō village life, Maracle provides a view of what we have lost: "Every single person served the community, each one becoming a wedge of the family circle around which good health and well-being revolved. A missing person became a missing piece of the circle which could not be replaced" (26). In *Ravensong*, Maracle gives a generalized, even polarizing image with her observations of the settler-Canadian community. She casts them within a sharply negative light, as there are people in "white town" who are dispensable, and as the coming and going of some individuals "didn't seem to have much value"; from Stacey's perspective, it was even frightening "how inessential the others were to one another" (ibid.). For the most part I tend to agree, as strict codes of silence, the mechanics of conformity, and inflexible norms within Canadian society are almost impenetrable barriers for those who struggle to think, act, and live by a different way. And we all experience these barriers and exclusions throughout our lives in one way or another. However absurd it is to have to say it, nobody likes a boat rocker, despite how fast the boat—which is also clearly on fire—is sinking.

Considering lessons of TEKW, economist and Aboriginal development specialist Ronald L. Trosper illustrates four common values that are key principles for respecting life within the holistic cosmological perspective of First Nations peoples on the coast of British Columbia. These are: 1) *community*, which includes the community-of-beings, 2) *connectedness*, 3) respect for future generations, which Trosper calls *seventh generation*, and 4) *humility* (67). While Kasser tells us that materialistic people invest less in both relationships and communities, this lack of connectedness has no parallel within these traditional Indigenous values (72). While many Indigenous cultures do exert a great deal of social control over their community, if the force of social order means to preserve a cohesive breadth of eco-logic within human logic, there may be ethics and principles within this system worth investigating. Yet Robert Bringhurst tells us that there is "a long-standing habit of ignoring Native American oral literature and at the same time blindly romanticizing [particular interpretations of] indigenous traditions," and this distorting routine continues today, caught as we are between postcolonial urgencies, political correctness, and multi-generational undercurrents of racism (*Everywhere* 332). Whether Indigenous or non-Indigenous, people on the North Coast live in communities where daily tensions require an adaptive flexibility and a careful attention to momentary presence, as well as a force of will that can survive the hard truths of isolation, poverty, and the lack of many cultural, employment, medical, and educational opportunities. For Indigenous peoples in particular, there are also the debilitating legacies of generations of colonialism, ongoing social exclusion and repression, and the constant industrialization and disruption of their Storied Lands.

The X̲aaydaa artist *Iljuwas* (Bill Reid) understood this situation well, and Bringhurst describes how he also became, "little by little, an ex officio member [of both cultures], an expert of both, a *creator* of both…and therefore inescapably a conduit between them, which in conditions of monumental mutual ignorance and mistrust cannot be an easy thing to do" (*Tree* 290). *Iljuwa* understood that if the cultural gifts and knowledges of Indigenous story work are never taken beyond their original contexts, they might be protected and made impervious to the homogenizing forces of commodification, yet there also exists the danger of turning them into museum pieces, where their power and usefulness may be defeated, along with the languages that created them. While he held a perspective that bridged certain elements of contrasting cultures and conflicting realities, back in 1985 *Iljuwas* also made provocative statements about the nature of being X̲aaydaa (Haida) during the public hearings organized in support of saving South Moresby:

> *As for what constitutes a Haida—well, Haida only means human being, and as far as I'm concerned, a human being is anyone who respects the needs of his fellow man, and the earth which nurtures and shelters us all. I think we could find room in South Moresby for quite a few Haida no matter what their ethnic background. (217)*

Although this sounds like a statement of tolerance and welcoming, *Iljuwas* was speaking as an individual within the context of his life experience, perhaps even speaking against the political and social will of the X̱aaydaa Nation. Today, cultural norms as well as bloodlines can be seen as being directed toward a regulated essentialism, where even to marry outside of the traditional system is to be denied certain privileges within the community. At the same time, these cultural regulations mean to protect what remains of the theoretical integrity of a culture that, just like most other Indigenous cultures around the world, was, has been, and is still in danger of being overwhelmed by the homogenizing force of Western culture.

There is no way that I can presume what the best solution may be for any individual living within this situation. On the one hand, there is the objective to protect and guard the physical survival of the people as well as the historical breadth of their cultural heritage, and an agenda of isolation does achieve this. On the other hand, there is the always circulating pressure to accept a place within twenty-first-century Canadian society, which means taking on the complex task of embracing both its positive and negative influences, which depends upon the degree of assimilation that can be tolerated by any distinct cultural group. Either way, through isolation or assimilation, here on the North Coast there is no way to predict the outcome, as both points of departure require a complex journey into a future that is as uncertain as it is tumultuous and wild.

Considering what analytics and statistics might offer, forest biologist Denise Lach points out that almost any idea of "certainty is a false idol," as there are hardly ever unanimous points of consensus located out of the challenges that exist within increasingly complex systems and societies (235, 234). Poet and ecocritic Henry David Thoreau presciently and humbly professes that, for humans, "the highest we can attain to is not Knowledge, but Sympathy with Intelligence" (26). What does all of this mean? Putting trust in the decision making of trees, shamans, and poets instead of our local cultural leaders and elected government officials? If we chose to look to the Real Work of wild ecosystems for some kind of answer, intelligence points most obviously to the lessons we've learned about who we should at least *not* trust, considering the destructive nature of foreign invasives and the fact that when people make mistakes, it often takes many generations to fix the problems. While education and critical thinking must always play a role, paying close attention to the fullest range of diversity within the spectrum of ethical ideas and wise opinions may be the best we can hope for. But how do we sort through all of this to find a path to follow? How can we take a compass bearing from a tree-ruffle liverwort that points us in fifty directions at once?

If we accept Lach's studied summary of there being a lack of definitiveness in critical enquiry and decision making, Thoreau's prescient insight points a grounded limb to illuminate the distracting busywork of our hubris, revealing that the human tendency toward unequivocal assertion is nothing more than our inability to differentiate between what is *trēowe* and "the lighting up of the mist by the sun" (ibid.). But Lach also tells us that the way to approach our differences is not to view them as untrustworthy or harmful but to embrace them within the concept of the outlier, which is an observation or a practice that "occurs a long way from other values; it's not necessarily a wrong observation, just one apart from the norm" (236). This is not the same as accepting the opinion of those you don't agree with, as to adopt the outlier view is more a case of accepting an opinion that almost no one seems to agree with.

Confirming *Iljuwa*'s personal position of welcoming new dimensions of productive diversity into X̲aaydaa culture, Lach's proposal does hold up against scrutiny, as the presence of outliers, outsiders, and dissidents is as beneficial for science as it is for a variety of other social systems and organizations, and, as these modes and behaviours are crucial for growing a healthy culture—as change is all—accepting outlier elements of diversity and adopting their experimental proposals tends to be how most productive new approaches and innovative ideas are created (235). Embracing diversity sounds great, but I must also not be found guilty, as Thoreau warns, of promoting the smoke of yet another pseudo-scientific paradigm, and professing any kind of certainty can be nothing more than claiming work from smoke. At the same time, there is much more to both *Iljuwa*'s statement about people of various ethnic backgrounds becoming X̱aaydaa and his statement's conflict with the X̱aaydaa Nation's policy of cultural restriction.

Considering my own conflicted history of forestry work in the North and how I continue to reach within it for a personal and creative life that is ethical, what I see around me, day to day, are myriad opportunities that pass us by for any number of legitimate reasons and flimsy excuses. Most of these are based on fear. Understandably, I can see why people find it difficult to trust something as vague as uncertainty or an oddball outlier view.

The daily cycle of educating ourselves about new viewpoints can also give life to Guattari's insistence that it is always possible "to organize new micropolitical and microsocial practices, new solidarities, a new gentleness, together with new æsthetic and new analytic practices" (34). While this idea comes close to a utopian theory for incremental revolution (perhaps limited to the realistic, eye-opening work of reading a page one day and writing on one the next), revolution can often be the key to success for cutting-edge business proposals, just as revolution is quite possibly the prime directive of the biosphere itself. Going along with the right-wing plan of refusing to acknowledge deeper values within the steady encroach of the leaf-by-smolt-by-thought-by-page-turning-crawl-from-sea-to-sky-to-soil, that which is the adaptive progress of life itself, is turning out to be as futile as it is destructive. Still, Lach asks us to embrace something that is unintuitive at its most basic level.

This, I think, is what *Iljuwas* meant about accepting people of non-Indigenous backgrounds in the X̱aaydaa Nation. In the context of the South Moresby logging blockades, he knew that standing before him were a group of like-minded peers who were all outliers of one kind or another. But what the outlier represents is potential, alternatives, fresh perspectives, and in a world where everything from government policy to members of our own families are potentially untrustworthy, it also means looking beyond the dualistic perspective of Western thought and turning to look more closely at things we tend to ignore, perhaps even the lessons of ground-truth that exist in the biomass that has been forming generously and productively for hundreds of thousands of years, right under our feet.

No less so than in the ancestral past, today there is nothing simple about encountering and negotiating the complex trials of life, but the personal example of X̱aaydaa artist *Iljuwas* is evidence of the fact that there are both non-Indigenous as well as traditionally minded First Nations people who are open to bridging the parallels that exist between cultures and individuals. But the somewhat arresting policy of the X̱aaydaa Nation to perpetuate itself in relative isolation with rules that restrict marriage to outsiders does not mean to challenge individual Canadian visitors who fall in love with these magical islands; instead it serves to resist the legislation of cultural erasure that hides within recent laws passed by the Canadian government. There is likely more to this X̱aaydaa policy than I can understand, but no doubt it is a partial response to section six of Bill C-31, whereby children born of particular designations of mixed marriage will permanently lose their official status of being X̱aaydaa—which is, after all, to lose the status of being a human being.

More optimistically, at the level of both community and the individual along the North Coast, there are productive examples of First Nations people who embrace and make the most of the productive elements of Canadian culture. In 2001, Charlene McLean, then deputy chief of the Tsimshian First Nation village of *Metlakatla*, told journalist Alex Rose something that sounds as if it were taken directly from the rhizomatic trail of an adventitious map: "We have to look back at those aspects of our traditional culture that have to do with independence and power. Then, we have to learn how to use them in today's society" (95). As they stand, sprawl, and blossom out of moss, the lives of the mountain hemlock tree, the rhizomatic devil's club, and the mycorrhizal blue chanterelle offer their own demonstration with their biotic lives as gifts to us while they work to fulfill their own interconnected community needs, just as the long history and experience of dwelling and interbeing by First Nations peoples reflects the knowledge and lessons they utilize today to negotiate the contemporary world. As nearly anyone can make a new family out of strangers by simply falling in love, communities also possess the potential to accept and embrace any number of chances for productive change.

And there are contemporary examples of individuals finding a renewed purpose and value by immersing themselves in traditional practices and a life lived closer to the Land. Beyond, above, and surrounding so many towns like New Hazelton, Smithers, Kitimat and Moricetown, Greenville and Masset, what the North Coast offers is big mountains, big trees, endless clouds heavy with rain, fierce winter storms, all cast along immense and often impenetrable distances. These giant things and the sense of isolation they bring also encourage the ability to relocate a sense of being that is separate from the distraction and intensity of the materialistic world, but they also disconnect people from some of the productive aspects of diversity, such as opportunities for education and other critical aspects of community health. But within every kind of life there is a series of trade-offs.

Back in 1990, *Maht* (Beverly Anderson), a Gitxsan Fireweed chief from the Hazeltons, told journalist Terry Glavin that she sees it as a priority for her people to leave the government-established reserves and return to a life of respectful connection with the Land (*Death Feast* 160). *Maht* points to the immense social problems that exist in Gitxsan communities, believing that they are partly perpetuated by the national reserve system, the result of which has become a cycle of confinement and welfare, poverty and alcoholism. (160–61). *Maht* told Glavin that the Gitxsan have almost completely abandoned the five "natural doctors" of *exercise, fresh air, nutrition, water,* and *rest* (160–61). As she outlines the basic function of the *halayt, Maht* describes how this secret society of shamans meant to look after the physical aspects of the individual as well as fostering overall health through the combined strength of personal and community spirituality (167).

Historically, *T'imlax'aamit* was the name of a mythical Gitxsan city state that once flourished along the valley of 'Ksan. Here, traditional teachings of respect and long-term thought were paramount to living a good life, as they are still accepted in much of Gitxsan society, not just as they affect the immediate lives of people, but more tragically, where they have been ignored or abused. And it is because of this abuse of nature that the destruction of *T'imlax'aamit* came about, happening first in the distant past, perhaps a few thousand years ago, and repeating numerous times since, always after the city had rebuilt itself through the work of subsequent generations. There were always one or two individuals who were outliers—those who didn't conform to the mainstream of thought and practice—and it was these few who were spared so that the Gitxsan themselves could try again. But as the population grew, most turned once more to the mainstream of selfish, lazy, destructive habits, and the sacred lessons of respect were abandoned. Each time, harsh repercussions were handed down from the powerful forces within the kincentric world that would no longer tolerate the disrespect for nature that human beings displayed. And, each time, a few outliers who resisted the mass hysteria of the ecology of bad ideas were allowed to survive.

In addition to the potential for larger cultural benefits to Gitxsan culture, *Maht*'s desire for her people to return to health and well-being by the path of traditional practices is a brave and profound statement of dissidence—it is a refusal to participate in the disrespect of nature, which is a contemporary habit that most of us conform to in one way or another with each compulsion we indulge ourselves with in our addiction to needless consumption. Mostly, *Maht*'s story of the hope for returning to traditional Gitxsan teachings, of re-establishing regular appointments with the five natural doctors, and of returning to a life of interconnection with the Storied Land confirms the necessity that we must, in one way or another, reengage with the deeper intangibles of life that persist beyond the material contamination zone of post-globalization and the mainstream values of Canadian society. Of course, this zone is internal as much as external.

Here in the West, social theorist and journalist Chris Hedges believes that *hope* and *love,* what he calls the "champions of the sacred," are two underestimated gestures that can create messages that "ripple outward over time" (192). It is also this hopefulness of love that Maracle believes will help each one of us climb "all the hills of complete misunderstanding" that are both the real and imaginary hurdles that exist between First Nations peoples, Canadian society, and the many diverse wild communities of the Indigenous rainforest (114).

Bringing together *Maht*'s, Hedges', and Maracle's recognition of the human potential for personal and community recovery through knowledge and direction found in the Wild, what we find is a staple proportion of an important concept that I have been slowly describing and writing about throughout this text. All of these ideas can be gathered together into the perceptual framework of a way of participating with the world called *ecosophical æsthetics.* This concept combines human understandings of ecological justice with the deeper lessons, ethics, and even morals that are revealed in the diversity of life processes that are expressed within the Real Work of the larger-than-human realm. Ecosophical æsthetics is part of the process through which we can learn to interpret and activate these values and principles.

Ecosophical æsthetics can be seen within the daily activities of those who work to nurture fruitful relationships of Real Work in either wild or human communities, and, most profoundly, as they do so within both. As Hedges asks, much more than rhetorically, just as Maracle and *Maht* do in their own ways, these are a few of the questions posed by ecosophical æsthetics: "Will we responsibly face our stark, new limitations? Will we heed those who are sober and rational, those who speak of a new simplicity and humility?" (145).

Considering these calls for a major shift in values, in her novel

Ravensong, Maracle describes the people in "white town" who pull "weeds" out of their flower gardens and how the Indigenous initiate Stacey observes their ignorance, struck by the "pathos of white folks discarding wild food growing:" "Comfrey root, dandelion, plantain and mullein...all being tossed of a heap to disappear in a strong black garbage bag" (31). Maracle repeatedly highlights the basic, individual but negative activities of the citizens of white town, not just in how they treat people from the Indian village but in how they treat their own, which is as a kind of garbage, and which is also how they treat the wild world that reaches up everywhere around them with gifts of food and medicine.

Revisiting *Maht*'s hopeful attempt for reclaiming a way of living by the new-old means of traditional Gitxsan practices, *Maht*'s husband Ian partly answers Hedges' questions about what can be found in embracing our new limitations and living humbly by a new simplicity and recognizing what there is to be gained: "You become stronger, the winds, the snow, all those things you're up against. You're healthier for it" (quoted in Glavin 168). Just as Kasser and so many other scholars repeatedly inform us that materialism values neither community nor environment, there is much more to be gained by participating in Real Work than the basics of physical health and personal satisfaction. Again, Maracle expresses her belief that "these others [the whites] had to be rooted to the soil of this land or all would be lost" (44). Maracle believes, as do many others, that every Indigenous living thing exists purposefully for us to utilize gratefully in order that we learn how to live properly by following its example. The Wild is not a leafy chaos that encroaches uselessly and even destructively upon private property; instead, it is a wealth of knowledge arising from the deeper, all but forgotten wellspring of our own human understanding, respect, and cooperation. As simple and eco-logical as it sounds, the productive force of the larger-than-human means to show us that, more than anything else, our lives are gifts, gifts that are not meant to be used up in self-indulgence by ourselves alone.

Although it has taken a while (which is how it goes when you follow the examples given by trees)—up here, up-coast, I try to follow the larger-than-human patterns that I have begun to recognize and decipher across the story map of a life spent working and watching within the Wild. For some people, the idea of engaging with deeper tangibles will unavoidably require a trial of immense proportions—perhaps a pilgrimage of one hundred thousand exhausting steps up into a mountain hemlock forest—perhaps the equally difficult reinvention of a life within a city that has no green spaces that inspire any ideas of the Wild. Yet these things can begin simply and directly within our minds as we sit in a chair, as we read and think and write, even as we consider what goes on in the puddle that drains out of the neglected strip of scrub that runs behind the store we visit every week, and with all of the moment-to-moment activities we undertake to initiate some kind of small change.

Admittedly, as they walk each day through the trees, most forestry field workers can't help but stumble and flail about themselves, raising their voices to curse at the sharp branches that stab their limbs or scrape their faces as they blunder along. It has taken me years, but I have finally learned that it is the ones who blunder who are to blame for their pain, not those wild entities upon which they blunder. These days, when I am out in the rainforest and a broad, wet leaf covered in quills flips up to whack me in the forehead, I no longer consider this a random violent attack but a direct and purposeful check to the head.

*I've been hunting keenly for twenty years and I've never seen
even one. I haven't given up, but it's like you have to have some
kind of special eyes or something. I'm from the city, so maybe
I think too many bad thoughts in traffic and so they just hide
when they feel me coming.*

—Aafke Leisbet Croockewit (2009)

Blue Chanterelle (view 3

EXUDING THE REDOLENCE OF EARTHY PURPLE-BLUE-BLACK LIQUORICE,
the fresh aroma of *Polyozellus* is rich, intoxicating, and sweet: a per-
fume as unique as the inky rainforest fruit itself. Quite often they do
just smell purple-blue, pure and simple. On the few occasions I find
blue chanterelles, I am usually lucky enough to come home with a
kilogram or more crammed into the back pocket of my cruiser's vest.
Out on Tow Hill, resource conservation technician Elin Price tells me
that in the lush, ideal habitats of *Xaaydaa Gwaay,* blue chanterelles
often develop into masses of hundreds, sometimes in clustered groups
up to a metre across.

True story: In 2009, as usual, I was working in the bush for a small
forestry consulting company in northwestern BC. From the end of
April until the end of August I had been spending five days a week in
the forest. On my very last day of bush work, I took along Lisa's dig-
ital camera, which was the only time I had brought it along. During
these last few weeks of work, I had been up in an area north of the
Morice River, just south of *Tazdii Wyiez Bin* Burnie-Shea Provincial
Park, and, as is so often the case, I was in the complex of transition
zones where the sub-boreal spruce, Engelmann spruce-subalpine fir,
mountain hemlock, and coastal western hemlock zones converge and
intertwine. And, of course, I found some blue chanterelles on this, my

last day of work in the bush, while I was walking out at the very end of the day, heading straight up a north-aspect slope of very old, late-successional fir entangled with looping snag fences of devil's club. To be expected, this was a dark, rather-difficult-for-human-movement kind of place, one that was plugged up even thicker with an understory of warped, serpentine hemlock trees. But these blue chanterelles were the only ones I had found in four years. Here I was and there they were, at the end of my last workday of the season, and on the one day that I had brought along a camera. Wonder. Validation. Providence. Photographic proof. Supper.

Apart from the private bliss of the few ecstatic mushroom hunters who type up their fungal bucolics with skillets and cameras, as far as my research has uncovered, blue chanterelles are too rare and obscure to merit attention from even the most persistent and cantankerous poets of the perhumid rainforest. Except maybe one.

Only, always to dream of erotic ghosts of the flowering earth;
to return to a decomposed ground choked by refuse, profit, & the
concrete of private property; to find yourself disinherited from
your claim to the earth.

—Daphne Marlatt (1974)

transect 13

forests, books, and texts,
a Third World in the First,
new affiliations and malingering oppressions.

ONCE, IN THE 1980S, PRESSED ALONG A PERSONALLY INTERESTING BUT otherwise forgettable art lark, I planted the seeds of various local tree species into the middle pages of a number of books and left them outside over winter. In the spring, I soaked the books thoroughly with water and attempted to sprout baby trees from *Candidates for the Natural Law Party of Canada* and Fowler's *Modern English Usage*, among others. No doubt the project is ongoing—at least I imagine it is: a few small trees still growing, unnoticed, under an audience of scrub aspen and spruce forest, somewhere out near a creek that runs behind a rural art school. Back then, I did the work alone, without telling anybody, and considered it a failure, not just because expressions of environmentalism were reviled by the general population of the 1980s, but mostly because the project germinated probably far less new fibre than went into the pulp used to make the original books. More than anything, I was young, human, impatient; and trees take their time—a long time.

Even though poet Gary Snyder tells us that the Wild is composed of countless varieties of languages and stories, he also believes that it should not be described in comparison to things such as books (*Practice* 69).

As he writes: "The world may be replete with signs, but it's not a fixed text with archives of variora" (ibid.). Books can be useful and do have certain advantages but they also restrict ideas with the fixed order of words on a page and the rigidness of their covers. As well, their contents are often perceived of or are even meant to be absolutes, while most of the natural wor(l)d is open, waiting for a gust of wind.

Books should be as materially and mentally transformative as the Wild, just as Emily Carr wrote in the early twentieth century after viewing a house in the long-abandoned village of *Cha'atl* on *X̱aaydaa Gwaay*, where the "trees had pushed the roof off and burst the sides" (64). Things can turn out this way, if only we could let the new-old dust of change blow in and allow some of the local, ever-present Indigenous concepts to take root, encouraging them to transform our Western ideas, just as a few old books can became points of germination for cottonwood, black spruce, and tamarack.

Historically, just as today, Indigenous Storied Lands are not viewed as static texts, although their lessons have retained their meanings for thousands of years. Historical oral narratives are continually adapted by individual storytellers to hold relevance in the present, just as the mountains, streams, coastlines, and rainforests are temporally and physically multidimensional and always evolving. Traditionally, truly local people recognize both the swift alterations and the slow transformations within ecosystems just as in their own communities, recognizing the patterns by which history, the present, and the future impact as well as reflect long- and short-term perspectives and daily concrete outcomes. As James Andrew McDonald writes, the Tsimshian of *Kitsumkalum* draw "on more than their Indigenous culture for values, and the Tsimshian culture is not a dead archive of traditions and customs frozen in the past…The people of *Kitsumkalum* enjoy a very rich cultural life as participants in the Canadian tapestry" (4–5). McDonald also points out that "those influences cannot be removed and should not be removed—they are a vital part of the cultural fabric that makes *Kitsumkalum* what it is," in combination with influences from the

Nisga'a, Gitxsan, Haisla, Tlingit, X̱aaydaa, and other non-Tsimshian cultures from up and down the coast (5). As Indigenous communities continue their long-standing ligatures with the Wild, they will also continue to be valued as unique and as important connectors within diverse cultures from around the globe.

Life in the rainforest is always moving within itself. Year after year, forces of change alter the waxy taste of salal and tamper with the generational songs of Steller's jays. Annual and seasonal changes will nudge the elusive silver-blue glacier bear out of *this* inaccessible inlet and into *that* almost inaccessible fjord, sending it to hunt down the scent trail of a vanguard salmon run that is, by chance, happening up a creek newly created by the shifting of a melting glacier. Echoes of the timelessness of these wild stories remain but with each season they will, invariably, express themselves as noticeably skewed. Even as local wild knowledges might appear as ephemeral as flowing water, their deeper lessons—of careful endurance, of responding appropriately to change, of embracing and utilizing the local and giving oneself wholly back in return—these will always be bursting forth somewhere with a vital potential.

It might be lack of sleep, exhaustion from work, fatigue of the mind and the spirit, perhaps just the grey world full of rain, but even though people can sometimes find it nearly impossible to find productive ways to engage the day, we all live surrounded by a wealth of possibilities. And every day that the raining rains rain, sliding in overhead after their last deep plumb and pass through the Pacific, they perform functions that we cannot do without. Coming down and down over this drenched archipelago of glaciers, rainforests, and lichen-dappled stone, water as both time and slippery wisdom covers the craggy slopes of stress-tolerant conifers and flows through the drenched swales of devil's club and alder—refreshing all, feeding and linking everything together—and, even though we might fail to appreciate it, people are always included.

Now imagine an unpeopled stretch of highway that climbs up and down through the vast forestlands of drenched mountains—a thread of asphalt obscured by a perpetual density of shifting grey cloud.

Imagine this narrow signifier punctuated every fifty or one hundred kilometres by a village or a town that has only one grocery store, one liquor store, one gas station, one motel, and perhaps one post office, where only one of these businesses draws enough income to do more than cover its expenses. Whether you are of Indigenous or non-Indigenous background, Highway 16 should already be a potent signifier, not just because of its notoriety as the "Highway of Tears" and the violence it facilitates against women but for the violence it allows to reach deep within the larger-than-human world. While Highway 16 provides access to schools, hospitals, employment, and other essential services, both it and the railway that twins the old westward dream of a trade route with Asia were not built to bring social welfare programs to local workers or an Indigenous population; the highway and the railway were built mainly for the efficiency and profitability of heavy industry. While this may be understood as a basic background concept, the visceral truth is that most of these small, remote communities built out in these very wild places are generally perceived by travellers as well as many local residents as forgettable outposts of backwardness—each a dull Podunk on a gravel scrape to nowhere.

As cultural geographer Sarah de Leeuw reflects and describes quite accurately, the general view of the North Coast is of "a place on the edge of nothingness," and, perhaps, as de Leeuw writes, a great place for hunting and fishing but no place to live a civilized life (9). And as I have experienced countless times, it is considered that people who live in northern communities can never be taken seriously as artists, as thinkers, or as meaningful agents of culture unless they make the smart decision to *move away*. On the surface, the practicalities of this problem may seem obvious—as I've been told straight to my face, time and again, always with a good-natured backwoodsy tone and a sideways grin: Why aren't you off in the big city, where anything and everything of importance happens?

How does a teenage human misfit attempt to live his or her own dissident and adventitious answer to such a marginalizing question?

Considering what the internet reveals is always happening every day in the largest urban centres of North America and beyond, after living his or her whole life in a small village on Highway 16 or out on one of its more remote gravel side roads, how does someone put the intense, technologically mediated lure of a seemingly exciting and often largely imagined world, with all of its supposed choices, anywhere but as a fixed dream to which they can aspire to someday reach?

So often, these perhumid rainforests, these Storied Lands, they are a very cold, dark, and wet place: unchanging, leaden, unmoving, even overwhelmingly non-human. There seems so much more death and decay here than life and vitality, which makes sense, as, from the human perspective, Indigenous growth takes so long to add up to anything substantial, especially if we measure the environment with the same state of impatience that we use to evaluate the speed of human activities on the internet and TV—as if a meaningful life were created with a flash of biotic paint that must dry the instant it is applied.

What we are faced with here is an entrenched cultural ecology of bad ideas. More than anything else, both the Wild and the Indigenous of the North are prized for their consumptive values over their productive values, which is a disparate imbalance between hard and soft values. Having lived here for about twenty-five years, I understand all too well the logistical hardships that are experienced anywhere that is labelled the North. But things here can be more challenging than elsewhere. As the climate, geography, contemporary culture, government, latitude, population, and infrastructure of Canada may be similar to those of the Scandinavian countries, the scale of Canada's land mass is nearly ten times greater. Here we also have a large Indigenous population and a series of unresolved issues in regards to land, cultural rights, and entitlement. And we have one giant southern trading neighbour instead of a dozen smaller ones. Despite the fact that western Canada is extremely rich with natural resources, neither industry nor government has been willing to commit to building the infrastructure and institutions required to transform the North. For the last hundred years the north has remained a string of disconnected, one-industry labour camps, where people are drawn for a short time to acquire a few fat paycheques. While many people do live out their lives here, giving birth to new generations, neither government nor industry has been doing much to transform northern BC into a network of desirable, thriving cultural centres. Being rich in natural resources could translate into an equally rich cultural life, but we have become accustomed over many decades to accept that this will never happen. During the summer of 2013, as I watched hundreds of industrial trailers being brought west along Highway 16 to house the thousands of workers being brought into the region for the current influx of temporary work, it seems clear that nothing has changed.

Considering the Indigenous rainforest, the intense pressures of industrial and cultural decisions made by government and industry have very few health-giving influences over the long-term planning strategies within which these wild communities operate. "Energy flow through an intricate conduit of this kind is dilatory and digressive," as urban planner and activist Jane Jacobs writes: "in the forest, energy flow is anything but swift and simple, because of the diverse and roundabout ways that the system's web of teeming, interdependent organisms uses energy" (46). From a human perspective, what meaning can things like interbeing and dwelling have in the contemporary situation of isolation and little opportunity, poor housing and lack of education, where the ecology of bad ideas is pervasive, dispersing with overwhelming transformative pressures that function with as much negative effect as a noxious alien invasive species? While so many are acted upon by destructive forces in their daily lives, what can be done about the fate of the wild ecosystems we have little if any power to protect? As Maracle told us earlier, the connections of family and community are vital for the health and strength of both people and the Land. But the fact remains here that too many of the brightest, most gifted and unique of our local young people leave the region and find few reasons or opportunities to return, while more and more temporary workers arrive daily to unwittingly continue to transform these Indige-nous Storied Lands in predominantly negative ways. Again, if workers are brought in for short periods of time, and if their experience is brief and even uncomfortable, they will neither remain nor hold fond memories of the place, and thus there will be no creation of a sense of respon-sibility or community, and industrialization can proceed without any passionate scrutiny.

Whether it is due to the ongoing residue of colonial-era racist policies or the perceived vast nothingness of this wild place itself, as sociologist Sennett explains, where the Other is missing or is purposefully denied, "there is no shared narrative of difficulty, and so no shared fate"—to which I would also add, no participation in the responsibility or work of transforming local negatives into productive renewals (147). When decisions that affect the local are made in distant power centres like Victoria, Vancouver, and Ottawa, or even farther away, in the United States, Korea, China, and elsewhere around the globe, the diminishing and devaluing of our environment, our cultures, our homes, and espe-cially ourselves becomes predictable and perhaps unavoidable.

Indeed, the perception of the North Coast as a remote scattering of "nowheres" spread over a beautiful wet tangle of impenetrable noth-ingness is the fairly general view I meet with and have lived with for years. This is a sad antithesis to the many alternate, living examples of beauty and joy that are actually experienced here each day. While so many other people in the North feel, as I do, that there is nowhere else on earth they could possibly live, the fact remains—grease or no grease, here in the coastal rainforest of the north, the squeaky wheel spins and rusts on into a wet silence. And, for some individual local First Nations people, the feeling of being wholly worthless in this worthless hole is an all too common reaction to the confusion and turmoil of long-standing policies and practices of colonial repression and cultural genocide. The sense of feeling part of a pointless existence can become a day-to-day routine after decades of being targeted by social and governmental assimilation, forces that work to fit dissident, outlier, non-conformist, or simply Indigenous people into a normative role within Canadian society—where we have a part to play as nothing more than a cog in an industrial machine, one that operates far and away from the largely urban cultural mainstream of the South.

In handling the brassiest of these tacks in the international sphere, philosopher Slavoj Žižek tells us that "for the last five centuries, the (relative) prosperity and peace of the "civilized" West [has been] bought by the export of ruthless violence and destruction into the 'barbarian' Outside" (4). This is a blunt and harsh assessment, and a shock to many, even within the highly mediated culture of our contemporary time. Even as we are bombarded day by day with a torrent of facts and information, if we consider the sentimentalized colonial version of Canadian history that most of us have been enculturated within, we have a lifetime of subtle imprints, rationalizations, and projections that may prevent us from accepting this parallax view of the place we live.

A very quick history: The conquest and transformation of the North Coast of Turtle Island began in 1741 with the first wave of Russian fur traders. Coming to the North Coast and Southeast Alaska in pursuit of sea otter pelts for the Asian and Russian markets, these earliest European capitalists enslaved and worked to death untold numbers of local Indigenous peoples, most of whom were kidnapped as needed from nearby coastal villages, a practice which continued for the duration of the slaughter. By this means, the market for furs committed the second corollary injustice of pushing the otter population to the brink of extinction. More recently, systems of largely unregulated and intense exploitation entered into the market field of fisheries, then whaling and forestry, and are at work today within mining and gas development. Today, the mountainous, rain-drenched and heavily forested "field" is open for whatever turns a buck, whether it be a growing raw log export sector, the expansion of an international port, even a pipeline for transporting bitumen and condensate through the most pristine wild salmon habitat remaining in North America.

As they have been for decades, all over the North Coast, many of our dilapidated port and mill towns are paradoxical refractions of Third World realities: atrophied, collapsing, abandoned within the lush rainforest growths. This abundance of green partly serves to disguise them from view, from appearing as glaring as they are, as perhumid refractions of ghost towns from the deserts of the southwest. Žižek describes how the First World and the Third World are split between "the opposition of leading a long satisfying life full of material and cultural wealth, and dedicating one's life to some transcendent Cause" (6). Here Žižek refers directly to current and ongoing global provocations between Western industrial political powers and the reactionary activities of a radicalized and racialized Other, as these distinct and marginalized cultures perceive themselves as threatened by foreign powers. Žižek's description is a luminous insight into the North Coast local, as it illustrates many of the conflicts that occur between capitalist entrepreneurs of the affluent First World and the impoverished Others of the Third World that persist within the social strata of small northern communities, clinging to peripheral enculturations as citizens of Canada. One might view the comparison of towns like the Hazeltons, Prince Rupert, *Kitwanga*, and others with overseas Third World locales as absurd, depending upon the scope of one's class consciousness and whether or not one has experienced these local communities with their eyes and mind truly open. Still, this provocative juxtaposition is one of the harder realities of North Coast life.

As Žižek describes, these *are* the de facto extraction sites of raw materials for the "prosperity and peace of the 'civilized' West," which is an idea affirmed by Guattari, who tells us that ongoing patterns of industrialization without reciprocal benefit leave the local "accompanied by a sort of Third-Worldization within developed countries" (4, 22). Each exhausted frontier of resource extraction—from crumbling canneries to vacated mills—has been and in many cases is still being "bought by the export of ruthless violence and destruction into the 'barbarian' Outside." This Outside is the local, represented by the Other of local Indigenous peoples and the rugged forests of their Storied

Lands, both of which are still considered, by colonial forces, as in need of being tamed, assimilated, and transformed. If we grasp a truly mordant perspective, we live within sites of extraction and dumping on a scale comparable to the Third World.

Examples are not hard to find. First, the environment: Natural resources consultant Ben Parfit writes that "analysis of log flows off Haida Gwaii [in 2001] suggests that more than 95 percent of all the trees logged on the islands go to off-island interests" (62). As well, UBC Forestry Advisory Council member Ian Gill, with *Hilistis* (Pauline Waterfall) and Doug Hopwood, tells us that, of the two-billion-dollar value of all timber in Heiltsuk territory logged to date, the Heiltsuk have received no royalties or other compensation other than a small number of seasonal jobs on a sporadic basis (118).

Next, there are the many unresolved issues of BC's Indigenous peoples: Relating 2006 figures, the Canadian Community Economic Development Network writes that in the small villages of the Upper Skeena there are extreme unemployment rates, at more than 90 percent in some communities and 60 percent on average; as well, there is a failed education system, with 28 percent having less than the equivalent of a high school diploma (CCEDNet). There are deteriorating infrastructures at quadruple the rate of the BC average and a health-care and wellness crisis in which residents die from treatable diseases at four times the normal rate (ibid.). Part of these statistics reflect the state of Indigeneity in a society dominated by predominantly white European values, but these figures also reflect the remoteness, the inaccessibility, and the physical restrictions of living in the North. Even as social structures and perspectives are changing with growing diversity, clear disparities remain, as critic Norah Bowman-Broz tells us: "new affiliations do not rule out malingering oppressions"; and, as First Nations scholar Craig Womack remarks: "simply being visibly identifiable as an Indian person sometimes subjects a person to racism and social stigma, no matter how assimilated he or she might be" (138, 41). What this adds up to is a social order of imbalanced equities across a spectrum of injustice, where neither the short-term workers nor the long-term residents of our remote northern towns reap benefits or lead a long and satisfying life full of material and cultural wealth. While local people face constant pressure to assimilate and conform to the dominant Canadian ideology, it is always with the caveat that to refuse this privilege is to shoot yourself in the foot, and that if you continue to be marginalized, silenced, and brushed aside, it is just your own fault.

Today, as we enter a boom cycle of port expansions and lique-fied natural gas (LNG) exploration all over the North Coast, many local people are being displaced from their homes and forced out of their communities, mainly by evictions from landlords who are ren-ovating their rental properties for the chance of the higher rates that the influx of temporary workers will pay. This is just the beginning of another series of short-sighted progressions that we have long been experiencing in the North. For decades, Terrace has been experiencing an unmanageably low housing vacancy rate. No one wants to build housing in a place where there is almost no certainty for the economic future. At this point, there is no plan by government or the private sector to do anything about this problem or about the related problems of social institutions, infrastructure, local skills training, etc. On a daily basis, so many stories of traditional culture will continue to decay and family ties across the diverse range of local cultures will fragment, dis-perse, and dissolve. As new bulldozers and ever-larger kinds of heavy equipment arrive, so many more story lives may fail to realize their potential—not just those of people but also so many voices within the Wild—those who speak with the green of reptilian leaves and the creak of mossy timbers, voices that sound with the flash of fins splashing from salt into fresh water, so many voices that, in the face of progress, human beings attempt to deny, ignore, and silence.

A chance:
The space and place to speak/write her own experience, without
encroaching, appropriating, taking over. We need to back off.
The world does not belong to me just because I am in it. And I
am not black or native, so as feminist or fictioneer I'm not sure
I should appropriate difference to aggrandize either my own
fiction or my own feminism:
And right now, it might be my job to shut up and listen, or
to try to do something concrete to create space for the silenced
other, feminist or fictional space to say our story. To know when
to back off:

— Aritha Van Herk (1991)

Devil's Club (view 3

CUKILANARPAK, AS THE ALUTIIQ OF KODIAK CALL DEVIL'S CLUB, IS A member of the ginseng family (*Araliaceae*) but could never be mistaken for the more common cultivated varieties. Devil's club is indeed the monster of the family and, appropriately enough, is found in one of the most extreme alternate realities of North American habitats. Being at home in the extraordinarily rugged tumble and sprawl of the temperate North Coast jungle, devil's club makes its communities in places that are regularly inundated by torrential runoffs and flash floods. The species snakes its long multiple limbs up the treacherous runs of unstable seepage lanes and is equally at home within the flat quagmires of soaked floodplains, especially those choked with the crisscrossing, rotting hulks of fallen trees. Devil's club tumbles its octopus limbs down rocky stream edges throughout the breadth of the CWH zone and into the sub-boreal spruce (SBS) zone that reaches east of the coast mountains, into the interior cedar-hemlock (ICH) zone that meets the

Rocky Mountains, and throughout the wettest, most inhospitable sites of the high-elevation Engelmann spruce-subalpine fir (ESSF) zones of the interior (Pojar and MacKinnon 82; Klinka, Krajina et al. 173).

Erect and yet also sprawling, devil's club effectively guards the saturated capillary waterways and fragile communities of its many symbiotic associates: three-leaved foamflower (*Tiarella trifoliata*), oak fern (*Gymnocarpium dryopteris*), sweet-scented bedstraw (*Galium triflorum*), baneberry (*Actaea rubra*), and lady fern (*Athyrium filix-femina*), among others. Climbing steep green with sturdy and flexible golden hoses full of medicine, every September devil's club adds vast quantities of compost to the heavily leached, often gleyed, acidic, calcareous organic soils when it drops its massive leaves (Klinka, Krajina et al. 173). Both its octopus limbs and the veins of its oversize maple-form leaves are covered in a constant excurrent overlapping of long, straw-coloured spines, which provide it with defensive weapons that are necessary for protecting its nutrient-rich foliage.

Heshkeghka'a, as it is called by the Outer Inlet Dena'ina of the *Kenai* Peninsula, grows a bright red terminal fruit cluster, as do most cultivated varieties of ginseng, except that the berries of devil's club are also armed with the same array of thorns that cover the rest of the plant. These hard red berries are poisonous to humans but perfect autumn food for grizzly bears.

Being quite literally "the drugstore of the north," *wi'qas*, as it is called by the Henaaksiala of the *Kitlope*, does not avoid reality, and neither does it allow this of any foolish human being who moves carelessly into its home (Reidy and Reidy-Zieglar). For nature writer Robert Michael Pyle, it was not love at first sting, as he seems to have given devil's club just one regrettable grasp, after which he compares its formidable leaves to the medieval torture device the Catherine wheel; and, as he adds, flippantly and disrespectfully, ahistoricizing thousands of years of carefully accumulated First Peoples knowledge of its important gifts: "devil's club has no life-giving properties; life-arresting might be more like it" (67). While the denigration of the hidden and misunderstood nature of Indigenous entities is the most common trope of power within the colonial frontier æsthetic, Pyle's statements reveal ignorance more than fear or hatred. Yet they still encourage destruction as they signify the Wild with negative qualities, which informs the reader to consider it with derision, which can lead a misinformed landowner to view it with suspicion and remove it from its habitat. Despite Pyle's appraisal (which I have heard repeated countless times out in the bush), I have also eventually come to realize, and not without some outside guidance and many often painful encounters, that a little effort toward understanding can go a long way to finding respect and admiration for the strange and the mysterious.

As forest biologist Robin Wall Kimmerer rightly explains: "to the attentive observer, plants reveal their gifts" (101). Ethnoecologist Johnson, who spent many years working with and studying medicinal plant uses with the Gitxsan, Witsuwit´en, and many other Indigenous peoples, writes about devil's club in a 2006 edition of the *Journal of Ethnobiology and Ethnomedicine*. Johnson describes the species as "the most frequently mentioned and widely used medicinal plant," explaining that 83 percent of Indigenous peoples west of the Rocky Mountains report an extensive and varied knowledge of its properties. Most commonly it was used as a tonic, but it was also applied in decoctions for the treatment of respiratory illnesses, tuberculosis, and arthritis, and as both a medicine of the heart and the blood. Johnson writes that colleagues McCutcheon and many others have demonstrated that the species has many antibacterial and other similar properties and is important for its effectiveness against respiratory viruses, and has been shown to completely inhibit certain forms of tuberculosis. Johnson also tells us that Kobaisy and others have found that devil's club bark has proven its potential for development as an anti-colon-cancer medication; as well, there are indications that it has the potential to regulate blood-sugar levels in diabetes patients. Wrongfully named in a fit by the European blunderers who arrived here only recently, *Oplopanax horridus* is, to say the very least, hardly mean-spirited. *Wi'qas* might be spiny and dangerous, yet when it is treated with care and investigated with respect, devil's club reveals that it is one of the most important-spirited plants in all of Cascadia.

After a time I could see
for a time in the green country;

I learned that the earliest language
was not our syntax of chained pebbles

but liquid, made
by the first tribes, the fish
people.

—Margaret Atwood (1970)

transect 14

ecological linguistics,
tawny grammar,
ecosophical æsthetics.

PHILOSOPHICALLY, SCIENTIFICALLY, CULTURALLY, AND HOPEFULLY, ANY-
one who understands the necessity for Real Work may also come
to recognize the *grammar of the Wild.* Spelling itself out of its leafy
aggregate lexicon, the grammar of the Wild has given itself freely for
millennia, with languages that constantly unfurl out of wood, water,
weather, and the pulsing growths of wild life. Starting with a personal recognition of the existence of these always changing permanent
communications, showing respect for their voices is the first part of
understanding them, but working to transform this mostly chaotic
information into knowledge may be no more productive than assum-
ing that just because we were born on this earth, we are then entitled
to do as we please, even live.

To remove ourselves from the asphalt of mainstream perspectives is a start, but the biggest challenge is comprehending the grammar of the Wild. Seeing a probable path through the rainforest is one thing, and negotiating it is another, but actually getting yourself where you imagine you want to go is something quite different. But, due to the nature of the activity of encountering and establishing an Other way of walking, thinking, and living, we open ourselves to the imprint, memory, and existence of the new-old neurological pathways of the past that can be transcribed into the present. Here we can find connections we once had to ancestral knowledges contained in a fog-shrouded ripple of stone or the pungency that fills our chest in a blue-shaded lowland. When we find these signs and signals perking up our ears and tuning our senses, we begin a process that can change our habits and lead us to places that are far more life-giving, or, if you prefer, far more culturally and politically sound.

As Ken Belford found out as he worked for decades, both on the land and in poetry, mainstream meanings tend to stump where they hit the trees. "I speak one of the many languages of the Nass," he writes, and "it's not possible to translate what I know into English" (*lan(d) guage* 35, 28). We heard a similar kind of statement at the very beginning of this text, from *Desskw*, Walter Blackwater, a Gitxsan Wolf elder who tells us that "to speak thoroughly and accurately about this countryside is impossible in English" (quoted in Glavin 86). Being much larger and far more complex than the often locally misleading English (which is a language of nouns, possessions, and boundaries), the linguistics of the ecological world speak mostly in terms of reciprocation, mutualism, dependence, and openness. Here, where innumerable lives stretch out within soil, water, and all kinds of flesh, thousands of dialects express objectives, not just of cooperation and competition, but articulating the strategies and histories of growths and deaths, the seasonal rounds of activities engaged within litter-level barter and nurse-log conference, the tension of the hunter-prey dialectic, and the regulatory relay system of mycelia, all of which express not just the health of the rainforest but also our own.

Bringhurst engages with these ideas in his consideration of ecological linguistics, a perception he brings back to the English language but which is still in practice within the Indigenous world (*Tree* 163). Bringhurst describes the "vocabulary of the wild" as all the individuals that exist within nature; its syntaxes are its ecosystems, species, and ecological processes; and its phonology, its essential material substances, are its hydrocarbons (268). Bringhurst tells us that wild languages speak first of all in stories of immediacy, of lives being lived: "*This, this, this, being, here, being here, you, me, us,*" but that there is much more to these stories than seasonal declarations of unfurling green and what can be interpreted as utilitarian by a scientist unpacking a carbon-sugar sequence in a lab (ibid.).

Language, as Bringhurst illustrates, "is a means of seeing and understanding the world, a means of talking with the world" (163). This is a definition that leaves plenty of room for healthy diversity. As Bringhurst tells us, the rainforest thinks in the form of trees and their associated life forms; it thinks with phrases and expressions of mosses, fungi, and the many creatures that link with and modify them—beings like annelids and deer, arthropods and thrushes (165). Bringhurst's vision of language is open and inclusive, encompassing human as well as larger-than-human languages—from the life stories of animals and plants to larger forces of hydrology and weather, and the ways in which we translate and utilize them. While some of these entities provide information that can be decoded and interpreted by human beings, all of them can be considered as possessing forms of recognizable language, even if we cannot understand them. After all, there is no rationale to demand that the limited capability of human language is the sole necessary condition for establishing anything else as being or not being a language. If Gitxsan Storied Lands require a Gitxsan language to properly understand them, then the many wild communities rightly require their own languages in order to achieve their objectives of Real Work.

Henry David Thoreau describes the work of a "wild and dusky

knowledge, *Gramática parda*, tawny grammar," a concept he takes from the Spanish but which likely existed at one time within every culture, as it is the plain "mother-wit" of life borne in the Wild and is the most fundamentally intuitive language form in the world (25, 24). Tragically, for everyone and everything involved, tawny grammar is also the one language form that we have weaned ourselves away from in our often forced haste to enter into more and more technologically advanced and insular societies. Even as we create more and more complex methods of communicating, these forms are usually meant only to include human ambition, and always at the cost of losing more and more of the grammar of the wild. Yet, no matter how much we try to remove ourselves from the earth, it becomes no less immense or any less real, and as we treat it with less and less respect, our necessary participation within its processes becomes only more and more critical to consider.

Gary Snyder is just one Western thinker who places a great deal of contemporary importance upon these older ideas of tawny grammar. As he tells us, the dialogue that the West now needs to reopen is with this older, nearly lost perspective, within which there exists the means to bring ourselves back "among all beings, toward a rhetoric of ecological relationships" (*Practice* 68). Being similar to Belford's lan(d)guage, tawny grammar is "a curl of breath, a breeze in the pines," and, as Snyder tells us, tawny grammar is all that speaks through and "belongs to our biological nature" (69). When we look at human languages, we can find its material representation within productions, documents, and texts. Texts, as Snyder points out, "are information stored through time. The stratiography of rocks, layers of pollen in a swamp, the outward expanding circles in the trunk of a tree, [all] can be seen as texts" (77). As language "belongs to our biological nature," whether oral or written, language can also be interpreted in the Wild when we decipher the meaning of such basic things as "moose tracks in the snow" (ibid.).

Philosopher Alphonso Lingis proposes a similar idea, his being that any person who comes to understand is one who listens not only to words of direct meaning but also to the internal noises of the body:

"the rasping or smouldering breath...the rumblings and internal echoes" as well as "the glossolalia of nonhuman things—the humming, buzzing, murmuring, crackling, and roaring of the world" (91, 84). "If we speak to another of a mountain vista," it is because, literally enough, "that mountain landscape spoke to us"; and, if "our words... have referents, it is because things address signals to us—or at least broadcast signals at large" (78). Whether heard as lan(d)guage, seen as tawny grammar, or conceived of as ecological linguistics, this communication is concrete and "takes place when the vibrancy of the land, the oceans, and the skies is taken up, condensed and unfurled in the hollows of one's body, then released," where it bounces off the rock and comes back into our ears as expressions of Wild thoughts and impulses similar to spoken words, which hold meanings that we all interpret emotionally, just as "when one hears [an] echo returning with the wind and the sea" (97–98).

As they work in wild exclusivity from contemporary human modes of fixing, owning, and locating, these seemingly unintelligible expressions of tawny grammar might appear to be overly difficult indirections that lead mostly to regression and chaos, yet lan(d)guages mean to express only what is true and real and necessary. Belford points to these abstract notations as he sees them running as reflections downstream, grasped with the eye as motions instead of with the ear as words: "My narrative is waves of meaning / crashing through a watery code" where "clusters of tiny, new perceptions shift / and turn at once and I don't know / how it works, but I can see it" (*lan(d)guage* 19, 11). Belford gestures here to personal revelations found in the free-circulating qualities of liquid as experience, translated out of the eco-logical nuances of cycling water. Belford's personal understanding of lan(d)guage may appear wild in nature, yet the necessity of the living processes of the earth are the most highly civilized expressions, offering us images of wisdom to aid in our resistance to the homogenizing forces of post-globalization, with its rootless, throwaway activities of exploitation, consumption, and destruction. I would propose that

Belford's epiphany of connection—his abstract glimpse of understanding within one small structure in life—seen through the flowing of wild water, reveals a kind of understanding that can come only with the unknowing of the many supposed truths that are forced upon us by the institutionalized mechanisms of empire and capital. The elusive but powerful sense of direction and purpose that can be grasped in tawny grammar can become our own individual ground-truth and remains as one of the many life-giving benefits that only some kind of Real Work in the Real World can encourage and nourish within us.

If we let them, the qualities, processes, and expressions we realize through understandings of the Wild can become principles and values for a productive life within a concept that I earlier referred to as *ecosophical æsthetics*. Principles of ecosophical æsthetics exist partly in the activities and knowledges we gain through education but also as crucially through our emotions and epiphanies—those intangible possessions of intimate experience that create personal and vital connections. These are the internal devices that give direction to our ability to understand the necessity to remain connected to untamed, unpredictable, larger-than-human ideas, concepts that exist beyond the vacuum sterility of purely rational thought—things like dirt, air, water, and love.

Ecosophical æsthetics can begin with the simplest of early steps—perhaps seeing the value of little things or grasping the need for cohesion and connectedness—abstract ideas that work over time to transform our outlook, inform our decisions, and direct our activities. If we let them, these abstractions can become everyday associations, then the normal routines that can carry us to realizing the means for participatism and Real Work.

As for the meaning of æsthetics, the ecocritic Allan Johnston writes that æsthetics "concerns nature, value, [and] judgement of beauty" (14). But the meaning-sense of æsthetics I deal with here works beyond these conventions, eclipsing a larger-than-human or *ecosophical* perspective (*eco* meaning life and environment, and *sophical* meaning relating to wisdom or knowledge). My own personal æsthetic is directed as much as possible through references of "ecointelligence," which psychologist and ecotherapist Norah Trace describes as social intelligence attuned to biotic needs, which creates "a scenario that includes individual value, diversity, healthier connectedness and shared valuing of life" (190).

To give one wild example that exemplifies ground-truth, let us consider a crumbling redrot stump upon the rainforest floor. We have already learned that this entity is connected to the soil by a thriving mycelial network, that it is infiltrated by dense microbial and bacterial communities, and that it has become the structural habitat for many other life forms, such as amphibians, birds, insects, and many smaller plants. As it accommodates innumerable living spaces and lives, this rotting stump is a city, one as complex in its own way as any made by humankind. The stump is the site for various industries; it has centres for health care and regulatory communication; it has transportation networks, a variety of housing centres, and more—all held together by lush mosses and filigrees of lichen, and crowned by plants that offer leaves, pollen, and fruit by season for shade, protection, food, and as venues for various industries. To me, this larger-than-human-community-as-ecosystem, in both concept *and* image, is more ethically beautiful than just about any piece of modern or historical art. Seriously. And this statement comes from someone who is an art-school and creative-writing graduate, someone who admires art and has spent more than thirty years developing a creative practice, but also someone, importantly, who has also spent just as many years living and working directly within and learning from the Wild.

The first reason I would chose a decaying stump in a rainforest over a Rembrandt or a Rothko lies in consideration of the fact that industrially manufactured art materials have likely gone into making the piece of "high art." Although there are ethical art materials, most of the products and services utilized in this process—whether they be through travelling gallery installations, ceramics manufacturing, metal foundries, big-budget Hollywood movies, or popular musical acts that tour the world—all can exist or operate only through the despoliation of an ecosystem or a portion of some larger-than-human community. The majority of industrially manufactured art materials, past and present, are poisons of one kind or another and are, undeniably, ethically unsound. If we consider their origins, their reason for existing in the world, and their downstream consequences, there is little to justify their use in just about any form of cultural production. And, when we participate in either the making of or the consumption of any kind of art or culture that utilizes unethically sourced materials, we become complicit with injustice, as we are giving personal permission for the ongoing destruction of the productive world that has privileged us with our very life.

Considering this criteria, all gestures that destroy, pollute, and waste can hardly be considered beautiful, as what is truly beautiful are gestures that give at least as much or more than they take. Locally, ecosophical æsthetics also draws a strong association with the long-standing worldviews and value systems held by traditionally minded Indigenous peoples, those who have created valued cultural works through sustainable processes of daily necessity. For the most part, these are works of art that are much more ethically sound than those we find, for example, that have been created through the last few hundred years of European and contemporary art history—where caustic resins, oils, raw chemical pigments, and turpentines were in constant use. Traditionally, First Nations cultural art objects were made out of either directly found, lightly extracted, or easily renewable objects, most of which were common to their local environment, all of which can also return back to their origin with the simple act of placing them back on the beach or under the tree where they came from—which is a practice that was also commonplace, as canoes, implements, and houses were all left to crumble back into the environment from which they originated.

Although we have looked briefly at human values, there are also values specific to the activity we are engaged with here—writing, reading, and thinking—and questions as to what ethical benefits or usefulness they hold. According to ecocritic Johnston, a value "suggests measurable degrees of æsthetic, ethical or other qualities" (14). Although it seems here that almost anything goes, the parameters of respect for nature and what constitutes Real Work draw relatively strict lines between what *does* and *does not* provide for biotic and social health and justice. Johnston's definition allows that ecosophical æsthetics are possible in works that focus not just on the natural world but also on the human wor(l)d, pointing to those works that embrace the interdisciplinary, works that "insist on the basic interrelation of humanity and nature, and show how people can open to and be healed by nature's beauty" (15). For those of us who are acculturated into mainstream society, the production of literature or any kind of "art" becomes subject to the same judgements, duties, and responsibilities that provide for what Gregory Bateson calls "an ecology of mind," from which there are outcomes that split two ways: into the "ecology of bad ideas" and the "ecology of good ideas."

This might be a hard statement for cultural institutions to hear— especially the humanities, which considers many of its productions to be culturally relevant and even crucial to the health of society, but I would propose this: if a cultural work does not transmit an ethic that reflects principles of Real Work or values similar to what we find in kincentrism, there is little to justify its production and consumption. I know I am being a total killjoy, but no form of art or expression can be defended if it does not meet guidelines and principles of eco-logic. This very page must pass through this same critical frame, and all of my words must demonstrate whether or not they reflect an ecology of mind, of action, and of consequence.

This does not mean that ecosophical æsthetics is impenetrably intellectual and philosophically arcane or that it exists in the privileged sphere of some self-righteous elite. These ideas are the simple ground-truth of respect for the Real World. For a local example, we can consider the ancient dwelling experiences of the Gitxsan, whose social laws and practical knowledges are gifts received from the kincentric entities of their Storied Land. The tripartite nature of the Gitxsan relationship with the world constitutes an inclusive vision, one that values the legacy of the past and realizes its debt to the future, brought together in the necessary tasks of the present, all synthesized within the simple idea that every living thing, no matter how small or seemingly inconsequential, should be treated with the same dignity, respect, and right to life that we would give our elders, our children, and ourselves. This kincentric morality, as ethnoecologist Leslie Main Johnson describes, "encompasses the broad æsthetic or cosmological sense of the local environment," as geographic, physiographic, and ecologic truths exist within the traditional features of Storied Land, gifting themselves to those who accept the selfless work of obeying them, all of which defines the very loci of power in Gitxsan territories (17).

For me, as a typical Canadian of European origin, one who lives within the bounds of but not as a privileged member of the Storied Lands of the North Coast's Indigenous peoples, these concepts and their lived human experiences are tentative thought experiments that can be nurtured and developed through education and a gradual awakening, just as TEKW itself has revealed its power and gifts through many thousands of years of the survival and thriving of Indigenous peoples. The adoption of an ecosophical æsthetic, whether found through new lessons provided by science or through older knowledges provided by TEKW, also demands taking on a life of eco-logical duty. This is a life in which the value, integrity, and authority of Wild processes—the very same processes that create, protect, and nurture human communities—become a large part of the practical focus and plain pleasures that we find in daily life, replacing our addiction to destructive Western values of consumption, those that offer not only the empty promise of an endless pursuit of extrinsic self-gratification but which also destroy life on the planet.

Environments are social and economic as well as physical, and all rather intricately bound up. The land and sea are the same land and sea as they were before the white man came but the total environment is as changed as day from night.

—Alan Fry (1970)

transect 15

medicines in the trees,
cultural experiments,
Native land claims.

ON THE NORTH COAST, WE HAVE TREES AND TREES AND TREES AND trees and trees and more trees and more trees and more and more and more and more and more and trees and trees and trees and trees and trees and trees and trees and trees and trees and trees and trees and trees and trees and trees and still more trees and more trees and more and more trees and more and more and more and more, and then still even more, which doesn't even begin to describe the extent of how well they thrive extravagantly within this rich green place. Even though the most obvious statement that any tree makes with its seven-hundred-year-old stand is a bold pronouncement of *Here*, trees do much more than speak of just more and more trees.

My philosophical perspective upon the roles that trees play for humans in the Indigenous rainforest would be to describe them as being endlessly giving and exceedingly generous, but also as being austere, rigorous, many-branched ascetics. Trees are almost impenetrably dense taskmasters that, both unfortunately and unwittingly, tend to shove most people out of the way with their rough-barked elbows. The conifer trees of the North Coast and our perhumid rainforests in general are most usually too cold, too wet, and too rough for most people to endure for very long, but these largest and most profound living residents of the North Coast are also our most venerable and stoic uprightstarters, and they have been pointing the most realistic way to tomorrow for enough time that their experience should, by this time, be recognized and respected.

Wayne Grady and David Suzuki tell us that gymnosperms have lived on earth for at least 235 million years (25). *Homo sapiens* have only been around for about two hundred thousand years, and quite a bit less here on the North Coast (Smithsonian). Not surprisingly, there is a large if not corresponding imbalance of quantity and complexity in the genetic material between trees and people. Gymnosperms possess at least seven times more DNA than human beings, and likely much more, as scientists have found that mapping their overlapping genomes is an extremely complicated process (Nystedt et al.). Although recent research reveals that the bulk of the genetic material in gymnosperms does not seem to be doing anything useful and is perhaps merely "in storage," the results of genome research are also poorly understood and even this hypothesis is, at best, specious (ibid.). On the other hand, there is ample and profound evidence that gymnosperms are the most successful organisms the earth has ever grown; in particular, conifer trees of the west coast of Turtle Island are the tallest, heaviest, most productive, and oldest things that have ever lived (Timmer). Any discussion of this kind cannot help but toss the concept of human superiority right where it belongs. Close to home, biologists Pojar and MacKinnon tell us that our own perhumid rainforests have existed in one incarnation or another for at least two million years, and that some of these individual species have been evolving for at least seventy million years (14).

Pojar and MacKinnon also explain that the earliest peoples of the North Coast "had an intimate relationship with the plants in their environment" (21). Interestingly enough, the foliage, fibre, and dust of all cedar species are actually irritants and serious allergens for many non-Indigenous peoples, yet this repellent effect is not a problem for the Indigenous people that have been living on Turtle Island for thousands of years.

Anishaanabeg cultural scholar Wendy Makoons Geniusz tells us quite plainly that trees are medicine, and whether material or mental, this is one of the definite truths of trees. As she recounts the historic time in which European-derived smallpox devastated her ancestors, elder Mary Geniusz describes how an entire village was moved into a cedar swamp to bring more direct aid to the people (146). As they lived hour by hour amongst *giizhikaatig* (grandmother cedar), the Anishinaabeg were connected to her physical and spiritual properties (quoted in Geniusz 146). Validating this traditional practice with ecological science, botanist and medical biochemist Diana Beresford-Kroeger tells us that when trees reach a particular temperature, they release aerosol chemicals that are almost always some kind of human medicine (80). Amongst gymnosperms, *Pinus* species in particular emit odours that are mixtures of various esters of *pinosylvin*, a natural antibiotic that has a stimulating effect upon breathing and is a mild narcotic that works as both a relaxant and anæsthetic (81). As Beresford-Kroeger writes, "a forest of pines acts as an air sweep, cleansing and soporifying the atmosphere…Other trees do likewise. In fact, the global forests exert an antiviral and antibacterial action on moving air masses, in general" (ibid.). Both Geniusz and Beresford-Kroeger reveal just a few of the many ways in which the stalwart and silent trees of our cold and inhospitable rainforests contribute to our health with gifts that biological science has only recently discovered but which ancient practices of TEKW have appreciated for millennia. Here we can realize the most obvious signs of ground-truth: that we must accept and embrace the ecologic, psychic, and spiritual realities that are presented to us from out of the natural systems that encompass our lives; as well, we must work to respect, adapt to, and reflect these models with working methods that benefit ecosystems as much as they benefit us—not just for today but for the long term of the unforeseeable future.

As Evelyn Fox Keller tells us, part of what is required in coming to adopt a biotic perspective is that we must take the time to look and have the patience to hear, which is precisely what Nobel Prize–winning geneticist Barbara McClintock asks, pointing out that we must not only hear "what the material has to say" but that we must also "have a feeling for the organism" (quoted in Fox Keller 198). And as forester Hellum points out: "we could do much better by listening to trees, getting to know what they need, and what they depend on" (91). In the same way that we always respectfully consider the people around us, whether we are at home, at work, or on the street, the wild realm that sprawls beyond our door requires just as much sensitivity, and for the very same reasons.

Ken Belford reveals a similar sense of this need for respect within his apt *lan(d)guage*. Belford not only refocuses an experiential value similar to that of a traditional First Nations perspective wherein he recognizes the vitality and necessity that persist within the Land but also represents his own contrary model of outlier dissidence, one that attempts to dispel the quiet acceptance and complacency that lies uncontested within the violence, fear, and denial that operate within mainstream Canadian culture. In Belford's poems, words and ideas sound with the same ecological integrity that we find in Geniusz, Beresford-Kroeger, Maracle, Bateson, Guattari, and so many others: "Plants plan / and make decisions we call medicines / and lipids but really they heal and create community / so that none of us are alone" (25).

For a great many of us, it is only personal will that keeps us from reading, thinking, and participating as productively as poet and defender of water Rita Wong instructs us: to "start in the middle of rupert's lament and work / out, start from the coasts and work in, start" (30). We can also consider what journalist and environmental writer Richard Manning imagines and hopes: "If we are to succeed as inhabitants it will be by recovering information: knowledge of the habits of salmon, the layers of meaning of the land, the complexities of genetics; the wisdom of stories, command of craft, sure hands on chisel, net and keyboard" (10). As day-to-day habits of personality, will, and ability, these simple gestures can bring us a long way to finding the ground-truth in our own version of Real Work. Perhaps there is power within a book, a phrase, or one word that lodges in the memory and moves the body to become a tool, hopefully for much more than the once-a-year, day-long community volunteer job of dragging tires, broken bicycles, shopping carts, and garbage out of the salmon streams that wind around the streets of Prince Rupert.

Robert Bringhurst tells us that "language increases as biomass increases," and it is well documented that North Coast rainforests have more biomass than just about any place on the earth (159). Ecocritic Patrick D. Murphy argues similarly, asking that we hold "an appreciat[ion of] cultural diversity as a physical manifestation of biological diversity" (74). Journalist Alex Rose writes that, while it "can hardly compete with the new high-tech economies of Vancouver, Seattle or Portland," even "Prince Rupert has become a kind of working laboratory for a racially integrated society—a prototype for a place where aboriginal and non-aboriginal people work and live together" (96). The integration of these two human elements of the North Coast triad can be helped along by the richness of the third partner—the larger-than-human realm. Despite positive local aspirations, Rose points to some of the unavoidable negative pitfalls of human activity left over from the short-sightedness of industrial profit taking and the many cycles of capital flight that the North Coast has endured. Rose describes quite accurately how "the area remains an unmitigated planning disaster where a long line of empty canneries obliterates the harbour view" (ibid.). Even if he hadn't died on the Titanic, would Charles Hays have achieved his vision of Prince Rupert becoming a global trade centre?

Despite varying opinions and perspectives on economic development, the main reason that the North Coast retains so much of its ecological integrity is because capital has generally stayed away, been scared away, or been diverted south to easier bets with more certainty for profit taking. Either inadvertently or directly, the fierce Indigenous power of this place has been one of the strongest means for retaining the integrity of its people and its landscape. Rose gives her opinion about the socio-political weather of today, noting that, for those who live in contemporary Prince Rupert, "accepting and understanding the structural causes of the harsh new economic reality has ushered in a time of critical self-reflection," which is exactly the process needed for those who wish to continue to call this place home (ibid.). "Some are asking big questions about the economy and their jobs," as Rose explains, and "at the same time they are beginning to examine their own culture and its historical relationship to its aboriginal neighbours" (ibid.). For many non-Indigenous locals who live within the eternal, perhumid echo of raven song and rain-dripping cedar, strong ideas of cultural change are not so much embraced as they are grimly accepted, as they hold the potential for becoming more than just the current day-to-day annoyance that they are, which is tolerated, just like the ceaseless rain.

In order for Rose's cultural experiment to work, the ideas for which are similar to what we heard earlier from artist *Iljuwas* (Bill Reid) about the nature of being X̲aaydaa, can communities across the North Coast continue to be the homes for a dozen different First Nations peoples as well as for many more new cultural varieties of immigrant Canadians, those who come from an increasing variety of cultural backgrounds? Can this phenomenon occur here, where Canadian political policies and mainstream social pressures presume themselves to be as strong and as large as the mountains, rainforests, and waters—those larger-than-human forces that are, after all, much, much larger and likely more powerful than any human decision could presume itself to be?

Sizing up a few perspectives from the larger-than-human realm, Bringhurst and Murphy tell us that both languages and biodiversity have the potential to increase under the right conditions, and Jacobs tells us that forest biomass is always expanding, which is a steadily burgeoning fact that is plain for anyone to see, from *SGang Gwaay Linagaay* to the *Tatshenshini* to *Sanskisoot* Creek. It's *trēowe*: "trees get larger, moss thicker, vines longer, seeds more abundant, mushrooms bulgier, earthworms fatter, squirrels more abounding, lichens lumpier" (Jacobs 45). Jacobs reminds us that it is only a well-balanced ensemble that can make such an environment rich as it expands (ibid.). Interconnectivity, participation, and unrestricted communication—these elements are key factors for health in rainforest ecosystems, as they must be in any kind of community. With this ideal as an objective, we should all seek out and share with people who value these same principles, and not just within a large population centre like Metro Vancouver but also within small towns like Prince Rupert, Masset, *Taant'a Ḵwáan*, the Hazeltons, Terrace, and *Gitlaxt'aamiks.* These kinds of people are there, often hiding in the woodwork of plain sight.

How, then, do we engage with such productive change? Paying both respect and dues would be the best place to start. But, aside from the initial accomplishments of *Delgamuukw v. British Columbia* and the landmark Nisga'a Treaty, all other outstanding Native land claims in northern BC suffer from perpetual neglect. Up and up the coast, these unresolved issues are in the largest part responsible for the lack of growth and the economic decline of both settler-immigrant Canadian and First Nations communities. Since 1929, both the federal and provincial governments have been holding their breath on four- to twelve-year cycles, doing anything and everything to avoid tabling (never mind settling) any of the issues that are important in the North. Despite the fact that a 2009 PricewaterhouseCoopers study funded by the BC Treaty Commission states that the settling of land treaties will lead to immediate and long-term benefits in the forms of investments, jobs, and economic development for both First Nations and other British Columbians, productive progress on any BC treaty seems futile (Government). Skeena-Bulkley Valley NDP MP Nathan Cullen recently commented that claims to original title are the first things that must be addressed in order to provide certainty for future economic development and diversity on the North Coast (quoted in Thomas 2).

To provide context, there are only two colonial-era treaties in BC: the Douglas Treaties (1850) on Vancouver Island, which include the areas of Victoria, Saanich, Sooke, Nanaimo, and Port Hardy; and Federal Treaty 8 (1899), which includes all of the plateau area beyond the Rocky Mountains, in BC's northeast (Province, Government). One of the reasons all other lands in BC have un-extinguished Aboriginal title is due to a purposefully repressive decision in 1929 by the federal government to make it illegal for First Nations to hire lawyers to support their claims. Although the government has never come to legally possess any portion of land along the North Coast, the failure to affirm and respect First Nations' legitimate rights and agency (both of which are clearly expressed within the Royal Proclamation of 1763 and reaffirmed later by Section 35 of the federal government's Constitutional Act of 1982) remains as a fundamental stumbling block that must be resolved for much more than the economic health of the region (Government).

Despite a repeated avoidance of these fundamental issues, each subsequent government manages to easily find both the resources and the political will to push through legislative and regulatory infrastructure that allows industry the power to liquidate and transform the resource wealth that dwells within these Storied Lands. And it has proceeded like this for more than a century because all that any government has to do to get around restrictions of Native title is to make the case that a development initiative is pressing and substantial, after which industrial activity can proceed without the approval of any First Nations group (Supreme Court of Canada).

Today, the irresolution of Native land claims has become a perpetual background pattern of white noise that fades in and out of our attention, day by month by year. Lately, I watch the mountains for quicker signs of movement, as the chance of an earthquake or a volcanic eruption is more likely to reform the North Coast than any government action.

the spruce, its spine
on the rock, fighting the salt wind
looks more like a mound of moss than a tree
until it lets go of its bark and needles
and reveals
    bone lightning
      —John Steffler (1985)

Mountain Hemlock (view 3

TRADITIONAL JAPANESE TEMPLE ARCHITECTURE IS THE MOST DIRECT human reflection of the elegant natural design of the native *Kometsuga* (*Tsuga diversifolia*), especially when we look at the design of Shinto shrines, where the venerated *Tsu-ga* hybridize with the delicate grace of wildflower blossoms and the rugged strength of mountain peaks: *Niijo, Kinkaku, Todaiji, Kiomizu.*

As slope-angled expressions of strength in organic form, the terse branch wings of mountain hemlock curve and droop to shed water and snow, the current year's growth always hooking upward in bright green feathers to snag whatever light might flash by, even within a rainbow. Shaped by wind, precipitation, and darkness, foliage projections are highly variable in their manifestation. Jutting branches express agility and lift, randomized by harsh weather within dense, explosive shags that reach up the dusky trunks, where the bark splits into furrowed scales that channel runoff down to the roots. On steep slopes, young hemlocks and other conifers sometimes fall over, their roots slumping with the sliding soils. But they continue to grow, first across the forest floor, then slowly arching back up through the canopy, eventually curving into a strong, tall "pistolbutt," their top aimed back into the sky while their overall length exhibits a bowed form that will manage to take them through a few hundred more winter storms and into a full, if sweeping, maturity.

Up the North Coast and still further, deep within the Tongass, mountain hemlock accept slow murk within squat, dense stands, embracing the windy shadow of the Alaskan gyre from sea level at the *Taku* and on up above Hoonah. They plough their way back under the winter drifts up to four hundred metres and higher, all the way down to *Kyuquot* and *Nuchatlitz* on the west coast of Vancouver and Nootka Islands, living and growing within the tiniest energy sinks of the subzone. Here, between four hundred and one thousand metres and even higher, mountain hemlock thin out into a mosaic of subalpine parklands, bogs, and heaths. Here, within the meadows and rocky seepages of their fringe communities, the ground is dominated by tree-ruffle, red bryum (*Bryum miniatum*), purple-worm liverwort (*Pleurozia purpurea*), crowberry (*Empetrum nigrum*), partridgefoot (*Luetkea pectinata*), and yellow mountain-heather (*Phyllodoce glanduliflora*). Higher up, these fragmenting stands become increasingly irregular and spare but continue to grow right up to the timberline, where they splinter into clumps of stunted spires. In lee pockets set against the wind, they hold on in isolated singles and pairs, roughed up with broken tops and wildly jagged foliage—reduced to horns of grey resilience with a few green winglets twisted up against the sky (BC MoF).

Where subalpine conditions meet the surf, further and further west and north around the coast (which is yet another version of up), beyond *Yakutat* and *Chilkat*, along the mnemonic fjord and river pegs of the *Eyak*, the *Tutchone*, and the *Dena'ina*, up and around the Gulf of Alaska, mountain hemlock continue to grow, grappling themselves to the stone in twisted shreds of gnomic bonsai. Here they persevere, surviving for 500 years on moderate ground, most typically only 250, but telling; rarely, up to 1,000 years lucky, and still growing (Pojar and MacKinnon 23, 31). Up, out, and ever more wild, mountain hemlock warp under the fierce wild equation of wind + rain ÷ age, which = beautiful.

As a miscellaneous western softwood, one that loggers on the North Coast have long considered to be either inaccessible or just in the way, *Tsuga mertensiana* is still viewed mainly as a junk wood. Still, although it is harder to find than in most other local conifers, a prime and sound log is highly prized. Not surprisingly, as the rate of industrial logging of lower elevation species concludes amidst the fundamentally illegal loopholes of technically legal overcuts, new investigations of *k̲'aang* (as the X̲aaydaa call hemlock) declare it an important timber resource (Turner *Plants* 93). Even as industry presses governments into altering existing regulations to better suit its needs, forest biologist K.C. Swedeberg states that in the higher-elevation discontinuous forests (1,670–1,770 m) of the Pacific Northwest, where mountain hemlock are the most successful, they are also the most ecologically important tree; and, back in 1993, it was included in a world list of threatened conifer species (36, Farjon et al. 12).

In the rugged coastal inlets and islands of Southeast Alaska that are home to the Tlingit, the CWH zone is a faint membrane of green that snakes in and out of sheltered inlets, right down to sea level. Here, *yán* reaches north as one of the last stoics of the extreme weather fringe of the *Kunai* peninsula, bracing themselves as stress-tolerant stanchions along the wildest, most northerly seacoasts where a tree might find a chance to grow (Thornton 206, Pojar and MacKinnon 31). Being the last holdouts in both upland bogs and the roughest subalpine and alpine terrain, mountain hemlock provide shade and windbreak for the elfinwood stagger of Sitka spruce and Pacific silver fir, and mountain hemlock are the last living uprights found at the bare, knobby headwaters of the *Kwinamass* and the *Kshwan*. What the Gitx̲san call *hlk̲uugan*, mountain hemlock grow high up and high, and just before they climb up and twist themselves into krummholz, their tops may tear off or shatter apart in violent winter storms, and much of their roots may become exposed by erosion, which leaves them appearing to launch themselves in naked fragments, out past the broken edge of the rock, into open air (Johnson 36). Yet they still manage to survive, their deformed, exiguous branches arching back against the gales, grasping for a sun that is almost always hidden in cloud somewhere near the southern horizon. As the species is forced upward into heath and rocklands by anthropogenic climate change, mountain hemlock communities have little alternative but to crawl upward into less hospitable terrain, where they will dwindle upon the extreme heights of the wildest precipices, places where lichen and wind fight over specks of dust.

On the way to that grove where the exemplary trees
Of "the working forests" make one last stand to stall
Their manufacture, dropping wakefulness upon us
Just as earlier the alarm had awoke us from our sleep
We drove along freeways, passing gloomy mill towns
Connected precariously to the information corridor
Without imagining we would find along the way
Anything that might trouble our progress.

—Roger Farr (2006)

transect 16

diversity, fruitility, and the pistolbutt forest.
Brazilian rubber tappers and Haitian deforestation.
culturally modified trees and the view from the stump.

DESPITE HOW MUCH ACTIVE COMPETITION THERE IS WITHIN THE PER-humid rainforest for available space, light, and nutrients, there is always an equally strong, wild green requirement to collaborate and to remain open (

Here on the North Coast, diversity is more than just a popular catchphrase dropped by human geographers, environmentalists, and left-leaning ecologists. Diversity is an everyday process as much as it is a state that transforms the lives of species whose communities and needs overlap and whose processes adapt to the needs of their neighbours as much as to the pressure of climate and geography. As more than the activity of different species fighting over resources, with winners *here* and losers *there*, diversity is also how so many local organisms tend to aggregate and puzzle themselves together in cooperative interdependent niches, forming long-standing tapestries of evolved community that cannot be untangled from one another. In describing what the intensely wild and often inhospitable coastal rainforests of Southeast Alaska still manage to create and give, Japanese wildlife photographer Michio Hosino freely combined the two English words, "fruit" and "utility," to come up with the brilliant "fruitility" (Schooler 165). Hosino's fruitility is the perfect idea for describing what the North Coast and the entirety of Cascadia expresses with its overall green-blue spectacle of weather, wood, and wildlife.

As for protecting the rich but fragile fruitility of the North Coast, many of us can do little more than write letters, protest, or partake in acts of civil disobedience in the hopes of altering the policies of government and the activities of industry. But as individuals and consumers we can do a great deal more. We can choose to adopt the principles and processes of ecologic diversity as the model of how we live our lives, which means that we can choose to work with others in mind, collaboratively, following the many examples given to us by the Indigenous larger-than-human locals, those that return all of their material value in rich fruitility back to the parent materials of their communities of origin. We can also choose to consider, as traditionally minded First Nations peoples do, that everything around us is as valuable and as worthy of respect as the most cherished members of our families— that is, we can love this land as we should love ourselves and strive to work for the benefit of all of its Indigenous inhabitants—human and larger-than-human.

However we choose to perceive it, we hold both a duty and privilege to protect and nurture the elements of life—the essential stuff of life on the North Coast that must always find its way back to the Pacific through the threading of the rain, where it must return through salt water into the mouths of whales, herring, crustaceans, halibut, sea lions, and more, where it will return up into the terrestrial habitats and back within the flesh of salmon and eulachon, working its way through the roots and leaves of conifer trees and riparian plants and back into the mouths of bears, hummingbirds, eagles and ravens, mink, blacktail deer, and people, around and around through ancestral time within cycles of constant rain.

While there is hardly enough flat space on the North Coast to pitch a tent, it is still here, reaching across the Mesozoic accretions and granitic batholithics that dominate the zone, where the most highly productive and diverse forests of Canada grow. Upon some of the most rugged terrain on Turtle Island, these forests have managed to bend and contort and survive, holding themselves not just against weather but also gravity, clinging to ground that is oftentimes closer to the vertical than the horizontal. With no choice but to endure and twist upward through the constant ordeal of their Sisyphean life's work, these pistolbutt stands of conifers curve their way up and up and up the roughest slopes, finding sustenance within soils whose nutrients are always being leached away by constant rain. Clenching their roots for firm holds around protrusions and within cracks of stone, these weather- and elevation-beaten stands grapple resolutely up the wildly pitching slopes to the narrowest ledges of bare stone, bashed by hurricane-force winds and bending under the most rainfall experienced anywhere on the planet. Eventually, some of them achieve the somewhat conditional solidity of stand dominance as they enter maturity, where at least the weight of sliding snow no longer has the power to budge their roots or distort their trunks. Yet there is still the potential for a rainfall-induced landslide or a hurricane-force gust that might toss them down the side of the mountain.

At the stand level: here, there, and everywhere we might learn to look, we can see that rainforests fall as much as they stand within the successional processes of small-scale patch dynamics. Appearing much more obvious to the eye than the slow drop and fall of select groups of trees under the randomized force of wind and decay over the slow accumulation of centuries, human beings have been clearcutting entire hillsides and whole valleys, knocking down two to three centuries' worth of windthrow in a few months or even just a few weeks.

Next, mills transform these denuded stands into rough logs and then into cants, boards, pellets, pulp, cardboard, toilet paper, magazines, and so many other products, especially the reams of office paper that forestry managers must diligently fill out requisition and approval forms upon and submit to the government, all in order to receive permission to log even more trees next season. And, no matter where you might be at this moment, millions of stumps have been required to get you and the rest of us to this stage of human development.

Within the circles that I keep, almost everyone has planted hundreds of thousands of conifer seedlings across the blurred memory of so many uncounted clearcuts, dodging stumps and then falling to rest upon them. While most every Canadian has climbed on top of a stump at one time or another to get a better view of the rate of progress, many environmental activists have been born the moment their boots climbed bark to bleeding sapwood and set them to stand bewildered upon a few hundred years of smoothly bifurcated growth rings. This is the kind of experience that often serves to locate the tiny human within the crisscrossing regions of history, the momentary, and causality, providing them a direct glimpse into the fundamental role we all play in what we earlier imagined was a detached, otherwise generalized transformation of the natural world. Of course, many lifelong loggers and career foresters have also been created this same way, yet there need not be such a gulf in either ethics or disparity in the manner of expressions of love for the earth between these two seemingly distinct avocations and vocations. It stands to reason, some of the loggers and forestry workers that I know have a much broader and more realistic understanding of the ramifications of logging and its consequences than some of the (most usually urban) environmentalists and eco-friendly nature lovers I have encountered, those who work tirelessly with the best of intentions, yet sometimes within a mostly fictionalized world of black and white absolutes. That being said, some of the loggers I have met over the years—to use their own language— have their heads up their asses.

From the point of view of the stump: This is where most Canadians perceive of a forest, although not usually right here, at the edge of the uneven floor of recently razed trunks, broken and bleeding roots, and tangled slash, where the wall of partly living green rises with its flush of biotic reverb, seeming like the living bars of a cage until you find your way inside, where things get easier or only much worse. Looking back, as frustrating and as plain and simple as it can be, almost all of us in BC live upon levelled, gravelled, and concreted grounds that are the ghostscapes of former old-growth forests. If we accept this as the cut-tree truth, we should also consider that we, as immigrant Canadians in BC, also live upon the illegally possessed and historically unceded Storied Lands of so many First Nations peoples.

Stepping back from this socio-political quagmire to the flat plane of a cut stump, logging itself as a human activity should not be a problem, as it remains (in theory) the most benign of the heavy industries. But alarms should ring when we consider the unsustainable practices of this global industry, where most of the power and decision making is centralized far beyond our borders. Aside from a few small-scale, community-run forests, offshore interests dictate unsustainable standards as necessary and normal within regimes that demand spiralling growth, all of which is mediated as necessary for economic health, which then provides the social licence for multinational corporations to campaign for massive targets for both production and profit. This reveals part of the motivation that allows the Prime Minister's Office (PMO) of Canada's Conservative government to allegedly label individuals and groups who work to protect the ecological health and diversity of the North Coast—for example, a group like the non-profit organization Forest-Ethics—as an "enemy of the government of Canada" and an "enemy of the people of Canada" (Frank). Directly enough, as former federal Natural Resources minister Joe Oliver writes in an open letter he published on January 9, 2012, wherein he stigmatizes predominantly ordinary BC citizens as dangerous radicals: "Their goal is to stop any major project no matter what the cost to Canadian families in lost jobs and economic growth. No forestry. No mining. No oil. No gas. No more hydro-electric dams" (Government of Canada). As enemies of Canada, we outliers, dissidents, and mainly average people now clearly see what we are up against when we do not wholly agree with projected plans for future government policy regarding industrial development.

Historically, both Ireland and Scotland (where many early Canadian immigrants came from) were once covered entirely with forest lands, as was much of the Middle East (where many of our most recent immigrants come from). Both of these regions were subject to complete deforestation and are now dominated by bare rock or desert due to eras of subsequent erosion. Within this same outcome, many of the immediate problems faced by the tiny nation of Haiti stem from the fact that the country was forced to liquidate its entire forest resource, worth about 90 million francs ($21 billion), which the French government demanded, in 1825, as payment for its independence.

Clearcuts, as poet George Stanley writes, "are not part of the 'views' we appropriate, / they are external / the scraped / slopes evidence value has been racked up somewhere, / some big account" (*Opening* 94). Here on the North Coast, as everywhere, the history of industrial forestry has hardly mimicked or reflected Real Work, and the volume of clearcuts from *Xaaydaa Gwaay* to the House of *Woos* is the physical evidence of a very brief but substantial legacy of injustice, all tucked way out here in the massive middle of nowhere, a place where it is believed that no one is watching except the complicit and where it is presumed that only the voiceless and powerless care.

As Gitxsan hereditary chief and artist 'Wii Muk'willixw (Art Wilson) writes, "our religion was written in our hearts and not on paper, [and] it didn't count" to white newcomers, who presumed that the Gitxsan and other First Nations had *nothing* of importance to say, especially about what happened within their lands (18). From a traditionally minded perspective, many millennia of First Nations history tell a different story of both the scale and kinds of engagement local people had with the original forests. As we know, traditional life centred upon means of dwelling and interbeing within Storied Lands through a kin-centric philosophy and the pragmatic local science of TEKW. Because the ecological footprint of First Nations peoples over many thousands of years was so small as to be nearly invisible, there was a false percep-tion amongst colonial-era newcomers that First Nations peoples *did* nothing, which added up to the people themselves being considered *as* nothing, which I believe is still very much the perception, not only for First Nations in Canada but for the almost 370 million Indigenous peoples that live around the world.

Tsimshian cultural scholar and anthropologist James Andrew McDonald prefaces his description of traditional *Kitsumkalum* activ-ities on the Land with this corrective aimed at contemporary society: "the popular sense of what [the] world was like [before colonization,] according to our current sense of history, is deeply mistaken" (50). True enough, as the Tsimshian landscape of 120 years ago was

> very different from what you see today. You may expect to have seen a wilderness where today there are farms, roads and settle-ments, but there was no wilderness. Prior to the settlement of Terrace, the Kitsumkalum Valley and nearby lands were under the land management of the people for the benefit and pros-perity of each Waap.... They had to ensure the conservation of the resources for future generations and they did so with management practices that enhanced the productivity of the laxyuup [the Tsimshian landed properties, their house territo-ries]. (McDonald 50–51)

And to give just one example of these practices: prized berry patches were tended, weeded, cleared of overgrowth, cleaned and pruned, and in many cases invigorated by seasonal controlled burns, the patches also made accessible by a series of well-maintained trails (53).

Research biologists Pojar and MacKinnon describe another aspect of the low-impact management practices of First Nations on the North

Coast, writing that "few redcedars were actually felled before European contact. Instead, fallen logs or boards split from standing trees were used. To split off cedar boards for house planks or half-logs for canoes, a series of graduated yew-wood or antler wedges were pounded into living trees along the grain," which facilitated the removal of necessary wood products without killing the tree (42). Afterwards, the culturally modified tree (CMT) remained standing, where it continued to grow and thrive. Today there are likely still tens of thousands of CMTs across the region and I have witnessed many hundreds myself over the length of a career in the field. As Nancy J. Turner and *Kii'iljuus* (Barbara Wilson) explain, the long, narrow scars that persist upon the boles of trees stripped for minor resources "reflect the removal of bark or wood from no more than one-third of the circumference," while larger trees often show the evidence of numerous activities decades or more apart, with removals on all sides of the tree, a process that allows the tree to remain living, eventually growing swollen layers of growth tissue and "reclaiming the area that was cut" (133). Heiltsuk scholar and educator *Hilistis* (Pauline Waterfall), together with Doug Hopwood and Ian Gill, tells us that the traditional "Heiltsuk concept of logging was to beachcomb for blow-down trees. A living tree was not used unless its dimensions met the criteria for building a canoe, long house, or other specific use. If a tree had to be cut down, a song was sung to empathize with the pain it was enduring" (121).

To emphasize the thoughts behind this practice, we must remember that the deeper, hidden values of the tree as a living entity, with its ties to the health of the whole ecosystem and thus the people themselves, were considered and paid respect. Turner and *Kii'iljuus* also draw attention to the most important aspect of traditional tree use: ceremonial recognition. This included demonstrations that reveal the tree as "a living and generous being, whose life would not be forfeited unnecessarily. The harvester would negotiate with the tree, through a respectful request, and an explanation as to the purpose of harvesting by those undertaking the task" (134). Today, although there is a great deal of registered history of First Nations low-impact forestry practices, with the access and control of Crown lands held by large timber licensees or mining interests, most traditional trails and other physical evidence have disappeared into the windthrow and the overgrowth or have been erased by clearcutting, road building, and other development. As McDonald laments, many sites previously under traditional management "have become very wild places" (53).

Bringing an international perspective to the importance of biocomplexity in wild forests, ethnoecologists K.H. Redford and A.M. Stearman studied the industrial production of rubber tappers in rural Brazil in the 1990s, analyzing the effects of clearcutting local old growth and replacing it with a target crop monoculture. Eventually, Redford and Stearman positioned this argument in theory: "If the full range of genetic species and ecosystem diversity is to be maintained in its natural abundance on a given piece of land, then virtually any significant activity by humans must not be allowed" (252). This being not an emotional activist plea but the outcome of critical analysis within a scientific study, Redford and Stearman's criteria of "any significant activity" applies to a specific scenario in sites particular to Brazil, yet their statement of "any significant activity" does ring true as a primary question for all of us: What forms and what levels of anthropogenic transformation (such as logging) have negative consequences upon the long-term health of an ecosystem?

Providing a local answer that is unsurprisingly similar to Redford and Stearman's, BC forest biologist Victoria Stevens writes that the process of "removing large portions of decaying wood may alter the components of a forest that are part of the place-specific evolutionary history that has resulted in process and interactions essential for maintaining that forest" (93). But as forest biologist Denise Lach told us earlier, science only scrapes the surface of incredibly complex processes. Just as physicists inform us that atoms do one thing when they are being watched by scientists and do another thing when they look away, we must also consider that our seemingly simple and benign intrusion within the study of a single drop of water may distort processes that are unimaginably complex.

When we consider the large volume of tree removal that happens within clearcut logging across BC, every stick taken from the woods is an incremental, permanent loss to the integrity, diversity, and health of the entire ecosystem, as well as serving to bring residual harm to those systems that overlap within its many interpenetrating relationships. Looking at the research, contemporary forestry practices in BC may very well leave neither human beings nor the larger-than-human realm with the intensely mediated promise of a future renewable resource but one that is actually substantially degraded. Unless a sufficient regime of analysis is undertaken to better determine the long-term consequences of high-impact industrial activities, the potential downstream effects and invisible hand processes they initiate will not be calculated—and, as it stands today, these are hardly even considered. Even though the assessments of Redford and Stearman and others may be waved aside as utopian idealism by those who believe that the economic activity generated by industry is of primary importance, these outlier viewpoints do resonate with an ethical depth that demands consideration. As 2014 marked the hundredth anniversary of the completion of the Grand Trunk Pacific Railway, the breadth of industrial activity experienced by these Storied Lands should be grasped within its proper context.

Stepping back into the clearcut, the most obvious thing we can see is a field of stumps and slash. Many career foresters will insist that, unlike the slowly changing state of a supposedly static old-growth forest, the fresh cutblock is not an ugly scar but is a dynamic pivot point of accelerating change and renewal. This could be a true statement, were it not for the fact that the largest source of energy that the forest requires for its renewal—the biggest trees—have all been removed. While not every cut stump represents a tree taken to the mill (as many are too small, rotten, broken, deformed—the junk left behind to be dragged together and burned in a slash pile), each tree that is trucked away from the site is a proportionate loss from the local nutrient pool that the forest needs for equivalent decomposition and subsequent regeneration. Just as a logging truck driver needs fuel in his gas tank to get the trees back to the mill, the cut forest needs fuel to regrow itself into a new forest. In BC, although both the logging industry and the Ministry of Forests, Lands, and Natural Resource Operations (MFLNRO) applaud themselves over the immediate visual success that treeplanting represents, each new seedling goes into a bed of soil that has been denied the bulk of an entire forest's generation of compost. More than this, after the multi-storied canopy has been removed, other important elements required for health and integrity within the old-growth system (such as sunlight and shade, hydrology, and various other factors) will have flared away from equilibrium into a range of inhospitable extremes that swing from all to nothing. As well, freshly exposed soil that was once anchored by roots and debris and protected by layers of moss and smaller plants will now be susceptible to erosion during the heavy rainfalls that will undoubtedly come. After a flash flood and a landslide, the site may be stripped to a barren, nearly sterile state of clean stone, one that resembles the situation experienced eleven thousand years ago, after the retreat of the glaciers. Even though an episode of erosion after a storm surge is a natural part of the geographic sequence, human activity should not play such a significant role in their frequency.

However much the figures below are presented within an agenda of environmental activism, no agency exists within government or industry in BC that compiles or makes public logging waste data or other similar data for scrutiny at the scale of the overall landscape. In terms of what has been removed, as historian Richard R. Rajala reveals, one recent audit by the David Suzuki Foundation and Forest Watch shows that "on 72 percent of 227 logging sites, 80 percent or more of the trees had been removed and only 4 percent of the plans provided buffers along small streams" (228). Looking at what remains of the 6,423,000 hectares within the North Coast timber supply area (TSA) (with 2009 Sierra Club figures), 75 percent remained intact, with 50 percent having been set aside for protection (9). At first glance, this is surprisingly positive and sounds more than reasonable, yet within these figures we find that only about 4 percent of what remains of these Indigenous rainforests falls within what the Ministry considers good-productivity-class timber (stands of the kind that contain rich ecosystems with the biggest trees and the complexity of forest structures that fulfill the demands of both loggers and public recreation use). Over 40 percent of what remains is classed as poor-productivity sites (mainly non-forested rocky bogs and muskegs, thin subalpine scrub, and vast areas of alpine tundra) (15). Going deeper into the numbers, we find that 60 percent of the remaining good-productivity-class forests on the North Coast are in line for logging in the near future, and few of the areas targeted include the abundance of low-quality hemlock surprise, most of which were strategically avoided during the high-grading sweeps that typified most earlier phases of logging (22). Economic pressure demands the targeting of the highest-quality stands, mainly those of redcedar and Sitka spruce, and so their downfall is clear and we will eventually be left with a patchwork of predominantly scrub stands of hemlock surprise.

As Rajala points out, the five companies of the Coast Forest Con-servation Initiative (CFCI) were charged by environmentalists in 2005 for masking business-as-usual logging practices within a vague conservation consensus agreement, a scheme that proposes a commit-ment to protected areas and adhering to standards of ecosystem-based management, yet which also finds fail-safe loopholes that allow for unethical logging practices (244). While each forest in line to be cut falls under the rules, prescriptions, and forensic scrutiny of the biogeo-climactic classification system of the provincial ministry, the real plans that drive industrialization are made in the US, China, Korea, and India by business graduates and accountants who are pressed to crunch numbers for the sake of finding only crunchier and crunchier numbers. Neither literally nor metaphorically, none of the large licensees in the local resource industry have any "roots in the community" but they do have powerful machines with highly efficient cutting blades—and not just for use in the bush.

After more than twenty years as an employee of a handful of small consulting companies, I can state that the only job security any of us has these days depends upon whether or not the phone rings on a week-to-week basis, hopefully with a call coming from one of maybe half a dozen different managers who come from as many different mills. And the likelihood of this call being made depends upon nothing more than a personal willingness to dole out what usually amounts to no more than a few weeks or even a few days of work. Luckily, a few managers do still pick up the phone, but there are no offers of multi-year contracts, no promises of any future work—not one gesture made to affirm the material sense of being a part of the local community with anything as trustworthy as roots.

He tries to stay ahead of me by reading books
he's hidden. I overhear him whispering the Latin and English
names in the TV room.

But it's the Indian names that quiet him. He says the most
peculiar thing after I tell him the secret names of Salal and the
story-trail they lead us to.

—Philip Kevin Paul, WSÁ,NEC, Saanich Nation
(2008)

POT (point of termination

mountains watching with a forest of eyes,
old-growth montane and krummholz,
stress tolerance and Indigenous experience.

MORE THAN ANY I HAVE EVER SEEN, NORTH COAST MOUNTAINS POS-
sess stunning profiles of both the elemental and of scale, bristling as
they also do with dark green skins of wood and leaf, all of which create
a million more tall wonderings within yet Other dimensions. Still, at
ts'i'winhl sga'nist (the mountain peak, in *Gitxsanimx*), the lessons of
First Nations peoples tell us that we should not gape vacantly or idly
but instead look thoughtfully down and respectfully away from certain
mountains (Johnson 45). These giant M and W words serrate immense
phrasal succession from ridge to valley to ridge, way over our heads
into the haze-shrouded distance, covering the extent of a Gitxsan *Wilp*,
a Tsimshian *Laxyuup,* and a Haisla *Wa'wais.*

As much more than concepts, these heritable house territories are
"known by the human activities and unique events peculiar to them,"
all of which are held under the ownership of the family affiliation

House group (McDonald 49). *Wilps, Laxyupps, Wa'wais,* and other similar institutions represent laws of responsibility for interconnected ecosystems of Storied Land, those that often include all of the valleys and peaks within a closed sequence of mountain ridges, usually including major watersheds and creeks, right up to the upland headwaters where snowmelt births into eventual rivers (Daly 243).

Up in the Hazeltons, just as traditionally minded Gitxsan people employ courtesy protocols by averting their eyes in the presence of their elders, they also do so in the presence of *Stikyoo'denhl,* "Home of the Mountain Goats" (Mount Rocher de Boule), which is one of the many mnemonic pegs that reside within their deeply Storied Lands (Daly 181). We learned earlier from *Sèdayà* of the *Yanyèdí* (Elizabeth Nyman) that some mountains were once people, and just as it is impolite to stare at a person, it is considered improper to stare at a mountain. Nancy J. Turner also tells us that, "even today, the mountains may reveal their human or supernatural traits and must be treated with special deference," and to point or even look directly at certain mountains is to demonstrate disrespect (*Earth's* 90).

With this in mind, we should also consider the amazing things that grow throughout the vast array of stories that are spread throughout the tusks, slumps and bergschrunds, saddles and hanging valleys, moraines, corries, and spires of North Coast mountains. These immense, rugged pitches where stone has shaped itself into awe are much more than the basic foundations upon which our rainforests, cultures, and communities cling. As Linda Hogan writes, the vast ecosystems of mountain and valley are "the containers for our lives," they are repositories for the mystery of the natural laws that precede our own, and they "rule us whether we acknowledge it or not" (45–46). Just as a blue chanterelle may be a hyperbolic model of the universe, holding its own breadth of singular purpose and minute process, and just as the prickly sprawl of devil's club encapsulates the essence of protection, adaptability, and health, so it is that even the smallest stones are mountains in microcosm—refractions of geologic upheavals that can be held in the palm of the hand, revealing the literal histories of the region's earliest processes.

On the North Coast, what the mountains and Indigenous rainforests should be best at is humbling people—humbling their acts, humbling their thoughts and words, humbling people through whatever syntactical or literal form in which we encounter them, from any abstract vantage of immediacy and from every fiercely intractable point of distance. If mountains fail to humble, it might just be time to go for a walk. Personally, I find that the closer I get to a mountain and the deeper I set myself within the rainforests that grow upon them, the smaller I become, the less I speak, the more I listen, the more I am held by the "sound of shushing cedar branches," as Stó:lō author Lee Maracle puts it perfectly, understanding as she does the gift meaning that rests in the perception and expression of reverence (64). Usually, whether up the mountain or down under the trees, if you try to move like you would in town, you will most likely be frustrated. None of these places were created for two-legged creatures in any kind of a hurry.

Crowding up and in and out to the laps of so many snaking lakes, waters formed by millions of rivulets trickle pencil-thin into spiralling valleys. Water, water, water, pearling down the bear-tooth faces of mountains that are slowly folding in upon themselves. From alpine to valley, the rainforests that grow within the laps, feet, and shoulders of these mountains are *all* green—green like most people can hardly begin to imagine that green can be green.

While slopes that are extreme can create adverse temperatures on the south aspect and too much shade and cold on the north, flatlands have their own downsides, as they can be either predominantly boggy or arid, and none of these scenarios will grow trees on the order of the superorganic. But here on the North Coast, consistently mild weather, plentiful rainfall, and optimal slopes create the situation where mountains shed water and absorb diagonally angled sunlight in a way that maximizes the growth of so many species of plants and trees.

Thinking in terms of the obvious upright restriction of mountains, Indigenous rainforests on the North Coast generally don't just start *here* and end *there*—valley to ridge, creek to river, rising and falling into distinct separations where ravine walls drop out of sight. Even though human beings are all too good at letting things drop out of mind, perhumid rainforests plan ahead along the natural designs of the past. Ending only where they can't quite begin, these green systems are always reaching beyond known projections of geological stature and biological limitation. Trees might not walk but they sure can fly. And mountains, even though they are unimaginably heavy, they are always crawling.

Along with the silky featherings of birds, the mud-packed grooves of cloven hoofs, and the tiny mandibles of insects, wind facilitates the greatest migration of trees as seeds up mountainsides and the most massive transport of soil in the form of dust. For hemlock, yellow-cypress, fir, spruce, and pine, climbing mountains is the easy part, as their massive, mature forms can be blown anywhere as tiny-winged capsules of potential, drifting on updrafts in the millions to become further examples of *here* and *there* and awe: upon the upper crests of barren ridges and plunging stone crevices, at the edge of nothing where the block and tackle of roots might find a bit of wet dust caught in a crack. As both potential rooting material and mineral source, dust that has yet to be washed away by the rain or sneezed out by a gust becomes a place for life to take a foothold.

Up and up, *there*, and *there*—look, where inhuman heights of elevation, ecology, and weather shrivel alpine trees into *hlḵuugan* (the *Gitxsanimx̱* term for scrubby bonsai mountain hemlock) and *sba ts'ex* (timberline krummholz)—miniaturized trees maximize the near-nothingness of treeline austerity with amazing attempts that redefine what it means to survive, grow, and reproduce (Johnson 36). A forest can also be the last green twig that punctuates the edge of a cliff, its coiled strong-arm showing more grey than green, functioning at the same scale as one of the ornamental junipers that hug the grime along the sidewalk in Smithers, where their roots are littered with McDonald's burger wrappings and cigarette butts.

Here, way up at the edge of the larger-than-human alpine, we might find only one torqued fence post of a tree trailing its few wiry limbs of silver coiled vine along every hundred metres of cracked stone. But then another: the frozen roil of a wooden octopus flailing over a halibut of stone. And there: the bottom half of a tree jammed like an anchor into the rock, encrusted with more lichen than foliage, its broken top having fallen two hundred metres down the rock face, looking like a smashed ribcage crammed into a dark crack. And dotted everywhere across the immense stone: more of the same along the leading edge of shifting, grinding, overlapping plates. Look—no bigger than a peregrine falcon or a glaucous-winged gull, trees that will still slowly spread their wooden wings for three hundred years, the knuckles of their roots wedged into the seam of one ledge or another that has yet to relent to the laws of gravity. Snow-polished and lee-compassing the prevailing winds of centuries, many of these silver weathervanes spiral point the way to either the next valley or to *Simoigetdamla ha*—the "First Man" or "Heavenly Father" of ancient Gitxsan narratives (*Hagbegwatku* 13).

Looking closer, down on your belly, imagine the grey-green crown of a pipe-cleaner forest under the palm of your hand—here, where every summer a few tiny, purple-brown seedcones will still manage to form on branches growing raggedly intertwined within their own roots. Eventually, the wind will rattle a tiny-winged legacy out of these hardy time capsules, breathing them out into the next valley, into the next millennium.

And as we squint, we should try to see what exists beyond the surface. As Lee Maracle reminds us, looking is "not just a matter of seeing what's there, but seeing what could be," which takes us to what poet Joseph Brodsky nudges us to grasp when he tells us that "geography blended with time equals destiny," which takes us to the abstract flush of truth that we would do better to realize and feel within the naturalness of our bodies more than recognize through the rational work of our brain and eye (*Ravensong* 65, 152). And rightly so, in this case, as the trees that have been evolving on the flanks of these North Coast mountains for hundreds of thousands of years possess the experience and knowledge we should aspire to ourselves if we wish to survive and thrive here beneath their eaves.

If we move and look a few more steps up and up, there, we will see where the lichen take over from the withered silver lightning of a tree that is as spare as a poem, where the forest is finally scoured entirely away before the inhospitable trivalence of stone, weather, and sky. Here, just before the crest of the ledge, on the)edge, lichen grow in minute expressions of texture and colour upon nothing but rock and a few grey antlers of polished wood. These collaborative communities on the micro-scale are forests in their own right. Lichen are one of the rainforest's most essential communities in miniature: they are the texts of alpine micropoetry, slowly crumbling stone into minerals that blow down and enrich the soil of somewhere in every direction below.

Up here, in their cooperative and generative materiality, algae and fungus work together and resolutely in interdependent reciprocity to speckle-colonize broad tracts of otherwise bare stone. Even though they appear as diminutive biotic scabs, lichen perform a very Real Work. Look: as arborist Julian Dunster and biogeographer Katherine Dunster describe, lichen utilize tiny rhizines (tufted, brushlike, filamentous hyphae, their typical organs of attachment) to invade the surfaces and crevices of stone, where they slowly disintegrate these surfaces and crevices into enough dust that, when wetted by rain, the seed of a mountain hemlock or a yellow-cypress can blow in and stick, perhaps sprouting to life within a new, thin layer of mineral soil (267).

As we make our own distinctions between the massive scale of a lower-elevation stand of old-growth rainforest—those that burst as herds of leviathan whales of wood out of drenched fern, moss, devil's club, and huckleberry; and these tiny forests of stunted gnomics, the lichens and the krummholz, hanging or jutting like a fierce ivy within lee pockets of alpine rocklands—the Indigenous rainforest makes its own distinctions and notices subtle differences between varieties of human activity. Although we don't give it much thought, the greater biotic community passes its own judgements, slowly diffusing outcomes at various trophic levels throughout the long-term processes of ecosystems. "There is no emptiness in the forest," as anthropologist Richard Nelson warns: "no unwatched solitude, no wilderness where a person moves outside moral judgement and law" (13). Sharing the lessons he has gathered from the Koyukon of Alaska, Nelson explains that "trees are aware of whatever happens around them, and like all living things they participate in a constant interchange of power," with some tree species in particular possessing "a heightened sensitivity towards humans" (ibid.). Anthropologist Berkes tells us that traditional Cree hunters believe that the grey jay (or whisky jack, *Perisoreus canadensis*) "hovers about hunting camps, checking to see that nothing is wasted," and anthropologist Turner reminds us that disrespected kincentric entities can and will punish "the greed of the unthinking" (87, *Earth's* 128). Anthropologist John Corsiglia observes, thinks, and types just as deeply about what comes out of the Indigenous soil, pointing to the wisdom from which all human innovation and cultural expression find their origin. As Corsiglia writes, "we live in a world of energies where appearances may not always reveal underlying realities; our thoughts represent a way of connecting with this world of energies; there are clues about us that we may see if we use our minds properly" (231).

Still, we know that it is most often Indigenous peoples or the larger-than-human realm itself who bear the brunt of the punishment and backlash of the mistakes of industrialization as a whole and the subsequent choices of individual consumers. Meanwhile, the elite players of industry who facilitate the transformation of ecosystems bask in the immediate flush of wealth accrued from profit-taking, enjoying their reward at a purposefully calculated distance from where the negative downstream effects have the worst impact. Bringing an international perspective to these hard issues of the *anthropocene* (the term scientists now give to our era, a time when human industry carries impacts significant enough to be registered around the globe), philosopher and author Vandana Shiva points out injustices from rural India within farmer's representative Niti Mai's statement about the industrialization of her people's lands: "Real development happens when the people exercise their rights. We shouldn't have to give up our rights for someone else's benefits. We want development, not destruction" (14). Back home, the Indigenous rainforest responds as strongly to processes and activities that give life as they do to those that do not. The former it can respond to creatively through transformation and renewal, while the latter brings various disruptions: failed salmon runs, depleted shellfish populations, landslides across logging road cutslopes, more and more erratic weather patterns, and other kinds of things that are potentially in store for us that are perhaps much worse—perhaps a poisoned water system as a result of pipeline ruptures, tanker spills, or fracking.

Healthy ecosystems also respond productively to the wild pragmatics of event opportunities that interface naturally with biotic functions, or those whose material changes operate within the scope of natural evolution. These would be natural events like forest fires, earthquakes, or the simple falling of a rainforest tree in a windstorm. But the introduction of noxious invasive species, the interjection of various industrial disturbances, or anything that does not mimic naturally occurring events, all become problems that the larger-than-human realm often cannot embrace, synthesize, and resolve in a time frame that safeguards the health of the species within its bounds—humans included. But what does this mean beyond a glaring abstraction of words, or—getting to the heart of the matter—what kinds of entities are best adapted to life on the North Coast? Again, trees reveal the most important answers.

One interesting quality that forest scientists Roberta Parish and Joseph A. Antos point to is that while tree species' composition in North Coast rainforests are near equilibrium, the temporal scale of this stability varies among species (573). What this means is that the ever-changing conditions within old-growth stands are matched by the abilities of its various species to adapt to the many opportunities and events they sustain. This variety of conditions creates optimal levels of biologic and age diversity, which is an overall situation that indicates heightened levels of biocomplexity. The profound diversity that is present in the stratifications of ages and species in perhumid rainforests arises out of the ecological wealth that is created within this specific kind of community. In the CWH zone, the greatest variety of unique possibilities exists within 1) the patch dynamic regime of small-scale windthrow disturbances, 2) the gift of a perpetual and optimal climate, and 3) the greatest variance of geological and biological factors.

Forest scientist Andrew B. Carey clarifies this ideal picture with his own analytic description of variety and variability in Pacific Northwest old-growth rainforests. Making plain sense with a simple equation, it turns out that when Carey multiplies the length, height, and width of its boundaries by the overall greater height of its trees, an old-growth rainforest actually produces a volume of space that contains a greater overall capacity to support life than second-growth forests with mature trees that grow after timber harvest (62). Within the old-growth configurations of maximum potential there does exist a deeper space-per-area dimension, one which comes to express itself over long periods of time within the inner structural workings of each individual tree. For example, old-growth perhumid rainforest trees attain greater branch sizes and acquire deeper spaces in the crevices of their bark; they achieve larger sizes of cracks and cavities behind plates of bark and under the masses of larger, elevated roots (ibid.). All of these subtle qualities are important to recognize, as they provide greater potential for larger successes in biocomplexity.

Thinking in terms of how they thrive and survive, Parish and Antos classify conifer trees of the ancient montane forests of coastal BC as having the "ability to grow extremely slowly," as they possess key adaptive features such as "an impressive ability to tolerate major stresses" and the ability "to persist in the face of adversity" (562, 572). As the research shows, the life of a montane conifer is "life in the slow lane"; additionally, Parish and Antos alter the general perception when they describe that montane conifers of the North Coast are not to be viewed as "competitors" within their communities but as "stress tolerators" (571). I can recontextualize and personalize this distinction, as this reflects how Tahltan elder Alex Jack describes his own people's continued persistence in the Storied Lands of the Upper Stikine. Here he speaks of periods of mere "survival, of winter winds so strong the caribou froze, of times when his people ate nothing but spruce bark," of times when his people were forced to settle for several years at a place where life was so difficult that Jack could not rightly characterize it as living: "Here," as he tells ethnobotanist Wade Davis, "is where we survived" (108). And today the Tahltan do remain and continue, some still remembering their connections to the Storied Land and maintaining their own contemporary adaptations of subsistence and TEKW, even as the mixed blessing and curse of technologically embedded consumerism reaches further and further into the last road-free regions of northern BC.

This is not just my own personal view, as so many others we have encountered carry similar assertions of will, resiliency, and even love to keep us all looking and trying, even, like poet George Stanley, just "writing—to see what turns up, or to keep going" (*Vancouver* 66). Exploring the story trail of her own Indigenous trust and faith, Tlingit Wolf Ernestine Hayes writes about Ohmer Creek, one of the vital watercourses in Southeast Alaska that pulses through red huckleberry and mossy deadfalls beneath old conifer trees: "The forest and muskeg have lived here longer than the residents of Little Norway. They have lived here longer than the carvers of the poles and longer than the petroglyphs. The forest and muskeg along Ohmer Creek Trail counsel us all to endure" (140).

True: trees and entire stands of them die every season of their own accord and from the greater biotic forces or will of weather patterns and biologic incursions, all of which work from both the outside and inside of ecosystems. But how have people utilized trees in a way that does not break from the Real Work of sustainability, subsistence, and respect?

From the outer edge of the Tongass, anthropologist Richard Nelson writes that Indigenous peoples have always "cut trees from this forest, but whatever they used remained here…A tree used in that way is little different from one thrown down in a storm: its own land will have it back, spirit and body, still rooted within its place on earth" (59). Today, many of the original peoples of the many Indigenous rainforests of the region still call them home and continue to consider the trees this way. Although some people have become as assimilated as the average Canadian, many also dwell in and out of varying degrees of Indigenous interbeing, still thinking of the Storied Land from the perspective of kincentrism, still utilizing local foods and materials and still holding the preference for a way of life that most other people would find impossible, distasteful, and beyond the pale.

This is what the "backwordsy" coastal writer and publisher Howard White points to with his reflection upon the history of Indigenous cultures along the coast, wondering how they could thrive so splendidly while so many of the early European newcomers failed so miserably. As we know, local reciprocal economies knowledgably utilized the wealth of what was available, but the difference between this history and how things changed with the arrival of Europeans "is how far / Indian is from White how far / learning is from knowing how / far we are from this ragged place" (62). Here White is referring to the aroma and taste of the grease of the eulachon (*Thalicthys pacificus*), a small fish that spawns in freshwater in early spring, a fish which also historically brought the first supply of nutrient-rich food to the people after a long, hard winter. Eulachon was repugnant to early European immigrants on the coast and is still alien to most people in Canadian society, as are most of the deeper workings of so many North Coast relationships—"and however far you are from loving that," White writes, "is how far you are / from arriving" (62, 63). While Thai mangoes, Mediterranean figs and olives, Chinese mandarin oranges, Ecuadorian chocolate, and California butter lettuce are all available any time of the year from the Overwaitea in Prince Rupert or the Safeway in Smithers, the eulachon come just once a year, in the early spring, where they spawn in vast quantities upon the banks of most North Coast rivers, as they should and as they must, and as I hope they continue to do for thousands of years to come.

In the Real World, one means we have to re-familiarize ourselves with what is eco-logical or true is to come to understand what social theorist Viktor Shklovsky means with his proposition that we must *defamiliarize* ourselves from the false truths we cling to, especially today within the ultra-mediated and hyper-technological society in which we live. We can do this by allowing and encouraging the disruption of our firmly established and perhaps unrealized negative perception habits. Defamiliarization can happen both consciously and unconsciously. Shklovsky focuses upon the disruptive capacities provided within the perceptual processes of the art experience, believing that the often dissident intentions behind some forms of art should be experienced and extended to their fullest in order to begin an internal revolution against our long-ingrained negative perceptions and the destructive habits they generate (6). Presenting a similar idea to defamiliarization, Rainer Maria Rilke believes that poets and artists can be the conscience of a society, and he writes of the perception-altering power and the disconcerting, potentially jarring naturalness of a lifelike form as it is represented in a stone sculpture. Rilke believes that when we see our human self represented in a fragment of lifeless rock that has been cut from the crust of the earth, we can imagine, maybe for the first time, what I think Linda Hogan insists we must always try to keep in mind, this being the idea that "we need to reach a hand back through time and a hand forward, stand at the zero point of creation" (95). In consideration of our themes, perhaps somewhere within the liminal space of idea and some activity of cultural expression we can find our own glimpse of the Indigenous philosophy of respect for the kincentric entities of the Storied Land, and perhaps we can also find our own version of Real Work—maybe we can even find our own personal meaning and sense from out of the ecological linguistics and tawny grammar that teems in green, everywhere around us. Rilke believes that there is a path to personal and cultural transformation through the power of art, as he presses Western thinking to realize the larger perceptions and everyday processes that inhabit Nature, realizing as he does that the most ancient lives of the earth are peering down upon us, even from out of a sculpted stone mirror, which sounds like one of the fundamental principles of ecosophical æsthetics, and of kincentrism, just as Rilke proposes: "for here there is no place / that does not see you. You must change your life" (61).

Thinking and writing toward the ideas of Shklovsky, Rilke, Hogan, and so many others we have sought wisdom from throughout this text, Maori decolonization theorist *Ngati Awa* and *Ngati Porou* (Linda Tuhiwai Smith) reminds us, quite plainly, to engage vigilantly and perform "a process of critical self-awareness, reflexivity and openness to challenge" (166). Although engagements with art and community and Wild bewilderment may serve to slowly crack open minds and initiate changes in our behaviour, *Ngati Awa* and *Ngati Porou* implores us to resist our human inclination to seek easy solutions to difficult problems; instead, we must respond to imperatives for change and justice with personal, social, and legal activities that demonstrate legitimate work within the interiority of the self as well as with a practical and equally hard work that is directed intensely within the Real World (ibid.).

As anthropologist Nelson recounts the lessons of his Koyukon teachers, he hopes that humans will live with an understanding of the "mutual regard and responsibility" that binds us to the larger-than-human realm, that which, as the Koyukon see it, observes and judges all of our actions, watching us "in a forest of eyes" (53). It is no surprise to me that these ancient traditional concepts link up with many vanguard modernist ideas, as they are also reaffirmed in a directly roundabout way by contemporary Western Apache elder Nick Thompson, who reminds anthropologist Basso how the "places around here keep stalking us… They make you remember how to live right, so you want to replace yourself" (59).

Ecologist Neil Everndon, another great defender of wonder and the Wild, writes that we immigrants and our descendants have become aliens with a self-identity that is distinct from the local world we have taken as our new home; also, that most ecologists and scientists have become such purely rational beings that they treat "nature as essentially non-living, a machine to be dissected, interpreted and manipulated" (20). To some degree, we have all been enculturated in this manner, if not trained outright into our adulthood by one of our higher institutions or through our working lives in the service of industry, community, and state. When we arrive at every unfamiliar new place, we make quick decisions and plan our efficient acts, and as we often admit, quietly, we do so many day-to-day things that leave a pang in our chests and a bad taste in our mouths. Automatically, we grow, learn, arrive, take our place, and begin to impose yet another version of an unrealistic and unsustainable imagination upon the world around us, whether by the force of social gesture, snowmobile, laptop computer, D9 cat skinner, speculative investment, tailings pond, prestigious display of wealth, or so many other misleading falsehoods marked out on so many pieces of wasted paper.

We would do better to slow down, to listen to and at the very least learn from the histories and cultures of those who have been living here for thousands of years, which includes not only the local First Peoples but also the trees, plants, animals, mountains, and rivers, the weather and the seasons, all of whom best represent and define the important Indigenous and Wild concepts of ground-truth. When we admit that we of immigrant descent are the aliens, and that it is we who hold the responsibility to learn these new-old languages, respect their new-old knowledges, and protect the new-old ways of this place, and that we have no rationale to displace, repress, or destroy the many objects and entities that have been thriving here for millennia, then and only then we can begin to engage productively and in likely collaboration with the rich Indigenous nature of our new home. Then and only then will we be able to understand the means by which to share with those around us, those that have always been quietly striving to fulfill and express themselves with lines of aromatic smoke rising from a waterside village and by means of green leaf root mycelia water microbe scale tooth and feather.

Bibliography

A Town Called Podunk. "Vicious Wind Storm Wreaks Damage Around North Coast." 10 Oct. 2010. Web. 5 May 2012.

Alexie, Sherman. *The Lone Ranger and Tonto Fistfight in Heaven.* New York: Harper Perennial, 2003. Print.

Alutiiq Museum Archaeological Repository. Web. 24 May 2011.

Armson, Kenneth A. *Forest Soils: Properties and Processes.* Toronto: University of Toronto Press, 1979. Print.

Armstrong, Chris. "Dwelling on Dreams." *Muskeg News* 4, 1 April 2011: 1. Print.

———. "Thanksgiving Windstorm Knocks Out Power in Rupert." *Muskeg Press.* Web. 5 May 2012.

———. "Gas Pipeline Fixed: Full Service By Wednesday Night." *Muskeg Press.* Web. 5 May 2012.

Arora, David. *All That the Rain Promises and More...: A Hip Pocket Guide to Western Mushrooms.* Berkeley: Ten Speed Press, 1991. Print.

Avison, Margaret. *The Dumbfounding.* New York: W.W. Norton, 1966. Print.

Bartemucci, Paula., K. Dave Coates, Karen A. Harper, and Elaine F. Wright. "Gap Disturbances in Northern Old-Growth Forests of British Columbia, Canada." *Journal of Vegetation Science* 13 (2002): 685–696. Print.

Bashō, Matsuo. *The Narrow Road to the Deep North: and Other Travel Sketches.* Nobuyuki Yuasa, trans. New York: Penguin, 1986. Print.

Basso, Keith H. *Wisdom Sits in Places: Landscape and Language Among the Western Apache.* Albuquerque: University of New Mexico Press, 1996. Print.

Bateson, Gregory. *Steps to an Ecology of Mind.* New York: Ballantine 1972. Print.

"Bearing." *Oxford Canadian Dictionary,* pbk. 2000 ed. Print.

Belford, Ken. *Ecologue.* Madeira Park, BC: Harbour Publishing, 2005. Print.

————. *Lan(d)guage: A Sequence of Poetics*. Halfmoon Bay, BC: Caitlin Press, 2008. Print.

Berkes, Fikret. *Sacred Ecology: Traditional Ecological Knowledge and Resource Management*. Philadelphia: Taylor & Francis, 1999. Print.

Boone, R.D., P. Sollins, and K. Cromack Jr. "Stand and Soil Changes along a Mountain Hemlock Death and Regrowth Sequence." D.G.W. Edwards and M.D. Meagher, eds. *Mountain Hemlock* (Tsuga mertensiana *[Bong.] Carr.*): *An Annotated Bibliography*. Info. Report BC-X-352. Victoria: NRC CFS PFC, 1994. 4–5. Print.

Bringhurst, Robert. *Everywhere Being is Dancing: Twenty Pieces of Thinking*. Kentville, NS: Gaspereau Press, 2007. Print.

————. *The Tree of Meaning: Thirteen Talks*. Kentville, NS: Gaspereau Press, 2006. Print.

————. Foreword. *He Who Hunted Birds in His Father's Village: The Dimensions of a Haida Myth*. By Gary Snyder. San Francisco: Shoemaker and Hoard, 2007. Print.

British Columbia Geographical Names Information System. "BCGNIS Query Results: Nass." Web. 8 June 2011.

British Columbia Ministry of Forests: Research Branch. *The Ecology of the Mountain Hemlock Zone*. Victoria: n.p., 1997. Print.

————. *A Field Guide to Site Identification and Interpretation for the Prince Rupert Forest Region, Part One*. *Land Management Handbook 26*. Victoria: n.p., 1993. Print.

Brockway, D.G., C. Topik., M.A. Hemstrom, and Q.H. Emmingham. "Plant Association and Management for the Pacific Silver Fir Zone." D.G.W. Edwards and M.D. Meagher, eds. *Mountain Hemlock* (Tsuga mertensiana *[Bong.] Carr.*): *An Annotated Bibliography*. Info. Report BC-X-352. Victoria: NRC CFS PFC, 1994. 14. Print.

Brodsky, Joseph. "Strophes." *Collected Poems in English*. New York: Farrar, Straus and Giroux, 2000. Print.

Brooke, R.C. "Vegetation-Environment Relationships in Subalpine Mountain Hemlock Zone Ecosystems." D.G.W. Edwards and M.D. Meagher, eds. *Mountain Hemlock* (Tsuga mertensiana *[Bong.] Carr.*): *An Annotated Bibliography*. Info. Report BC-X-352. Victoria: NRC CFS PFC, 1994. 5. Print.

Canadian Broadcasting Corporation. "Queen Charlotte Islands Renamed Haida Gwaii in Historic Deal." *CBC News Canada*. 11 Dec 2009. Web. 17 May 2011.

Carey, Andrew B. "Maintaining Biodiversity in Managed Forests." *Old Growth in a New World: A Pacific Northwest Icon Reexamined*. Thomas A. Spies and Sally L Duncan, eds. Washington: Island Press, 2009. 58–69. Print.

Carlson, Roy. "The Native Fishery in British Columbia: The Archaeological Evidence." Unpublished paper. 1992. Print.

Carr, Emily. *Klee Wyck*. Vancouver: Clarke, Irwin & Co. Ltd., 1941. Print.

Corsiglia, John. "Traditional Wisdom in Northwestern British Columbia." Charles R. Menzies, ed. *Traditional Ecological Knowledge and Natural Resource Management*. Lincoln: University of Nebraska Press, 2006. 221–35. Print.

Cruikshank, Julie. *Do Glaciers Listen? Local Knowledge, Colonial Encounters, and Social Imagination*. Vancouver: UBC Press, 2006. Print.

Daly, Herman E. "In Defence of a Steady-State Economy." *American Journal of Agricultural Economics* 54.5 (1972): 945–54. Print.

Daly, Richard. *Our Box Was Full: An Anthology for the Delgamuukw Plaintiffs*. Vancouver: UBC Press, 2005. Print.

Daniels, L.D., J. Dobry, M.C. Feller, and K. Klinka. "*Determining Year of Death of Logs of* Thuja plicata *in Southwestern Coastal British Columbia.*" *Canadian Journal of Forest Research* 27.7 (1997): 1132–41. Print.

Dauenhauer, Nora, Richard Dauenhauer, and Lydia Black., eds. Gazetteer. *Anóoshi Lingít Aaní Ká: Russians in Tlingit America, The Battles of Sitka, 1802–1804*. Seattle: University of Washington Press, 2008. 454. Print.

Davis, Wade. "British Columbia's Outback: Deep North." *National Geographic* magazine 205.3 (2004): 102–21. Print.

de Leeuw, Sarah. *Unmarked: Landscapes Along Highway 16*. Edmonton: NeWest Press, 2004. Print.

Deleuze, Gilles, and Félix Guattari. Brian Massumi, trans. *A Thousand*

Plateaus: Capitalism and Schizophrenia. Minneapolis: University of Minnesota Press, 2005. Print.

Derksen, Jeff. *Transnational Muscle Cars*. Vancouver: Talonbooks, 2003. Print.

Dirr, Michael A. *Manual of Woody Landscape Plants: their Identification, Ornamental Characteristics, Culture, Propagation, and Uses*. 5th ed. Champaign, IL: Stipes Publishing, 1998. Print.

Douglas, G.W. "The Alpine-Subalpine Flora of the North Cascade Range." D.G.W. Edwards and M.D. Meagher, eds. *Mountain Hemlock* (Tsuga mertensiana *[Bong.] Carr.*): *An Annotated Bibliography*. Info. Report BC-X-352. Victoria: NRC CFS PFC, 1994. 9. Print.

Du Bois, W.E.B. *A W.E.B. Du Bois Reader*. Andrew G. Paschal, ed. New York: Macmillan, 1971. Print.

Dum *Baal*-Dum. March 2008. Web. 31 March 2009.

Dunsmore, Roger. *Earth's Mind*. Albuquerque: University of New Mexico Press, 1997. Print.

Dunster, Julian, and Katherine Dunster. *Dictionary of Natural Resource Management*. Vancouver: UBC Press, 1996. Print.

Emmons, R.A. "The Personal Strivings Approach to Personality." L. A. Pervin, ed. *Goal Concepts in Personality and Social Psychology*. Hillside, NJ: Erlbaum, 1989. Print.

Everndon, Neil. *The Natural Alien: Humankind and Environment*. 2nd ed. Toronto: University of Toronto Press, 1993. Print.

Farjon, A., C.N. Page, and N. Schellevis. "A Preliminary World List of Threatened Conifer Taxa." D.G.W. Edwards and M.D. Meagher, eds. *Mountain Hemlock* (Tsuga mertensiana *[Bong.] Carr.*): *An Annotated Bibliography*. Info. Report BC-X-352. Victoria: NRC CFS PFC, 1994. 12. Print.

Feather, N.T. "Values, Valences, Expectations, and Actions." *Journal of Social Issues 48*. (1992): 109–124. Print.

First Peoples Cultural Foundation. "Nisga'a." *First Voices*. 2010. Web. 18 May 2011.

Fortuine, Robert. "The Use of Medicinal Plants by the Alaska Natives." *Alaska Medicine 30*, 6 (1988): 185–226. Print.

Fox Keller, Evelyn. "A Feeling for the Organism: The Life and Work of

Barbara McClintock." San Francisco: W.H. Freeman and Co., 1983. Print.

Frank, Andrew. "Whistleblower's Open Letter to Canadians." Web. 20 Feb. 2014.

Franklin, J.H., and F.L. Swanson, et al. "Effects of Global Climatic Change on Forests in Northwestern North America." D.G.W. Edwards and M.D. Meagher, eds. *Mountain Hemlock* (Tsuga mertensiana *[Bong.] Carr.*): *An Annotated Bibliography*. Info. Report BC-X-352. Victoria: NRC CFS PFC, 1994. 15. Print.

Frye, Northrop. *The Bush Garden*. Toronto: House of Anansi, 1971. Print.

Geniusz, Wendy Makoons. *Our Knowledge is Not Primitive: Decolonizing Botanical Anishinaabe Teachings*. New York: Syracuse University Press, 2009. Print.

Gill, Ian, *Hilistis* (Pauline Waterfall), and Doug Hopwood. "People and the Land." *North of Caution: A Journey Through the Conservation Economy on the Northwest Coast of British Columbia*. Vancouver: Ecotrust, 2001. 101–26. Print.

Glavin, Terry. *A Death Feast in Dimlahamid*. Vancouver: New Star Books, 1990. Print.

———. "The Waters." *North of Caution: A Journey Through the Conservation Economy on the Northwest Coast of British Columbia*. Vancouver: Ecotrust, 2001. 17–52. Print.

Golumbia, Todd E. "Introduced Species Management in Haida Gwaii (Queen Charlotte Islands)." *Proceedings of a Conference on the Biology and Management of Species and Habitats at Risk, Kamloops, B.C. 15–19 Feb 1999*. L.M. Darling, ed. BC Ministry of Environment, Lands and Parks, Victoria, and University College of the Cariboo, Kamloops. 327–32. 2000. Print.

Government of Canada. "Fact Sheet: British Columbia Treaty Negotiations." *Aboriginal Affairs and Northern Development Canada (AANDC)*. Web. 24 Jan. 2013.

———. "An open letter from the Honourable Joe Oliver, Minister of Natural Resources, on Canada's commitment to diversify our energy markets and the need to further streamline the regulatory process in order to advance Canada's national economic interest." *Natural*

Resources Canada: The Media Room. 9 Jan. 2012. Web. 20 Jan. 2014.

————. "Treaty Texts – Douglas Treaties," *Aboriginal Affairs and Northern Development Canada (AANDC).* 30 Aug. 2013. Web. 16 Jan. 2014.

Grier, C.C., and A.A. Vogt, et al. "Factors Affecting Root Production in Subalpine Forests of the Northwestern United States." D.G.W. Edwards and M.D. Meagher, eds. Mountain Hemlock (Tsuga mertensiana [Bong.] Carr.): *An Annotated Bibliography.* Info. Report BC-X-352. Victoria: NRC CFS PFC, 1994. 17. Print.

Guattari, Félix. *The Three Ecologies.* 2008 ed. New York: Continuum, 2010. Print.

Gyug, Les W. *Timber Harvesting Effects on Riparian Wildlife and Vegetation in the Okanagan Highlands of British Columbia.* Wildlife Bulletin No. B-97. BC Ministry of Environment, Lands and Parks, Wildlife Division. March 2000. Web. 15 May 2012.

Hagbegwatku (Chief Kenneth B. Harris) and Frances M. Robinson. *Visitors Who Never Left: The Origin of the People of Damelahamid.* Vancouver: UBC Press, 1974. Print.

Haida Gwaii Observer. "Big Storms Lash Islands, Another Expected Wednesday Evening." *QCIObserver.com.* Web. 5 May 2012.

Hammond, Herb. "Water and Connectivity." *Ecoforestry: The Art and Science of Sustainable Forest Use.* Alan Drengson and Duncan Taylor, eds. Gabriola Island, BC: New Society Publishers, 1997. Print.

Hayes, Ernestine. *Blonde Indian: An Alaska Native Memoir.* Tucson: University of Arizona Press, 2006. Print.

Hebda, Richard J., and Cathy Whitlock. "Environmental History." *The Rain Forests of Home: Profile of a North American Bioregion.* Peter K. Schoonmaker, Bettina von Hagen, and Edward C. Wolf, eds. Covelo, CA: Island Press, 1997. 227–54. Print.

Hedges, Chris. *Empire of Illusion: The End of Literacy and the Triumph of Spectacle.* New York: Nation, 2009. Print.

Hellum, A.K. *Listening To Trees.* Edmonton, AB: NeWest Press, 2008. Print.

Henley, Thom. *River of Mist, Journey of Dreams.* N.p.: Rediscovery International Foundation, 2009. Print.

Hogan, Linda. *Dwellings: A Spiritual History of the Living World.* New York: Touchstone, 1996. Print.

Hutchins, Robert. *The Learning Society*. Chicago: University of Chicago Press, 1968. Print.

Hwang, J.S., K.S. Song, W.G. Kim, T.H. Lee, H. Koshino, and I.D. Yoo. Abstract. "Polyozellin, a New Inhibitor of Prolyl Endopeptidase from *Polyozellus multiplex*." *The Journal of Antibiotics* 50.9 (1997): 773–77. Print.

Iljuwas (Bill Reid). *Solitary Raven: Selected Writings*. Robert Bringhurst, ed. Vancouver: Douglas & McIntyre, 2000. Print.

Imazeki, Royuka. "*Polyozellus multiplex* and the Family Phylacteriaceae." *Mycologia* 45.4 (1953): 555–61. Print.

"Indigenous." *Oxford Canadian Dictionary*, pbk. 2000 Ed. Print.

Ingold, Tim. *The Perception of the Environment: Essays in Livelihood, Dwelling, and Skill*. London: Routledge, 2000. Print.

———. "Hunting and Gathering as a Way of Perceiving Environment." *Ecology, Culture and Domestication—Redefining Nature*. Roy Ellen and Katsuyoshi Fukuki, eds. Berg: Oxford and Herendon, VA, 1996. 117–55. Print.

Jacobs, Jane. *The Nature of Economies*. Toronto: Random House, 2000. Print.

Johnson, Leslie Main. "Gitxsan Medicinal Plants: Cultural Choice and Efficacy." *Journal of Ethnobiology and Ethnomedicine*. 2006. Web. 22 June 2011.

———. *Trail of Story, Traveller's Path: Reflections on Ethnoecology and Landscape*. Edmonton: University of Alberta Press, 2010. Print.

Johnston, Allan. "Ecology and Aesthetics: Robinson Jeffers and Gary Snyder." *ISLE: Interdisciplinary Studies in Literature and Environment* 8, 2 (2001): 13–38. Print.

Kasser, Tim. *The High Price of Materialism*. Cambridge: MIT Press, 2002. Print.

Kim, H-J., and H. Jung. Abstract. "Chemoprevention Effect of *Polyozellus multiplex*, a Wild and Edible Mushroom." *Korean Journal for the Society of Food Science Nutrition*. 1126–331, 1.29 (2000):161–67. Print.

Kim, J.H., J.S. Lee, K.S. Song, C.S. Kwon, Y.K. Kim, and J.S. Kim. "Polyozellin Isolated from *Polyozellus multiplex* Induces Phase 2

Enzymes in Mouse Hepatoma Cells and Differentiation in Human Myeloid Leukaemic Cell Lines." *Journal of Agricultural and Food Chemistry* 52.3 (2004): 451–5. Print.

Kimmerer, Robin Wall. *Gathering Moss: A Natural and Cultural History of Mosses.* Corvallis, OR: Oregon State University Press, 2003. Print.

Kline, Thomas C. Jr. "Trophic Level Implications When Using Natural Stable Isotope Abundance to Determine Effects of Salmon-Derived Nutrients on Juvenile Sockeye Salmon Ecology." *Nutrients in Salmonid Ecosystems: Sustaining Production and Biodiversity.* John G. Stockner, ed. American Fisheries Society Symposium 34 (2003): 229–36. Print.

Klinka, K., V.J. Krajina, A. Ceska, and A.M. Scagel. *Indicator Plants of Coastal British Columbia.* Vancouver: UBC Press, 1989. Print.

Kovel, Joel. "Ecosocialism as Holistic Health Care: Redefining our Role as Environmental Agents." *Canadian Dimension* 44.5 (2010): 14–17. Print.

Krajina, V.J., K. Klinka, and J. Worral. "Distribution and Ecological Characteristics of Trees and Some Shrubs in British Columbia." D.G.W. Edwards and M.D. Meagher, eds. *Mountain Hemlock* (Tsuga mertensiana *[Bong.] Carr.*): *An Annotated Bibliography.* Info. Report BC-X-352. Victoria: NRC CFS PFC, 1994. 24. Print.

Lach, Denise. "Moving Science and Immovable Values: Clumsy Solutions for Old-Growth Forests." *Old Growth in a New World: A Pacific Northwest Icon Reexamined.* Thomas A. Spies and Sally L. Duncan, eds. Washington: Island Press, 2009. 233–43. Print.

Lee, H-J., I-K. Rhee, K-B. Lee, I-D. Yoo, and K-S. Song. Abstract. "Kynapcin-12, a New P-Terphenyl Derivative from *Polyozellus multiplex*, Inhibits Prolyl Endopeptidase." *Korean Journal of Antibiotics* 53.7 (2000): 714–19. Print.

Leslie, John. *The Historical Development of the Indian Act.* 2nd ed. Ottawa: Department of Indian Affairs and Northern Development, Treaties and Historical Research Branch, 1978. 114. Print.

Lincoff, Gary H. *The Audubon Society Field Guide to North American Mushrooms.* New York: Knopf, 1992. Print.

Lingis, Alphonso. *The Community of Those Who Have Nothing in Common.* Bloomington: Indiana University Press, 1994. Print.

Ljunggren, David. "*Every G20 Nation Wants to be Canada, Insists PM.*" Reuters. Leslie Alder, ed. 25 Sept. 2009. Web. 17 May 2011.

Luba, Frank. "Windstorm Wreaks Havoc in North." *The Province.* Web. 5 May 2012.

Mander, Jerry. *In the Absence of the Sacred: The Failure of Technology & the Survival of the Indian Nations.* San Francisco: Sierra Club, 1991. Print.

Manning, Richard. "The Speaker's Post." *North of Caution: A Journey Through the Conservation Economy on the Northwest Coast of British Columbia.* Ecotrust Canada. Vancouver: Ecotrust, 2001. 6–12. Print.

Maracle, Lee. *Ravensong: A Novel.* Vancouver: Press Gang, 1993. Print.

———. *I am Woman: A Native Perspective on Sociology and Feminism.* Vancouver: Press Gang, 1996. Print.

Marcot, Bruce. G. "Wood Decay in Healthy Forests." *Western Forester* 49, 4 (July–Aug.) 2004: 4–5. Web. 10 Jan. 2011.

Matthews, Caitlin. *The Elements of Celtic Tradition.* New York: Barnes & Noble, 1989. Print.

Matthews, J.S. "Conversations with Khahtsahlano, 1932–1954," Vancouver City Archives, 1955. 74. Print.

McDonald, James Andrew. *People of the Robin: The Tsimshian of Kitsumkalum.* n.p.: Alberta ACADRE Network, 2003. Print.

McDonald, James Andrew, and Jennifer Joseph. "Key Events in the Gitksan Encounter with the Colonial World," *Potlatch at Gitsequkla: William Beynon's 1945 Field Notebooks.* Margaret Anderson and Marjorie Halpin, eds. Vancouver: UBC Press, 2000. 193–214. Print.

Menzies, Charles R., and Caroline Butler. Intro. *Traditional Ecological Knowledge and Natural Resource Management.* Lincoln: University of Nebraska Press, 1–20. 2006. Print.

Minnis, Paul E., and Wayne J. Elisens, eds. Intro. *Biodiversity and Native America.* Norman, OK: University of Oklahoma Press, 2000. Print.

Molina, Randy, Thomas O'Dell, Daniel Luoma, Michael Amaranthus, Michael Castellano, and Kenelm Russell. *Biology, Ecology, and Social Aspects of Wild Edible Mushrooms in the Forests of the Pacific Northwest: A Preface to Managing Commercial Harves*t. USDA report: PNW-GTR-309. Portland, 1993. Print.

Money, Nicholas P. *Mr. Bloomfield's Orchard: The Mysterious World of Mushrooms, Molds, and Mycologists*. New York: Oxford University Press, 2002. Print.

Moore, Patrick. *Pacific Spirit: The Forest Reborn*. West Vancouver: Terra Bella, 1995. Print.

Muckle, Robert J. *The First Nations of British Columbia: An Anthropological Survey*. Vancouver: UBC Press, 1998. Print.

Muhley, Tyler. "Human Activity Creates 'Refuge' for Prey: Study." *CBC News: Technology and Science*. 3 Mar. 2011. Web. 10 Mar. 2011.

Murphy, Patrick D. *Farther Afield in the Study of Nature-Oriented Literature*. Charlottesville: University of Virginia Press, 2000. Print.

Nelson, Richard K. *The Island Within*. San Francisco: North Point, 1989. Print.

Ngati Awa and *Ngati Porou* (Linda Tuhiwai Smith). *Decolonizing Methodologies: Research and Indigenous Peoples*. 4th ed. New York: Zed Books, 2001. Print.

Noon, Barry R. "Old-Growth Forest as Wildlife Habitat." *Old Growth in a New World: A Pacific Northwest Icon Reexamined*. Thomas A. Spies and Sally L. Duncan, eds. Washington: Island Press, 2009. 44–57. Print.

NWAC (Native Women's Association of Canada). "Implementing Bill C-31: A Summary of the Issues." 1988. Web. 10 Dec. 2014.

Nystedt, Björn., Nathaniel R. Street, Anna Wetterbom, et al. "The Norway Spruce Genome Sequence and Conifer Genome Evolution." *Nature* 497 (May 2013): 579–84. 22 May 2013. Web. 17 Feb. 2014.

O'Clair, Rita M., Robert H. Armstrong, and Richard Carstensen. *The Nature of Southeast Alaska: A Guide to Plants, Animals, and Habitats*. Seattle: Alaska Northwest Books, 1992. Print.

Olrik, Axel. "Epic Laws of Folk Narrative." *The Study of Folklore*. Alan Dundes, ed. Inglewood Cliffs, NJ: Prentice Hall, 1965. 129–41. Print.

Pacific Analytics Inc. "Revitalizing British Columbia's Coastal Economy: A New Economic Vision for the North and Central Coasts and Haida Gwaii." 2004. Web. 26 April 2012.

Parfit, Ben. "The Lands." *North of Caution: A Journey Through the Conservation Economy on the Northwest Coast of British Columbia.* Vancouver: Ecotrust, 2001. Print.

Parish, Roberta, and Joseph A. Antos. "Structure and Dynamics of an Ancient Montane Forest in Coastal British Columbia." *Oecologia* 141 (2004): 562–76. Web. 10 Jan. 2011.

Patel, Raj. *The Value of Nothing: How to Reshape Market Society and Redefine Democracy.* London: Portobello Press, 2009. Print.

Pojar, Jim and Andy MacKinnon. *Plants of Coastal British Columbia, including Washington, Oregon & Alaska,* eds. Vancouver: Lone Pine Publishing, 1994. Print.

Province of British Columbia. *Ministry of Aboriginal Relations and Reconciliation.* "Treaty 8 First Nations." 2013. Web. 16 Jan. 2014.

Pyle, Robert Michael. *Wintergreen: Rambles in a Ravaged Land.* Seattle: Sasquatch Books, 2001. Print.

Pynn, Larry. *Last Stands: A Journey Through North America's Vanishing Ancient Rainforests.* Vancouver: New Star Books, 1999. Print.

Rajala, Richard. *Up-Coast: Forests and Industry of British Columbia's North Coast, 1870–2005.* Victoria: Royal BC Museum, 2006. Print.

Redford, K.H., and A.M. Stearman. "Forest-dwelling Native Amazonians and the Conservation of Biodiversity." *Conservation Biology* 7 (1993): 248–55. Print.

Reeves, Gordon H., and Peter A. Bisson. "Fish and Old-Growth Forests." *Old Growth in a New World: A Pacific Northwest Icon Reexamined.* Thomas A. Spies and Sally L. Duncan, eds. Washington: Island Press, 2009. 70–82. Print.

Reidy, Cheri and Sheena Reidy-Zieglar. "Ethnobotany and the Kitlope Research Paper." *Living Landscapes Project: Royal BC Museum.* Web. 24 May 2011.

Robbins, William G. "'The Great Raincoast': The Legacy of European Settlement." *The Rainforests of Home: Profile of a North American Bioregion.* Peter K. Schoonmaker, Bettina von Hagen, and Edward C. Wolf, eds. Covelo, CA: Island Press, 1997. 313–28. Print.

Robertson, Lisa. *The Weather.* Vancouver: New Star Books, 2001. Print.

Roorda, Randall. "Antimonies of Participation in Literacy and Wilderness."

ISLE: Interdisciplinary Studies in Literature and Environment 14, 2: (2007) 70–87. Print.

Rose, Alex. "Diversity." *North of Caution: A Journey Through the Conservation Economy on the Northwest Coast of British Columbia.* Vancouver: Ecotrust, 2001. 84–99. Print.

Schooler, Lynn. *The Blue Bear.* London: Random House, 2002. Print.

Scidmore, Eliza R. "The Discovery of Glacier Bay, Alaska." *National Geographic* 7, April (1896): 199–213. Print.

Sèdayà of the *Yanyèdí* (Elizabeth Nyman) and Jeff Leer. *Gágiwduł.àt: Brought Forth to Reconfirm: The Legacy of a Taku River Tlingit Clan.* Yukon Native Language Centre and Alaska Native Language Center, 2003. Print.

Seidel, K.W., and R. Cooley. "Natural Reproduction of Grand Fir and Mountain Hemlock after Shelterwood Cutting in Central Oregon." D.G.W. Edwards and M.D. Meagher, eds. *Mountain Hemlock* (Tsuga mertensiana *[Bong.] Carr.*): *An Annotated Bibliography.* Info. Report BC-X-352. Victoria: NRC CFS PFC, 1994. 34. Print.

Sennett, Richard. *The Corrosion of Character: The Personal Consequences of Work in the New Capitalism.* New York: W.W. Norton, 1998. Print.

Sept, Duane. *Common Mushrooms of the Northwest.* Sechelt, BC: Calypso Publishing, 2006. Print.

Septer, D., and J.W. Schwab. *Rainstorm and Flood Damage: Northwest British Columbia 1891–1991.* Victoria: BC Ministry of Forests, 1995. Print.

Shiva, Vandana. *Soil Not Oil: Environmental Justice in an Age of Climate Crisis.* Cambridge: South End Press, 2008. Print.

Sierra Club BC. "State of British Columbia's Coastal Rainforest: Mapping the Gaps for Ecological Health and Climate Protection." Dèc. 2009. Web. 25 May 2011.

Simenstad, Charles A., Megan Dethier, Colin Levings, and Douglas Hay. "The Terrestrial/Marine Ecotone." *The Rainforests of Home: Profile of a North American Bioregion.* Peter K. Schoonmaker, Bettina von Hagen, and Edward C. Wolf, eds. Covelo, CA: Island Press, 1997. 149–87. Print.

Smith, Alexander H. *The Mushroom Hunter's Field Guide: Revised and*

Enlarged. Ann Arbor: University of Michigan Press, 1970. Print.

Smithsonian National Museum of Natural History. *Human Evolution Evidence.* Web. 17 Feb. 2014.

Snyder, Gary. "Ecology, Literature, and the New World Disorder." *ISLE: Interdisciplinary Studies in Literature and Environment* 11.1 (2004): 1–13. Print.

———. *Practice of the Wild: Essays.* New York: North Point, 1990. Print.

———. *Proceedings of the Right To Remain Wild, a Public Choice.* Missoula: University of Montana Press, 1975. Print.

———. *The Real Work: Interviews & Talks,* 1964–1979. Scott McLean, ed. New York: New Directions, 1980. Print.

Spies, Thomas A. "Science of Old Growth, or a Journey into Wonderland." *Old Growth in a New World: A Pacific Northwest Icon Reexamined.* Thomas A. Spies and Sally L. Duncan, eds. Washington: Island Press, 2009. 31–43. Print.

Stamets, Paul. *Mycelium Running: How Mushrooms Can Help Save the World.* Toronto: Ten Speed Press, 2005. Print.

Stanley, George. *Opening Day.* Vancouver: Oolichan Books, 1983. Print.

———. *Vancouver: A Poem.* Vancouver: New Star Books, 2008. Print.

Stevens, Victoria. "The Ecological Role of Coarse Woody Debris." *Ecoforestry: The Art and Science of Sustainable Forest Use.* Alan Drengson and Duncan Taylor, eds. Gabriola Island, BC: New Society Publishers, 1997. Print.

Supreme Court of Canada. *Tsilhqot'in Nation v. British Columbia 2014 SCC 44.* 26 June 2014. Web. 27 Dec. 2014.

Sutton, Peter, Christopher Anderson, et al. *Dreamings: The Art of Aboriginal Australia.* Peter Sutton, ed. Exhibition catalogue. New York: George Braziller, 1988. Print.

Suzuki, David, and Wayne Grady. *Tree: A Life Story.* Vancouver: Douglas & McIntyre, 2004. Print.

Swedeberg, K.C. "A Transition Coniferous Forest in the Cascade Mountains of Northern Oregon." D.G.W. Edwards and M.D. Meagher, eds. *Mountain Hemlock* (Tsuga mertensiana *[Bong.] Carr.*): An Annotated Bibliography. Info. Report BC-X-352. Victoria: NRC CFS PFC, 1994. 36. Print.

Thomas, Shaun. "Land Dispute: Cullen Speaks on Watson Island Aboriginal Title Dispute." *Prince Rupert Northern View*. 9 Mar. 2011: 2. Print.

Thoreau, Henry D. *Essays and Other Writings*. Will H. Dircks and Walter Scott, eds. London, n.d. Print.

Thornton, Thomas F. *Being and Place Among the Tlingit*. Seattle: University of Washington Press, 2008. Print.

Timmer, John. "Pines Punched a 'One-Way Ticket toward Genetic Obesity.'" *Ars Technica*. 22 May 2013. Web. Feb. 2014.

Trace, Norah. "Ecointelligence and Hope." *Wild Foresting: Practicing Nature's Wisdom*. Alan Drengson and Duncan Taylor, eds. Gabriola Island, BC: New Society Publishers, 2009. 188–91. Print

Trosper, Ronald L. "Traditional American Indian Economic Policy." *American Indian Culture and Research Journal* 19 (1995): 65–95. Print.

"True." *Webster's Twentieth-Century Dictionary*. J. Devlin, ed. New York: Publishers Guild, 1939 ed. Print.

Turner, Monica Goigel. "Landscape Ecology: The Effect of Pattern on Process." *Annual Review of Ecology and Systematics* 20 (1989): 171–97. Print.

Turner, Nancy, J. *Plants of Haida Gwaii*. Winlaw, BC: Sono Nis Press, 2004. Print.

———. *The Earth's Blanket: Traditional Teachings for Sustainable Living*. Vancouver: Douglas & McIntyre, 2005. Print.

Turner, Nancy J., and *Kii'iljuus* (Barbara Wilson). "The Culture of Forests—Haida Traditional Knowledge and Forestry in the 21st Century." *Wild Foresting: Practicing Nature's Wisdom*. Alan Drengson and Duncan Taylor, eds. Gabriola Island, BC: New Society Publishers, 2009. 130–37. Print.

Tyler, Mary Ellen. "Spiritual Stewardship in Aboriginal Resource Management Systems." *Environments* 22.1 (1993): 1–8. Print.

Umeek (E. Richard Atleo). *Tsawalk: A Nuu-chah-nulth Worldview*. Vancouver: UBC Press, 2004. Print.

United Nations Permanent Forum on Indigenous Issues (UNPFII). "Indigenous Peoples, Indigenous Voices: Fact Sheet." Web. 10 Dec. 2013.

University of Northern British Columbia. *Sm'algyax Living Legacy Talking Dictionary.* April 2011. Web. 18 May 2011.

Vickers, Roy Henry. Foreword. *River of Mist, Journey of Dreams.* By Thom Henley. N.p.: Rediscovery International Foundation, 2009. 8–10. Print.

Vogt, K., E. Moore, et al. "Productivity of Upper Slope Forests in the Pacific Northwest." D.G.W. Edwards and M.D. Meagher, eds. *Mountain Hemlock* (Tsuga mertensiana *[Bong.] Carr.*): *An Annotated Bibliography.* Info. Report BC-X-352. Victoria: NRC CFS PFC, 1994. 39. Print.

Wade, Nicholas J., and Josef Brožek. *Purkinje's Vision: The Dawning of Neuroscience.* Mahwah, NJ: Lawrence Erlbaum Associates, 2001. Print.

White, Howard. *Ghost in the Gears.* Madeira Park, BC: Harbour Publishing,1993. Print.

'*Wii Muk'willixw* (Art Wilson). *Heartbeat of the Earth: A First Nations Artist Records Injustice and Resistance.* Gabriola Island, BC: New Society Publishers, 1996. Print.

Wilson, Shawn. *Research Is Ceremony: Indigenous Research Methods.* Winnipeg: Fernwood, 2008. Print.

Wishart, Bruce. "The Red Maple." *Bruce Wishart.* Web. 5 May 2012.

Womack, Craig S. *Red on Red: Native American Literary Separatism.* Minneapolis: University of Minnesota Press, 1999. Print.

Wong, Rita. *Forage.* Gibsons, BC: Nightwood Editions, 2007. Print.

Wood, Paul M. *Biodiversity and Democracy.* Vancouver: UBC Press, 2000. Print.

Wood, Paul M., and Laurel Waterman. "Sustainability Impeded: Ultra Vires Environmental Issues." *Environmental Ethics* 30 (2008): 159–74. Print.

Žižek, Slavoj. "Welcome to the Desert of the Real: Reflections on WTC—Third Version." *European Graduate School* EGS. 2010. Web. 23 Feb. 2010.

Epigraph Permissions

PHOTO LISA FUNK

BORN ON THE BC COAST, DERRICK STACEY DENHOLM HAS SPENT MOST of the last twenty years living and working in northern and coastal forests. Having come out of the trees just long enough to complete a bachelor and a masters in English, his literary work concerns respect for the wild, social and environmental justice, and the problems of ongoing industrialization within Indigenous lands. Denhlm won the 2011 Barry McKinnon Chapbook Award for *Dead Salmon Dialectics*, which was published in full form by Caitlin Press in 2014. Denholm also has poetry, prose, and visual art published in *Canadian Literature*, the *Capilano Review, CV2, Dreamland, Drunken Boat, filling Station, The Goose*, and *::stonestone::*.